How to Prepare BIBLE Messages

James Braga

MULTNOMAH

Portland, Oregon 97266

Foreign language editions of *How to Prepare Bible Messages*:
Arabic (Kmeel Kilada of Gospel Missionary Union)
French (Life Publishers International, Vernon, France)
Indonesian (Penerbit Gandum Mas, Malang, Indonesia)
Korean (Word of Life Press, Seoul, Korea)
Portuguese (Life Publishers International, Editorial Vida Ltda., Sao Paulo, Brazil)
Russian (International Correspondence Institute, Asslar, Germany)
Spanish (Kregel Publications, Publicaciones Portavoz Evangelico, Barcelona, Spain)
Swedish (Internationella Korrespondensinstutet, Stockholm, Sweden)

This book is also available in braille and on cassette tape from the Assemblies of God Library for the Blind, Springfield, Missouri.

Unless otherwise indicated, all Scripture quotations are from the Holy Bible: New International Version, ©1978 by the International Bible Society. Used by permission of Zondervan Bible Publishers.

HOW TO PREPARE BIBLE MESSAGES
©1969, 1981 by Multnomah Press
10209 SE Division Street
Portland, Oregon 97266

Multnomah Press is a ministry of
Multnomah School of the Bible
8435 NE Glisan Street
Portland, Oregon 97220

Printed in the United States of America.

Revised edition, December 1981

Library of Congress Cataloging-in-Publication Data
Braga, James
     How to Prepare Bible Messages
     Bibliography.
     Includes index.
1. Preaching.   I. Title.
BV4211.2.B674   1982   251'.01   81-14132
ISBN 0-930014-71-5   AACR2

          98 99 00 01 - 32 31 30 29 28 27 26 25

How to Prepare BIBLE Messages

Affectionately dedicated to
ANNE
my devoted and beloved wife

"In the presence of God and of Christ Jesus, who will judge the living and the dead, and in view of his appearing and his kingdom, I give you this charge: Preach the Word; be prepared in season and out of season; correct, rebuke and encourage—with great patience and careful instruction" (2 Timothy 4:1-2).

FOREWORD

If the Christian church is to maintain an aggressive witness in this generation, and if believers in Christ are to grow and to develop into mature and effectively functioning Christians, then it is of the utmost importance that pastors, teachers, and other leaders in the church provide "the sincere milk of the Word" through Bible-centered and Bible-derived messages for their people.

It is a pleasure, therefore, to commend to the Christian public the excellent volume of the Rev. James Braga, *How to Prepare Bible Messages*.

This is not the usual book on sermon preparation which simply describes types of sermons and includes a sampling of the author's best, but a true "how-to" manual which guides the individual or class in the step-by-step process of building the sermon.

The book is divided into two major portions, the first of which presents a definition and discussion of each of the principal types of sermons—topical, textual, and expository—with basic principles and illustrations to guide the prospective sermon builder. The second division of the book deals with the mechanics of sermon construction, considering homiletical structure, the title, the introduction, the proposition, the divisions, the discussion, the use of illustrations, the application, and the conclusion. Throughout the work, basic principles are stressed and interestingly illustrated, so that the volume lives up to its title as a "how-to" tool intended to aid the worker in his own preparation of messages.

A set of exercises at the close of each chapter makes the book more useful as a classroom text or in personal study. A bibliography at the end of each chapter further enhances the value of the work for the student who wishes to broaden his knowledge in this field.

As one reads this volume, the impression comes repeatedly that here is a work which reflects a lifetime of personal study of the Word combined with a deep reverence for the sacredness of a task and a desire to help God's people understand and communicate the precious truths of the Book.

Having known the author since 1949 as a fellow faculty member and personal friend in the ministry of the Word in our school, I have come to respect him deeply as a careful student of the Bible whose life and testimony have been a blessing to all on our campus. His book deserves careful consideration on the part of all who seek to improve their skills in preparing Bible messages.

Portland, Oregon   Ted L. Bradley
June 3, 1968   Multnomah School of the Bible

PREFACE

Because numerous books have been written on the preparation and delivery of sermons, it may seem superfluous to add another to the extensive literature on the subject. But after nineteen years of teaching homiletics in a Bible school, I am convinced of the need of a textbook which applies the principles of homiletics to the construction of discourses in such a manner that the student may learn from the outset how to prepare messages directly from the Bible. I am also impressed with the need in a work of this kind of an adequate number of examples which clearly illustrate the step-by-step processes in building sermons. I hope that in the writing of this manual I have been able in some measure to meet these needs and that the book may prove of value to students of Bible schools and to all who desire to learn how to prepare Bible messages.

I do not claim originality for the methods which are given in the chapters which follow. Some of the features in the first three chapters were gathered from a class in homiletics taught by the late Dr. James M. Gray when he was president of the Moody Bible Institute in Chicago. The material on the mechanics of sermon construction includes some useful suggestions from Dr. Charles W. Koller, former president of Northern Baptist Theological Seminary in Chicago, under whom I had the privilege of studying expository preaching. Many other helpful suggestions have come from various writers of homiletics, and I have also drawn upon the practical knowledge I have gained in teaching the subject.

A series of exercises at the close of several chapters will enable the student to put into practice the techniques he has learned. He should not be expected to do all the exercises, but only such as his instructor deems necessary. If the student finds difficulty in doing an exercise, he should review the chapter and then try again to do the work.

In connection with the construction of sermons I would encourage the use of a Bible which has the verses arranged in paragraphs, a topical Bible such as Nave's, an unabridged concordance, and the *Treasury of Scripture Knowledge*.

However, while the student should feel free to use reference books in the preparation of his messages, he should do his main studying in the Scriptures. He should never borrow outlines from reference books or commentaries, but should formulate his own sermon outlines. This may be hard and tedious work at first; but, as the beginner diligently applies the principles contained in this book, he will find himself becoming more and more adept in the preparation of Bible messages which will be homiletical in structure.

It needs to be stated, and to be stated emphatically, that the most important factor in the preparation of sermons is the preparation of the preacher's own heart. No amount of knowledge or of learning or of natural endowments can take the place of a fervent, humble, devoted heart which longs for more and more of Christ. Only the man who walks with God and who lives a holy life can inspire others to grow in the grace and knowledge of Christ. Such a man will spend much time in secret with Jesus, holding daily, uninterrupted, unhurried communion with Him in His Word.

The preacher must also be a man of prayer who has learned the art of holy warfare upon his knees. Like Daniel, he must have the habit of prayer and find the time, nay, take the time, to pray daily and regularly in his closet. His sermons then will not be the product of mere intellectual effort but will be heaven-sent messages—sent to him in answer to prayer. E. M. Bounds, the mighty man of prayer, said in truth, "Prayer puts the preacher's sermon into the preacher's heart; prayer puts the preacher's heart into the preacher's sermon."

But the man who is to preach the message of the Book must also be a man of the Book. He must study the Scriptures not just to get a message for his congregation. He must live in the Book. The Word of God must become his meat and drink. Throughout his life he must spend hours every week in diligent study of the Bible. He must saturate himself with it until it grips his heart and soul so that with Jeremiah he may say, "His word is in my heart like a burning fire, shut up in my bones. I am weary of holding it in; indeed, I cannot" (Jeremiah 20:9).

May God give to us in these days of unprecedented need men of God who love the Lord Jesus Christ supremely and who will so preach

His Word that others may be attracted and won to Him.

James Braga

"Let the prophet who has a dream tell his dream, but let the one who has my word speak it faithfully. For what has straw to do with grain?" declares the LORD. "Is not my word like fire," declares the LORD, "and like a hammer that breaks a rock in pieces?" (Jeremiah 23:28-29).

PREFACE
To the Second Edition

It is thirteen years since this volume first went to press. The book was written under the pressure of a busy teaching and preaching ministry, and after it was published I realized that there were areas which needed revision or amplification.

I desired for a long time to make the necessary revisions and additions to this work. When the publishers requested recently that I update the bibliography at the end of each chapter I saw this opportunity to make these changes as an indication of the good hand of God upon this task.

The first three chapters were originally written to provide the beginner with certain elementary principles which would enable him to construct a basic sermon outline without having to go into the intricacies of the proposition and other complicated homiletical procedures. I have chosen to retain this approach; therefore, instead of making many revisions in Part I of the book, I added a number of items which I trust will make the preparation of Bible messages simpler and more challenging to the student. At the same time, I hope the contents of these chapters may offer more mature students some valuable insights into the ways in which sermon outlines can be built from various portions of Scripture.

I also wish to point out that the methods of sermon preparation discussed in this book are by no means the only valid forms of discourse. There are other ways by which truths may be communicated. In accordance with the objective which he may have in mind when he is preparing his message, the preacher must determine for himself the most effective way of communicating biblical truth. Whatever method he decides to adopt, he should make his message plain and simple so all may understand what God has to say through his lips. Then he will follow the noble example of those Levites in the days of Ezra and

15

Nehemiah who "read from the Book of the Law of God, making it clear and giving the meaning so that the people could understand what was being read" (Nehemiah 8:8).

I send out the revised edition of my book with the prayer that the Lord may be pleased to use it to enable many of His servants to learn how to prepare messages from the Word of God.

Portland, Oregon   James Braga
July 31, 1981

TABLE OF CONTENTS

PART I

Principal Types of Biblical Sermons

PART II

The Mechanics of Sermon Construction

17

PART I
Principal Types of
Biblical Sermons

"So that in everything he might have
the supremacy."
(Colossians 1:18b)

1. THE TOPICAL SERMON

Classification of Sermons

There are many kinds of sermons and various ways of classifying them. In an attempt to classify sermons, writers of homiletics use different definitions, and in using these definitions there is considerable overlapping in classification. Some writers classify sermons according to their content or subject matter, others according to their structure, and others according to the psychological method used when presenting messages. There are other methods of classifying sermons, but perhaps the least complicated method is to classify them as topical, textual, and expository. We shall study the preparation of Bible messages by considering these three main types.

Definition of a Topical Sermon

We begin our discussion of the topical sermon with a definition, for if this definition is fully grasped the student will gain a mastery of the basic elements of a topical discourse.

A topical sermon is one in which the main divisions are derived from the topic, independently of a text.

Note this definition carefully. The first part states that the main divisions must be drawn from the topic itself. This means that the topical sermon begins with a topic or theme and that the main parts of the sermon consist of ideas which come from that subject.

The second part of the definition declares that the topical sermon does not require a text as the basis of its message. This does not mean that the message will not be biblical, but merely indicates that a text of Scripture is not the source of the topical sermon.

However, to insure that the message will be thoroughly biblical in content, we must start with a biblical subject or topic. The main divisions of the sermon outline must be drawn from this biblical topic, and each main division must be supported by a Scripture reference. The verses which support the main divisions should usually be drawn from portions of the Bible which are more or less widely separated from one another.

Example of a Topical Sermon

To understand the definition more clearly, let us work together on a simple topical outline.

We shall select as our topic, reasons for unanswered prayer. Note that we have not used a text but a biblical topic. From this topic we must now draw our main divisions. Therefore, we need to discover what the Bible states as reasons for unanswered prayer.

As we meditate and call to mind various parts of Scripture which refer to our topic we may find such texts as the following, all of which indicate why prayer often remains unanswered: James 4:3; Psalm 66:18; James 1:6-7; Matthew 6:7; Proverbs 28:9; and 1 Peter 3:7. It is here that a good reference Bible, an unabridged concordance, or a topical Bible, such as *Nave's Topical Bible,* may prove to be an invaluable aid.

With the help of these references we find the following causes behind unanswered prayer:

     I. Asking amiss, James 4:3.
    II. Sin in the heart, Psalm 66:18.
   III. Doubting God's Word, James 1:6-7.
   IV. Vain repetitions, Matthew 6:7.
    V. Disobedience to the Word, Proverbs 28:9.
   VI. Inconsiderate behavior in conjugal relationships,
       1 Peter 3:7.

Here we have a Biblical topical outline with each main division drawn from the topic, reasons for unanswered prayer, and each division supported by a verse of Scripture.

Unity of Thought

It will be observed from the example given above that the topical sermon contains one central idea. In other words, this outline deals with only one theme; namely, reasons for unanswered prayer. We may think of many other important facts concerning prayer, such as the meaning of prayer, the importance of prayer, the power of prayer, the methods of prayer, and the results of prayer. However, in order to conform to the definition of a topical sermon, we must draw the main parts of the outline from the topic; that is, we must limit the entire outline to the one idea contained in the topic. Such items as the meaning of prayer and the importance of prayer must be omitted from this particular message because our topic limits us to deal only with the factors which hinder the answer to our prayers.

Kinds of Topics

The Scriptures deal with every conceivable phase of human life and activity. They also reveal God's purposes in grace toward men both in time and in eternity. Thus the Bible contains an inexhaustible storehouse of topics from which the preacher may obtain material for topical messages suited for every occasion and condition in which men find themselves. Through constant and diligent digging into the Word the man of God will enrich his own soul with precious nuggets of divine truth and will also be able to share his spiritual wealth with others so that they too may become rich in the things that count for time and eternity.

Out of the vast treasure house of sacred writ we can find such themes as these: influences for good, little things God uses, blunders of God's saints, blessings which come through suffering, the results of unbelief, divine absolutes which mold character, the imperatives of Christ, the Christian's delights, the lies of the devil, conquests of the cross, birthmarks of a Christian, problems which baffle us, the glories of heaven, anchors of the soul, remedies for spiritual maladies, the riches of the Christian, biblical concepts of child training, and dimensions of Christian service.

Subsequent pages in this chapter will show the student the basic principles for the construction of the main divisions of topical outlines. As the reader considers these outlines he will observe that each outline not only has a theme or topic, but also a title which differs from the topic. A full explanation of the subject, topic, theme, and title is given in Chapter 5. For our present purposes, however, it is well to note that the subject, topic, and theme are synonymous. The title, on the other hand, is the name given to the sermon, stated in an interesting or attractive manner.

Choices of Topics

As the student gives himself to topical study of the Bible he will discover such a great variety of topics that he may wonder how to make his choice of a suitable theme for a message.

If we are to know which topic to select, we must seek the leading of the Lord. This will be given as we spend time in prayer and in meditation in the Word of God.

Other factors may also enter into the choice of a subject. The choice may be determined by the theme on which the minister is asked to speak or by the specific occasion on which the message is to be delivered. Again, certain conditions within a particular congregation may indicate the necessity or desirability of selecting a topic suited to the circumstances.

Although a topical sermon is not based directly upon a text, a verse of Scripture may be the starting point for an idea from which we can construct a topical outline. For example, Galatians 6:17 reads, "Finally, let no one cause me trouble, for I bear on my body the marks of Jesus." We are arrested by the words, "I bear on my body the marks of Jesus." By comparison, the New American Standard Bible translates this verse, "I bear on my body the brand-marks of Jesus." No doubt Paul refers here to the scars left by wounds inflicted on his body by his persecutors for Christ's sake, scars which were self-evident marks that he belonged to Christ forever.

Extra-biblical sources reveal that when Paul wrote these words, not only was the branding iron inflicted on animals, but also on humans —leaving marks on the flesh which could never be erased or removed. At least three classes of individuals wore scars of this kind—slaves who were owned by their masters, soldiers who sometimes branded themselves with the name of the general under whom they served as a token of their wholehearted devotion to his cause, and devotees who were attached for life to a temple and to the deity who was worshipped there.

As a result of this information, we put together the topical outline shown below:

    Title: "The Marks of Jesus"
    Topic: Life-long marks of a dedicated Christian.
       I. Like the slave, a dedicated Christian bears the mark of ownership of the Master to whom he belongs, 1 Corinthians 6:19-20, Romans 1:1.
      II. Like the soldier, a dedicated Christian bears the mark

of devotion to the Commander whom he serves,
2 Timothy 2:3, 2 Corinthians 5:15.
III.   Like the devotee, a dedicated Christian bears the
mark of a worshipper of the Lord whom he adores,
Philippians 1:20, 2 Corinthians 4:5.

Basic Principles for the Preparation of Topical Outlines

1. The main divisions should be in logical or chronological order.

This means that we should aim to develop the outline in some form of progression, either logical or chronological, but whether we should follow a logical or chronological order must be determined by the nature of the topic. We choose as our theme, vital truths concerning Jesus Christ, and thus construct the following outline:

Title: "Worthy of Worship"
Topic: Vital truths concerning Jesus Christ.
  I.   He is God manifest in the flesh, Matthew 1:23.
  II. He is the Savior of men, 1 Timothy 1:15.
  III. He is the coming King, Revelation 11:15.

Observe that this outline is in chronological order. Jesus Christ, the Son of God, first became incarnate, then He went to the cross and gave His life to become our Savior, and some day He is coming to reign as King of kings and Lord of lords. Also observe that in accordance with the definition of a topical sermon, the divisions are not derived from the title but from the topic or subject. The same is true of all the subsequent topical outlines in this chapter.

Another example of progression in an outline is shown below, with the divisions arranged in logical order. The theme deals with characteristics of the believer's hope, but we shall employ the three words, "The Believer's Hope," as the simple title for the outline:

Title: "The Believer's Hope"
Topic: Characteristics of the believer's hope.
  I.   It is a living hope, 1 Peter 1:3.
  II. It is a saving hope, 1 Thessalonians 5:8.
  III. It is a sure hope, Hebrews 6:19.
  IV. It is a good hope, 2 Thessalonians 2:16.
  V.   It is an unseen hope, Romans 8:24.
  VI. It is a blessed hope, Titus 2:13.
  VII. It is an eternal hope, Titus 3:7.

Note that the outline reaches its climax in the last division.

2. *The main divisions may be an analysis of the topic.*

To analyze a topic we must break it down into its component parts with each part of the outline contributing to the completeness of the discussion of the topic. We shall take the main facts about Satan in the Bible as our topic, and using "Satan, Our Archenemy" as the title, we can thus analyze the theme:

> Title: "Satan, Our Archenemy"
> Topic: Main facts in the Bible about Satan.
>   I. His origin, Ezekiel 28:12-17.
> II. His fall, Isaiah 14:12-15.
> III. His power, Ephesians 6:11-12; Luke 11:14-18.
> IV. His activity, 2 Corinthians 4:4; Luke 8:12;
>   1 Thessalonians 2:18.
>   V. His destiny, Matthew 25:41.

Note that if we were to omit, e.g., the second main division of this outline, we would not have a satisfactory analysis of the topic because one of the basic features of the topic would be missing. It is possible, however, that a further study of the subject of Satan in the Bible may result in one or two other important points being added to this outline. Also observe that in accordance with the previous rule, the divisions are arranged in logical order.

3. *The main divisions may present the various proofs of a topic.*

The outline shown hereunder is so constructed:

> Title: "Knowing God's Word"
> Topic: Some values of knowing God's Word.
>   I. Knowing God's Word makes one wise unto salva-
>   tion, 2 Timothy 3:15.
> II. Knowing God's Word keeps us from sin,
>   Psalm 119:11.
> III. Knowing God's Word produces spiritual growth,
>   1 Peter 2:2.
> IV. Knowing God's Word results in successful living,
>   Joshua 1:7-8.

It will be seen that each of the main divisions in this outline confirms the topic; that is to say, each statement in the main divisions shows one of the values of knowing the Word of God.

4. The main divisions may treat a subject by analogy or contrast with something else in Scripture.

In a topical outline of this type a subject is compared or contrasted with something to which it is connected in the Bible. For instance, we read in Matthew 5:13 that the Lord Jesus said: "You are the salt of the earth. But if the salt loses its saltiness, how can it be made salty again? It is no longer good for anything, except to be thrown out and trampled by men." An examination of the context in which this verse is found clearly indicates that Christ refers to the testimony of the believer and likens his testimony to salt. We can therefore construct an outline with the title, "An Effective Testimony," by making each division consist of a comparison between the testimony of the believer and salt:

> Title: "An Effective Testimony"
> Topic: A comparison between the testimony of the believer and salt.
> I. Like salt, the believer's testimony should season, Colossians 4:6.
> II. Like salt, the believer's testimony should purify, 1 Thessalonians 4:4.
> III. Like salt, the believer's testimony should not lose its savor, Matthew 5:13.
> IV. Like salt, the believer's testimony should create thirst, 1 Peter 2:12.

5. The main divisions may be expressed by a certain fixed word or phrase of Scripture repeated throughout the outline.

The phrase, "God is able" or "he is able" (where the pronoun "he" has reference to the Lord) occurs a number of times in the Scriptures. Using this phrase as the basis for each main division, we obtain the following outline:

> Title: "The Ability of God"
> Topic: Some things which God is able to do.
> I. He is able to save, Hebrews 7:25.
> II. He is able to keep, Jude 24.
> III. He is able to help, Hebrews 2:18.
> IV. He is able to subdue, Philippians 3:21. (KJV)
> V. He is able to give grace, 2 Corinthians 9:8.
> VI. He is able to do beyond what we ask or think, Ephesians 3:20.

6. The main divisions may be supported by an identical word or phrase of Scripture throughout the outline.

This means that the same word or phrase of Scripture is employed, not in the outline as in the case of the previous rule, but in substantiation of the statement of each division. As an example, we give an outline developed from a study of the expression "in love" which occurs six times in the Epistle to the Ephesians. By using the theme, facts concerning the life of love, and by noting each Scripture reference in the outline, it will be seen that this expression supports each one of the main divisions:

> Title: "The Life of Love"
> Topic: Facts concerning the life of love.
>   I. It is founded upon God's eternal purpose, 1:4-5.
>   II. It is produced by Christ's indwelling, 3:17.
> III. It should manifest itself in our Christian relation-
>   ships, 4:1-2; 4:15.
>   IV. It will result in the edification and growth of the
>   church, 4:16.
>   V. It is exemplified by Jesus Christ Himself, 5:1-2.

The diligent student will find that the repetition of significant words and phrases occurs frequently in the Bible. Sometimes significant expressions may occur repeatedly within a given book, as in the case above. These repetitions are not accidental but are no doubt recorded in the Word of God that we may take special notice of them. The Book of Psalms, as well as the epistles of Paul and the Epistle to the Hebrews, is especially rich in reiterations of significant words and phrases. Careful study of the context in which these words or phrases are found will yield many interesting and helpful messages.

7. *The main divisions may consist of a word study showing the various meanings of a certain word or words in the Scriptures.*
     The word study may be an examination in the original languages of a word used in the English Bible. By this means the preacher is able to show various shades of meaning of which the reader of the English Bible may not be aware. The verb rendered "to walk" in the English version of the New Testament, e.g., may be one of six different words in the Greek, and these six words suggest as many ways in which the verb "to walk" can be understood.
     Such a word study may be an examination in the original in order to discover the nuances of that word in Greek or Hebrew. For example, the noun "honor" (τιμή, in Greek) is used in four different senses in the Greek New Testament, and from a study of its usage in the original text we obtain the following outline:

Title: "Estimates of Value—God's or Man's"
Topic: Meanings of the word "honor" in the Greek New
Testament.
  I. A price that is paid, 1 Corinthians 6:20.
  II. The value which some men put on human ordi-
nances, Colossians 2:23.
  III. Esteem or respect given to another, 1 Timothy 1:17;
Hebrews 2:9.
  IV. The preciousness of Christ to the believer, 1 Peter
2:7.

It is not necessary to possess a knowledge of Hebrew or Greek
in order to make a word study. The unabridged concordance by Robert
Young or the one by James Strong, the *Expository Dictionary of New
Testament Words* by W. E. Vine, as well as other grammatical aids
available today, will enable the student who does not know the original
languages of the Scriptures to do valuable research in semantics.

Similarly a word study may trace a significant biblical word or
phrase through the Scriptures, noting it in its contextual relationships
and studying it inductively. In other words, we check every specific
reference to a particular word or phrase and then compare, analyze,
and classify our observations with the purpose of arriving at valid conclusions regarding that word or phrase.

For example, consider the phrase, "I have sinned." With the use of
an unabridged concordance, we discover a total of twenty-two occurrences of this expression in the Old and New Testaments. By observing the contextual relationships of every one of these references, as
well as by comparing and analyzing them, we find that the phrase, "I
have sinned," is not necessarily an expression of true confession. We
then classify our observations and place them in outline form. Under
the title, "Confessions—True or False," we show that the expression
"I have sinned" when used by various individuals in the Bible could
mean any one of various things:

  I. An expression of fear.
Note the case of Pharaoh, Exodus 9:27; 10:16; of
Achan, Joshua 7:20; of Shimei, 2 Samuel 19:20.
  II. An expression of insincerity.
Note the case of Saul, 1 Samuel 15:24, 30.
  III. An expression of remorse.
Note the case of Saul, 1 Samuel 26:21; of Judas,
Matthew 27:4.
  IV. An expression of true repentance.
Note the case of David, 2 Samuel 12:13; Psalm 51:4;

of Nehemiah, Nehemiah 1:6; of the prodigal son,
Luke 15:18, 21.

*8. The main divisions should not be undergirded by proof
texts wrested out of context.*

There is always the danger in topical studies that we might wrench a text out of its context; therefore, the preacher must constantly exercise care that each Scripture reference cited to support a statement in his outline is used accurately and in keeping with the evident purpose of its author.

Doctrinal Sermons

Topical study is admirably suited to the construction of the doctrinal sermon. The doctrine selected furnishes the topic. We may limit the topic to just one aspect of a doctrine. For example, we can choose the meaning of redemption as the theme, and select a few key passages to form the basis of the outline. But if we are to learn the whole truth regarding a given doctrine, it is necessary to cover the entire range of Scripture, noting all the pertinent references to that doctrine. Having studied each one of these references in its proper relationship to the context, we collate, analyze, and classify our findings and thus should be able to obtain a sound Biblical basis for our conclusions.

Series of Topical Messages

The preparation of topical outlines makes possible a set of messages on some broad subject. Here again there is almost no limit to the variety of series which may be developed, but space will allow no more than a few examples.

"Portraits of the Perfect Man" provides the heading for the following series of sermons:

> "The Love of Jesus"
> "The Face of Jesus"
> "The Hands of Jesus"
> "The Tears of Jesus"
> "The Cross of Jesus"
> "The Blood of Jesus"
> "The Name of Jesus"

From the examples of topical outlines already given in this chapter, it should be clear that the main divisions for the messages in a series such as this will not be derived from the titles but from specific themes which are related to these headings. For instance, to construct a topical discourse with the title, "The Love of Jesus," we can use any one of these topics: characteristics of His love, manifestations of His love, or the objects of His love.

In case a pastor should find a need for his people to become acquainted with certain forms of error, he may choose the general heading of "Common Spiritual Delusions" and use the following for titles in the series:

> "The Delusion of Jehovah's Witnesses"
> "The Delusion of Mormonism"
> "The Delusion of Christian Science"
> "The Delusion of Seventh Day Adventism"
> "The Delusion of 'Unity' "
> "The Delusion of Spiritism"

"Life on the Highest Plane" may form the basis of a succession of sermons with titles such as those given below:

> "The Disciplined Life"
> "The Consecrated Life"
> "The Contented Life"
> "The Prayerful Life"
> "The Abundant Life"

Another excellent series may be called "Successful Christian Living," using titles like the following:

> "How to Be a Growing Christian"
> "How to Be a Spiritual Christian"
> "How to Be a Useful Christian"
> "How to Be a Restful Christian"
> "How to Be a Happy Christian"
> "How to Be a Victorious Christian"

A plan which could be of special significance in these times may be called "The Christian Home" and include titles like the following:

> "The Foundation of a Christian Home"
> "The Wife's Relationship to Her Husband and to
> Christ"
> "The Husband's Responsibility to His Wife and to
> Christ"
> "The Privileges of Parenthood"

> "Discipline in the Home"
> "Family Devotions"
> "Threats to a Christian Home"
> "Happy Family Life"

"The Bible Examined" can be the general heading for yet another group of related messages, with titles like these:

> "Is the Bible True?"
> "Does the Bible Contradict Itself?"
> "Is the Bible Relevant?"
> "How Can We Understand the Bible?"
> "Can We Trust Our English Translations of the
> Bible?"

A study of major subjects in a book or group of books in the Bible will also suggest a series of discourses. Let us consider the First and Second Epistles to the Thessalonians as an example. These epistles contain several doctrinal subjects, and from them we may learn what Paul taught those early Christians concerning God, Jesus Christ, the Holy Spirit, the gospel, the way of salvation, the second coming of Christ, believers, and Satan. Each of these eight items could be traced through one or both epistles.

We select the second coming of Christ as an illustration, and as we study the First Epistle we observe that the second coming of Christ is referred to in each chapter of the epistle. Thus we derive the following outline:

> Title: "The Blessedness of the Believer's Hope"
> Topic: Effects on the believer of the hope of Christ's second
>   coming.
>   I. It produces patience, 1:10.
> II. It assures a reward for labor, 2:19.
> III. It satisfies the longings for holiness, 3:13.
> IV. It comforts in sorrow, 4:13.
>   V. It enriches prayer, 5:23.

We draw attention to one more subject found in First and Second Thessalonians. The word "brothers" occurs no less than twenty-four times in the two epistles—seventeen times in the first and seven times in the second. An examination of the use of this word in its contexts could form another interesting group of related messages.

Before we leave the subject of series of topics, it should be stated that there are two important rules which must be observed in the presentation of any series of messages. In the first place, the series should be brief. Even though the series may be well treated with considerable variety, the congregation is liable to lose interest if one major theme is presented over an extended period of time. In the second place, the series should show evidence of order or progress. A haphazard arrangement of related sermons is generally not as effective as one in which the messages are carefully planned in an appropriate order. When the series is properly arranged, it will be easy for the congregation to observe the relationship of the messages to one another. It will also serve to heighten interest as the series moves toward a climax.

Conclusion

The full development of the topical outline must await further instruction, but if the student has followed the discussion in this chapter he may, by careful application of the principles contained herein, learn to prepare the basic outline of a Biblical topical message.

EXERCISES

1. Prepare a topical outline using one of the themes listed under the section, *Kinds of Topics*. Make sure that each of your divisions is derived from the theme and that it has sound scriptural support.

2. Prepare a topical outline, using your own topic, and support each main division with appropriate Scripture. Be careful to follow the principles suggested above.

3. List seven suitable topics for a Mother's Day service and make a topical outline on one of them.

4. Find a significant word or phrase which occurs repeatedly in a book in the New Testament and develop a topical outline from the repetitions of that word or phrase.

5. Take a broad subject and list six suitable titles for a series of messages on that subject. Arrange the entire list in an order which may make for the most effective presentation. Then develop an outline on a theme relating to one of these six titles.

6. In accordance with Rule 4 under the *Basic Principles for the Preparation of Topical Outlines,* develop a topical outline on "God's Jewels" in which your divisions will consist of a comparison between God's children and jewels.

7. Examine the Epistle to the Philippians and make a list of five doctrinal features. Formulate a topical outline from the same epistle on any one of these five items.

8. With the help of an unabridged concordance, prepare a word study on the word "forgive."

BIBLIOGRAPHY

Baumann, J. Daniel. *An Introduction to Contemporary Preaching*. Grand Rapids, Michigan: Baker Book House, 1972, pp. 101-102.

Broadus, John A. *On the Preparation and Delivery of Sermons*. Revised by Jesse B. Weatherspoon. New York: Harper & Brothers, 1944, Part II, Chapter 3.

Caemmerer, Richard R. *Preaching for the Church*. St. Louis, Missouri: Concordia Publishing House, 1959, Chapters 22, 24, and 26.

Etter, John W. *The Preacher and His Sermon*. Dayton, Ohio: United Brethren Publishing House, 1902, pp. 178-200.

Gibbs, Alfred P. *The Preacher and His Preaching*. Third Edition. Ft. Dodge, Iowa: Walterick Printing Company, n.d., Chapter 21.

Macpherson, Ian. *The Burden of the Lord*. Nashville, Tennessee: Abingdon Press, 1955, pp. 87-88.

Pattison, T. Harwood. *The Making of the Sermon*. Philadelphia: The American Baptist Publication Society, 1898, Chapter 4.

Perry, Lloyd M. *A Manual for Biblical Preaching*. Grand Rapids, Michigan: Baker Book House, 1965, pp. 83-89, 95-105, 125.

Riley, W. B. *The Preacher & His Preaching*. Wheaton, Illinois: Sword of the Lord Publishers, 1948, Chapter 7.

Torrey, R. A. *How to Study the Bible for Greatest Profit*. London: James Nisbet & Co., Ltd., 1908, Chapter 3.

Unger, Merrill F. *Principles of Expository Preaching*. Grand Rapids, Michigan: Zondervan Publishing House, 1955, pp. 48-52.

White, Douglas M. *The Excellence of Exposition*. Neptune, New Jersey: Loizeaux Brothers, Inc., 1977, pp. 63-66.

Whitesell, Faris Daniel. *Evangelistic Preaching and the Old Testament*. Chicago: Moody Press, 1947, Chapter 12.

2. THE TEXTUAL SERMON

Definition

As we take up the textual sermon we deal with a type of discourse which is different from the topical sermon. In a topical sermon we begin with a theme, but in a textual sermon we begin with a text. Note carefully the definition of a textual sermon:

A textual sermon is one in which the main divisions are derived from a text consisting of a brief portion of Scripture. Each of these divisions is then used as a line of suggestion, and the text provides the theme of the sermon.

As we examine this definition, it becomes apparent that in the textual sermon the main lines of development are drawn from the text itself. In this way the main outline is kept strictly within the limits of the text.

The text may consist of only one line of a verse of Scripture, or it may be a whole verse or even two or three verses. Writers of homiletics do not specifically define the extent of a passage which may be used for a textual sermon, but for our purpose we shall limit the text in a textual outline to a maximum of three verses.

The second portion of the definition states that each main division derived from the text "is then used as a line of suggestion." This means that the main divisions suggest the features to be discussed in the message. Sometimes the text is so rich and full that we may obtain many truths or features from it which will serve as a development of the thoughts contained in the outline. At other times, however, it may be necessary to draw from other portions of Scripture to develop the main divisions. In other words, the main divisions in a textual outline must come out of the text itself, but further development may come either from the text or from other portions of Scripture.

The definition states further that "the text provides the theme of the sermon." In contrast to the topical sermon, in which we begin with a topic or theme, we now begin with a text, which will indicate the dominant idea of the message.

Examples of Textual Sermon Outlines

For our first example, let us take as our text Ezra 7:10 which reads: "For Ezra had devoted himself to the study and observance of the Law of the LORD, and to teaching its decrees and laws in Israel." It will often be helpful to consult a modern translation to obtain a clearer meaning of a passage. By referring to the New American Standard Bible we find that the expression "devoted himself" is translated "set his heart."

By carefully examining the text we may observe that the whole verse centers around Ezra's purpose of heart, and we thus draw the following divisions from the verse:

> I. It was set on knowing the Word of God, "Ezra had devoted himself to the study . . . of the Law of the LORD."
> II. It was set on obedience to the Word of God, "and observance of the Law of the LORD."
> III. It was set on teaching the Word of God, "and to teaching its decrees and laws in Israel."

A suitable theme, drawn from the ideas suggested in the text, may then be, Ezra's purpose of heart.

Each of the main divisions, according to the definition, is now used "as a line of suggestion." They indicate what we are to say about the text.

According to the first main division, we are to speak about Ezra's purpose of heart to know the Word of God. However, Ezra 7:10 is not detailed enough to enable us to gather sufficient information to develop the first main division out of the text, so we need to resort to other sources of Scripture for that development.

By noting the context of Ezra 7:10 we find that verse 6 of the same chapter reads: "He [Ezra] was a teacher well versed in the Law of Moses, which the LORD, the God of Israel, had given." Verses 11, 12, and 21 also refer to Ezra as a "teacher of the Law of God." Verses 14 and 25 indicate further that Ezra's knowledge of the law of God was even recognized by Artaxerxes, the king of Persia. Here then is a man who, although knowing the law of God well, was not content with all the knowledge he possessed, but gave himself to diligent study to know it even better. And this he did in the midst of the allurements and depravity of a heathen court where, it is evident, he was held in high esteem.

As Ezra read the Word of God, certain passages from the historical books and the Psalms no doubt impressed themselves upon him. From Joshua 1:8 he would have read: "Do not let this Book of the Law depart from your mouth; meditate on it day and night, so that you may be careful to do everything written in it. Then you will be prosperous and successful." From Proverbs 8:34-35 he would also have noted: "Blessed is the man who listens to me, watching daily at my doors, waiting at my doorway. For whoever finds me finds life and receives favor from the LORD." Then from Jeremiah 29:13 he would have heard the Lord challenge his heart: "You will seek me and find me when you seek me with all your heart." Surely passages such as these must have gripped the "well versed teacher" from Babylon and inspired him, with all his knowledge of the law of God, to seek with all his heart to know it even more intimately.

We may sum up what we have said in connection with the first main division in two brief subdivisions. Note the first main division in the outline once more, "It was set on knowing the Word of God," and see how it leads our thoughts to the subdivisions, or offers a suggestion as to what to say in connection with the text:

1. In the midst of a heathen court.
2. In a thorough manner.

The second main division of the outline on Ezra 7:10 reads, "It was set on obedience to the Word of God." In accordance with the definition of the textual outline, this second main division now becomes a line of suggestion, indicating what should be discussed under this heading. Thus, we must in some way discuss the obedience of Ezra to the Word of God, and we therefore present the following subpoints:

1. To render a ready obedience.
2. To render a complete obedience.
3. To render a continual obedience.

Ezra 7:10 does not describe the kind of obedience which Ezra had purposed to render to the Word of God, but these ideas can be gathered from other parts of the book of Ezra, especially from chapters 9 and 10.

Under the third main division, which reads, "It was set on teaching the Word of God," the following subdivisions may be developed:

> 1. With clarity.
> 2. To the people of God.

The text does not say that Ezra planned to teach the Word of God to make its meaning understandable, but this becomes obvious from Nehemiah 8:5-12.

By writing the outline on Ezra 7:10 in its entirety it should become even clearer to the reader how each main division drawn from the text serves as a line of suggestion. The subdivisions are simply a development of the ideas contained in their respective main divisions, but the material for these subpoints is obtained from other portions of Scripture.

> Title: "Putting First Things First"
> Subject: Ezra's purpose of heart.
>   I. It was set on knowing the Word of God.
>   1. In the midst of a heathen court.
>   2. In a thorough manner.
>   II. It was set on obedience to the Word of God.
>   1. To render a ready obedience.
>   2. To render a complete obedience.
>   3. To render a continual obedience.
>   III. It was set on teaching the Word of God.
>   1. With clarity.
>   2. To the people of God.

Observe that the title and theme in this outline are different from each other. For a full explanation of sermon titles see Chapter 5. It should be mentioned here, however, that when the theme of the sermon outline is sufficiently interesting it may also serve as the title.

For a second example of a textual sermon outline, we use Isaiah 55:7. The verse reads: "Let the wicked forsake his way and the evil man his thoughts. Let him turn to the LORD, and he will have mercy on him, and to our God, for he will freely pardon." In this outline, the development of the subdivisions has not been made wholly from the text for, as the reader will see below, the third subpoint under the last main division is drawn from other portions of Scripture.

Title: "The Blessing of Forgiveness"

Subject: Divine pardon.

    I. The objects of God's pardon, "Let the wicked . . . thoughts."
- 1. The wicked (literally, those who are outwardly vile).
- 2. The evil man (literally, those who are "respectable" sinners).

    II. The conditions of God's pardon, "forsake . . . turn to the LORD."
- 1. The sinner must forsake evil.
- 2. The sinner must turn to God.

    III. The promise of God's pardon, "He will have mercy . . . and freely pardon."
- 1. A merciful pardon.
- 2. An abundant pardon (literally, He will be great to pardon).
- 3. A complete pardon, Psalm 103:3; Micah 7:18-19; 1 John 1:9.

The examples of textual outlines given above should be sufficient to show that the main divisions in a textual outline must be derived from the verse or verses which form the basis of the message, while the subdivisions may be drawn either from the same text or from any other part of Scripture, provided that the ideas contained in the subdivisions are a proper development of their respective main divisions.

When all the main divisions and subdivisions are drawn from the same text and properly expounded, such a text is treated expositorily.

We shall now leave the discussion of subdivisions for the present and consider the main aspects of the textual sermon. The method of developing main divisions and subdivisions, along with additional examples of textual outlines, is presented thoroughly in Chapter 8.

Basic Principles for the Preparation of Textual Outlines

1. The textual outline should be centered around one main thought in the text and the main divisions must be derived from the text so as to amplify or develop that one theme.

One of the first tasks of the homilist in the preparation of a textual sermon is to make a thorough study of the text, discover a dominant idea, and then derive the main divisions from the text (see Chapter 9). Each division then becomes an amplification or development of the subject. In the example given above on Ezra 7:10, the theme is Ezra's purpose of heart, and each of the main divisions, drawn from the text, develops that one dominant idea.

Dr. James M. Gray once gave to his class a textual outline on Romans 12:1, "Therefore, I urge you, brothers, in view of God's mercy, to offer your bodies as living sacrifices, holy and pleasing to God —which is your spiritual worship." Using the believer's sacrifice as his theme, Dr. Gray derived the following main divisions from the verse:

> I. The reason for sacrifice, "Therefore, I urge you, brothers, in view of God's mercy."
> II. The thing to be sacrificed, "offer your bodies."
> III. The conditions of sacrifice, "as living sacrifices . . . to God."
> IV. The obligation of sacrifice, "which is your spiritual worship."

The following outline on Psalm 23:1 is developed from the dominant idea of "the Lord's relationship to the believer":

> Title: "Jesus is Mine"
> I. It is an assuring relationship, "The Lord is my *shepherd.*"
> II. It is a personal relationship, "The Lord is *my* shepherd."
> III. It is a present relationship, "The Lord *is* my shepherd."

As we attempt to prepare a textual outline the main divisions in some texts are so obvious that we may experience little or no difficulty in discovering them and then seeing their relationship to one dominant idea. But generally speaking, it is best to find the subject of the text first, for then it is usually easier to discern the main divisions.

2. The main divisions may consist of the truths or principles suggested by the text.

The outline of a textual sermon does not have to consist of an analysis of the text. Instead, the truths or principles suggested by the text may be used to form the main divisions.

Read John 20:19-20 and then observe from the outline below that the spiritual truths expressed in the main divisions are drawn from the text.

> Title: "The Joy of Easter"
> Subject: Likenesses of God's people to the disciples.

   I. Like the disciples, God's people are sometimes in distress without the conscious presence of Christ, v. 19a.
     1. They are sometimes in deep distress because of adverse circumstances.
     2. They are sometimes in unnecessary distress in the midst of adverse circumstances.
   II. Like the disciples, God's people experience the comfort of Christ, vv. 19b-20a.
     1. They experience the comfort of Christ by His coming to them just when they need Him most.
     2. They experience the comfort of Christ through the words which He speaks to them.
  III. Like the disciples, God's people are made glad through the presence of Christ, v. 20b.
     1. They are made glad although their adverse circumstances remain unchanged.
     2. They are made glad because Christ is in their midst.

Applying the same rule to Ezra 7:10, and with the theme of essentials of effective Bible teaching, it is possible to derive four main truths from the text:

   Title: "Bible Teaching That Excels"
   Subject: Essentials of effective Bible teaching.
     I. It demands resolute determination. "Ezra had set his heart" (NASB).
    II. It demands diligent assimilation, "to the study . . . of the Law of the LORD."
    III. It demands complete dedication, "and observance of the Law of the LORD."
    IV. It demands faithful propagation, "and to teaching its decrees and laws in Israel."

3. It may be possible to find more than one theme or dominant thought in a text, depending upon the point of view from which we regard the text, but only one subject should be developed in an outline.

By means of the method of "multiple approach" we may view the text from various angles, using a different central idea in each case, and thus have more than one outline on any given text. We shall illustrate this principle with John 3:16 as our text. Using distinctives of the gift of God as our main point of emphasis, we obtain the following outline:

    I. It is a love gift, "God so loved the world."
   II. It is a sacrificial gift, "that he gave his one and only Son."

    III. It is an eternal gift, "shall not perish but have eternal
         life."
    IV. It is a universal gift, "whoever."
    V. It is a conditional gift, "believes."

Looking at the same text from another point of view, namely, with vital features relating to eternal life as the dominant thought, the outline drawn around this idea will then be:

    I. The One who gave it, "God."
    II. The reason He gave it, "so loved the world."
    III. The price He paid to give it, "that he gave his one and only Son."
    IV. The part we may have in it, "that whoever believes in him."
    V. The certainty of our possessing it, "shall not perish but have eternal life."

For the beginner who may experience difficulty in developing an outline on any given text by the use of a main idea, it may sometimes be best to try more than one approach to the text. In other words, let him look at the verse, as we have done, from other points of view and attempt to develop an outline with a different theme.

4. The main divisions should be in logical or chronological sequence.

It is not always necessary to follow the order of the words in the text, but the main divisions should indicate a progressive development of thought.

Taking the first part of John 3:36 as our text: "whoever believes in the Son has eternal life," we begin with the subject of important facts concerning salvation and discover the following divisions from the text:

    I. Its provider, "the Son."
    II. Its condition, "believes."
    III. Its availability, "whoever believes."
    IV. Its certainty, "has."
    V. Its duration, "eternal."

We may give this outline the title, "The Life That Never Ends." Note that the title differs from the subject, but the former is nevertheless suggested by the text.

5. The very words of the text may form the main divisions of the out-

*line, provided that these divisions are gathered around one main
theme.*

There are numerous texts of this kind which lend themselves to an
obvious outline. Here is one illustration of this, based on Luke 19:10,
"For the Son of Man came to seek and to save what was lost."

> Title: "Why Jesus Came"
>   I. The Son of Man came to seek the lost.
> II. The Son of Man came to save the lost.

It is evident that in this outline the title and theme are essentially the
same. This is also true of the next example, based on John 14:6, "Jesus
answered, 'I am the way and the truth and the life. No one comes to the
Father except through me.' "

> Title: "The Only Approach to God"
>   I. It is through Jesus, the way.
>   II. It is through Jesus, the truth.
> III. It is through Jesus, the life.

In the course of our ministry we should not fail to make full use of
texts such as these which are so obvious in their structure. However,
for the student who is seeking to acquire the ability to construct textual
sermons it would be wise for him to avoid such "easy" outlines and to
concentrate his efforts upon texts which, to build the outlines, will
challenge his thinking.

6. *The context from which the text is taken must be carefully observed and related to the text.*

The relationship of a text to its context is basic to a right interpretation of Scripture. The importance of this cannot be over-estimated, for
a disregard of this rule may result in serious distortion of the truth or a
complete misapprehension of the passage.

Let us take Colossians 2:21 as an example. It reads, "Do not han-
dle! Do not taste! Do not touch!" If we wrest this verse from its context
we are likely to fall into the error of believing that Paul is urging a form
of strict asceticism. But read in its context, Colossians 2:21 is seen to
refer to the rules and regulations which false teachers were seeking to
impose upon the Christians at Colossae.

Texts drawn from the historical portions of Scripture also lose their
proper significance unless their relationship to the context is carefully
studied. This is apparent in connection with Daniel 6:10, "Now when

Daniel learned that the decree had been published, he went home to his upstairs room where the windows opened toward Jerusalem. Three times a day he got down on his knees and prayed, giving thanks to his God, just as he had done before." The prayer and thanksgiving of Daniel on this occasion assume their proper significance only in relation to the threat to his life which is described in the previous verses of Daniel, chapter 6.

7. *Some texts contain comparisons or contrasts which can be treated best by pointing out their purposeful similarities or differences.*

The treatment of texts of this type will depend upon a careful observation of the contents of the verse or verses involved.

In Hebrews 13:5-6 we have a designed comparison between what the Lord has said and what we may say in consequence. A glance at these verses makes this comparison obvious: "God has said, 'Never will I leave you; never will I forsake you.' So we say with confidence, 'The Lord is my helper; I will not be afraid. What can man do to me?' "

Note the triple contrast in Proverbs 14:11. The text reads, "The house of the wicked will be destroyed, but the tent of the upright will flourish." There is evidently a purposeful choice of words in the text in order to emphasize the difference between the wicked and the upright, the house and the tent, and the overthrow of that which would seem to be the stronger structure of the wicked in contrast to the endurance of the lighter structure of the upright.

Also observe the contrasts in 2 Corinthians 4:17, "For our light and momentary troubles are achieving for us an eternal glory that far outweighs them all." In this verse we find a purposeful contrast between present trial and future reward, between troubles in this life and the bliss hereafter.

In Psalm 1:1-2 we read: "Blessed is the man who does not walk in the counsel of the wicked or stand in the way of sinners or sit in the seat of mockers. But his delight is in the law of the LORD, and on his law he meditates day and night." The following outline will suggest how we may treat a text containing a contrast such as we find here:

> Title: "The Blessed Man"
> Subject: Two aspects of a godly character.
>   I.   The negative aspect, separation from evil doers, v. 1.
>   II. The positive aspect, devotion to the law of God, v. 2.

8. *Two or three verses, each taken from different parts of Scripture, may be put together and treated as though they are one text.*

Instead of using one of the verses to support one main division and the next verse to undergird the second main division, the verses are put together as though they compose a single text, and the main divisions are drawn indiscriminately from the combined verses.

The combination of verses in this manner should be made only when the verses have a definite relationship to one another. When done properly, a textual message of this kind becomes a valuable means of enforcing spiritual truth. Take, for instance, Acts 20:19-20 and 1 Corinthians 15:10. Note how both of these references deal with the ministry of the Apostle Paul:

> "I served the Lord with great humility and with tears, although I was severely tested by the plots of the Jews. You know that I have not hesitated to preach anything that would be helpful to you but have taught you publicly and from house to house" (Acts 20:19-20).

> "But by the grace of God I am what I am, and his grace to me was not without effect. No, I worked harder than all of them—yet not I, but the grace of God that was with me" (1 Corinthians 15:10).

    I. It should be a humble ministry, "I served the Lord with great humility."
    II. It should be an earnest ministry, "with . . . tears."
    III. It should be a teaching ministry, "have taught you publicly."
    IV. It should be a divinely-empowered ministry, "I worked . . . the grace of God."
    V. It should be a faithful ministry, "I have not hesitated to preach anything . . . to you."
    VI. It may have to be a laborious ministry, "I worked harder than all of them."

A suitable title for this outline would be, "The Ministry That Counts."

Series of Textual Sermons

With a little thought, textual messages can easily be arranged in a series. We may select a general topic and choose several texts which deal with it. Each text then becomes the basis of a textual message. For our first example we choose the word "come" as the basis of a series on "God's Best Secrets." Observe that each text in the series contains the word "come":

> "The Secret of Discipleship," based on Matthew 19:21, "Jesus answered, 'If you want to be perfect, go, sell your possessions and give to the poor, and you will have treasure in heaven. Then come, follow me.' "

> "The Secret of Rest," based on Matthew 11:28, "Come to me, all you who are weary and burdened, and I will give you rest."

> "The Secret of Confidence," based on Matthew 14:28-29, " 'Lord, if it's you,' Peter replied, 'tell me to come to you on the water.' 'Come,' he said. Then Peter got down out of the boat and walked on the water to Jesus."

> "The Secret of Satisfaction," based on John 7:37, "On the last and greatest day of the Feast, Jesus stood and said in a loud voice, 'If a man is thirsty, let him come to me and drink.' "

Another series of textual messages may be entitled, "The Praises of Christ's Enemies." As we note the statements concerning Christ which were made by His enemies as recorded in the Gospels, it is significant that some of the most remarkable declarations about Christ were made by men who either opposed or rejected Him. We list four such statements with sermon titles for a series on "The Praises of Christ's Enemies."

> "This man welcomes sinners and eats with them" (Luke 15:2). Title: "Jesus, the Friend of Sinners."

> "Here is this man performing many miraculous signs" (John 11:47). Title: "Jesus, the Worker of Miracles."

> " 'He saved others,' they said, 'but he can't save himself!' " (Matthew 27:42). Title: "Jesus, the Savior Who Could Not Save Himself."

> " 'I find no basis for a charge against this man' " (Luke 23:4). Title: "Jesus, the Perfect Man."

There are at least seven occasions in the Bible where the Lord addresses an individual by name twice in succession. Repetition in Scripture is a means of emphasis, and the preacher may utilize some or all of these calls for a series of interesting messages. Here are four of these double calls of God:

> "But the angel of the LORD called out to him from heaven, 'Abraham! Abraham!' 'Here I am,' he replied. 'Do not lay a hand on the boy,' he said. 'Do not do anything to him. Now I know that you fear God, because you have not withheld from me your son, your only son' " (Genesis 22:11-12). Title: "The Call to Trust."

> "When the LORD saw that he had gone over to look, God called to him from within the bush, 'Moses, Moses!' And Moses said, 'Here I am.' 'Do not come any closer,' God said. 'Take off your sandals, for the place where you are standing is holy ground' " (Exodus 3:4-5). Title: "The Call to Service."

> " 'Martha, Martha,' the Lord answered, 'you are worried and upset about many things, but only one thing is needed. Mary has chosen what is better, and it will not be taken away from her' " (Luke 10:41-42). Title: "The Call to Communion."

> "He fell to the ground and heard a voice say to him, 'Saul, Saul, why do you persecute me?' " (Acts 9:4). Title: "The Call to Surrender."

Every minister should be familiar with the "Seven Last Words," that is, the statements made by Christ as He hung upon the cross. It is important for the homilist to have at least two or three messages based upon these statements of Christ, and as time permits he should try to develop a series of pre-Easter messages on all of these "Seven Last Words." The series may be headed, "Words from the Cross," with sermon titles such as these:

> "Intercession at the Cross," based on Luke 23:33-34, "When they came to the place called The Skull, there they crucified him, along with the criminals—one on his right, the other on his left. Jesus said, 'Father, forgive them, for they do not know what they are doing.' "

"Salvation at the Cross," based on Luke 23:42-43, "Then he said, 'Jesus, remember me when you come into your kingdom.' Jesus answered him, 'I tell you the truth, today you will be with me in paradise.' "

"Affection at the Cross," based on John 19:25-27, "Near the cross of Jesus stood his mother, his mother's sister, Mary the wife of Clopas, and Mary of Magdala. When Jesus saw his mother there, and the disciple whom he loved standing nearby, he said to his mother, 'Dear woman, here is your son,' and to the disciple, 'Here is your mother.' "

"Forsaken at the Cross," based on Matthew 27:46, "About the ninth hour Jesus cried out in a loud voice, *'Eloi, Eloi, lama sabachthani?'*—which means,'My God, my God, why have you forsaken me?' "

"Thirst at the Cross," based on John 19:28-29, "Later, knowing that all was now completed, and so that the Scripture would be fulfilled, Jesus said, 'I am thirsty.' A jar of wine vinegar was there, so they soaked a sponge in it, put the sponge on a stalk of the hyssop plant, and lifted it to Jesus' lips."

"Triumph at the Cross," based on John 19:30, "When he had received the drink, Jesus said, 'It is finished.' With that, he bowed his head and gave up his spirit."

"Commitment at the Cross," based on Luke 23:46, "Jesus called out with a loud voice, 'Father, into your hands I commit my spirit.' When he had said this, he breathed his last."

The book of Psalms will provide appropriate texts for a succession of sermons on "Common Ills of Humanity." For a sermon on depression, we may choose Psalm 42:11; for one on fear, Psalm 56:3; for another on guilt, Psalm 51:2-3; for a discourse on trouble, Psalm 25:16-17; and for a message on disappointment, Psalm 41:9-10. The same book can supply material for a group of messages on "The Benedictions in the Psalms," each based on the phrase "blessed is the man." One message may be called "The Blessedness of the Godly Man" from Psalm 1:1; another, "The Blessedness of the Forgiven Man" from Psalm 32:1-2. Reference to an unabridged concordance will provide the necessary information for other beatitudes in the Psalms.

Another series may be on "The Claims of Christ," drawn from the "I AMs" of the Lord Jesus in the Gospel of John, such as, "I am the bread of life," "I am the good shepherd," and "I am the way and the truth and the life."

The examples given above should be sufficient to indicate to the student how it is possible to formulate a plan of textual sermons from the Scriptures. Preaching in serial order gives continuity of thought to the preacher's sermons and is likely to stir much interest when the sermons are properly arranged and developed.

Conclusion

As we finish our discussion of the textual sermon, let us note one more textual outline. This one is based on 2 Corinthians 5:21 which reads: "God made him who had no sin to be sin for us, so that in him we might become the righteousness of God." The reader will observe in this example that in accordance with the definition of a textual outline the main divisions are drawn wholly from the text itself whereas the subdivisions are not necessarily taken directly from the text but are based on other scriptural sources.

Title: "The Savior of Sinners"
Subject: Characteristics of our Savior.
  I. He is a perfect Savior
     1. Who never sinned against God or man, John 18:38; 19:4, 6; Matthew 27:3-4; 1 Peter 2:22.
     2. Who was inwardly as well as outwardly perfect, Matthew 17:5; Hebrews 10:5-7; 1 Peter 1:19.
  II. He is a vicarious Savior
     1. Who bore our guilt upon the cross, Isaiah 53:6; 1 Peter 2:24.
     2. Who died to save us from our sins, Romans 4:25; 1 Peter 3:18.
  III. He is a justifying Savior
     1. Who is the means by grace of our justification before God, Romans 3:24.
     2. Who becomes our righteousness through faith in His redemptive work, Romans 3:21-22; 5:1; 1 Corinthians 1:30.

The beginner usually finds considerable difficulty in preparing textual outlines. This is due to the fact that formulating a textual outline often requires careful examination of the natural divisions of the text. However, any such difficulties should not be a deterrent to the student but should rather be a challenge to him to acquire the ability to develop textual sermons. As he applies himself to his task he will gain, perhaps imperceptibly, skill in discovering the outline which seems to be hidden in the text, and he will also become more and more intimately acquainted with precious portions of the Word of God.

But there is another rewarding feature for the diligent worker in textual sermons—a compensation which comes at the time of delivering the message. As the young preacher unfolds the riches contained in his text he will observe how it delights the spiritually-minded among God's people to receive the spiritual nourishment which even a single verse of Scripture provides.

EXERCISES

1. Prepare a textual outline on 1 Thessalonians 2:8, giving the title, subject, and main divisions. In this, and all other textual outlines to be prepared, write after each main division that portion of the text which supports each main division.

2. Prepare a textual outline on Titus 2:11-13, giving the title, topic, and main divisions. As instructed above, quote after the main divisions the portions of the text which apply to the respective main divisions.

3. Find your own text and, by use of the method of multiple approach (see p. 41), construct two outlines from the same text. Write out your text in full and indicate the title, theme, and main divisions in each outline.

4. Use only the second half of Psalm 51:7 as your text and formulate an outline from it, stating the title, subject, and main divisions.

5. Find suitable texts (the texts should not be more than three verses) for each of the following occasions:

    1. A New Year's day sermon.
    2. A Father's day sermon.
    3. A dedicatory service for a baby.
    4. A funeral message for a Christian parent.
    5. A wedding service.
    6. An evangelistic service.
    7. A missionary message.
    8. A young people's meeting.
    9. A Sunday morning worship service.
    10. A message for Christian workers.

Write out each text in full, in the order given above, and give a suitable title for each.

6. Construct a textual outline on Daniel 6:10, indicating the title, subject, and main divisions.

7. In Genesis 39:20-21 there is a purposeful contrast between verses 20 and 21. Make an outline on the passage, stating the title, subject, and main divisions.

8. The first part of Exodus 33:11 reads, "The LORD would speak to Moses face to face, as a man speaks with his friend"; Deuteronomy 34:10 reads, "Since then no prophet has risen in Israel like Moses, whom the LORD knew face to face." Combine these two texts as though they were one and prepare a textual outline, giving the title, subject, and main divisions of the combined verses.

9. This chapter contains the titles for a series of four messages on "The Praises of Christ's Enemies"; copy these titles and add three more such "praises," giving the text and a title for each.

10. List a series of five texts suitable for communion services. Quote each text in its entirety and give an appropriate title for each. Prepare a textual outline, using the first text in your series of communion messages, giving the title, subject, and main divisions.

BIBLIOGRAPHY

Baumann, J. Daniel. *An Introduction to Contemporary Preaching*. Grand Rapids, Michigan: Baker Book House, 1972, pp. 102.

Broadus, John A. *On the Preparation and Delivery of Sermons*. Revised by Jesse B. Weatherspoon. New York: Harper & Brothers, 1944, Part II, Chapter 3.

Etter, John W. *The Preacher and His Sermon*. Dayton, Ohio: United Brethren Publishing House, 1902, pp. 201-202.

Gibbs, Alfred P. *The Preacher and His Preaching*. Third Edition. Ft. Dodge, Iowa: Walterick Printing Company, n.d., Chapter 20.

Macpherson, Ian. *The Burden of the Lord*. Nashville, Tennessee: Abingdon Press, 1955, pp. 88-89, 95-97.

Pattison, T. Harwood. *The Making of the Sermon*. Philadelphia: The American Baptist Publication Society, 1898, Chapter 5.

Perry, Lloyd M. *A Manual for Biblical Preaching*. Grand Rapids, Michigan: Baker Book House, 1965, pp. 146-197.

Riley, W. B. *The Preacher & His Preaching*. Wheaton, Illinois: Sword of the Lord Publishers, 1948, Chapter 7.

Unger, Merrill F. *Principles of Expository Preaching*. Grand Rapids, Michigan: Zondervan Publishing House, 1955, pp. 52-54.

White, Douglas M. *The Excellence of Exposition*. Neptune, New Jersey: Loizeaux Brothers, Inc., 1977, pp. 66-68.

Whitesell, Faris Daniel. *Evangelistic Preaching and the Old Testament*. Chicago: Moody Press, 1947, Chapter 11.

3. THE EXPOSITORY SERMON

Definition of an Expository Sermon

The expository sermon is the most effective form of pulpit address because, above all other types of discourse, it eventually produces a Bible-taught congregation. By expounding a passage of holy writ the minister fulfills the primary function of preaching, namely, to interpret Biblical truth to men (which cannot always be claimed for other types of sermons).

An expository sermon is one in which a more or less extended portion of Scripture is interpreted in relation to one theme or subject. The bulk of the material for the sermon is drawn directly from the passage and the outline consists of a series of progressive ideas centered around that one main idea.

As we examine this definition, we note in the first place that the expository sermon is based on "a more or less extended portion of Scripture." The passage may consist of a few verses or it may extend through a whole chapter or even further. For our purposes, we shall use throughout the discussion of the expository sermon a minimum of four verses, but we shall not place any limit on the maximum number of verses.

The definition also declares that a more or less extended portion of Scripture is interpreted "in relation to one theme or subject." The group of verses which forms the basis of an expository sermon is termed by Dr. James M. Gray, "an expository unit." More specifically, the expository unit consists of a number of verses out of which a central idea emerges. The expository sermon then, like the topical and textual, is centered around one dominant theme, but in the case of the expository message this comes from a number of verses instead of emerging from a single verse or two.

The definition states further that "the bulk of the material for the sermon is drawn directly from the passage." Not only should the leading ideas of the passage be brought out in an expository discourse, but the details should also be suitably explained and be made to furnish the chief materials of the sermon. It follows therefore that when we derive all the subdivisions, as well as the main divisions, from the same portion of Scripture and when all these divisions are properly expounded or interpreted the whole sermon outline is thereby based directly upon the passage.

The theme of the passage must ever be kept in mind throughout an expository sermon, and as that one main idea is developed out of the passage there should follow in the outline a series of progressive ideas all related to the theme. This will no doubt become clearer to the reader as he observes the examples in this chapter.

There is a significant expression in our definition which must not be overlooked. Note the first part of the definition again: "an expository sermon is one in which a more or less extended portion of Scripture is interpreted." Consider the last few words carefully. In exposition we are to unfold the meaning or elucidate the Scriptures. This is the very genius of expository preaching—to make the meaning of the Scriptures clear and plain. To accomplish this, however, we need to study the details thoroughly in order to master them (see Chapter 9). But always remember that the elucidation of a passage of Scripture must have as its objective the relating of the past to the present, or showing the relevance of the truth to the contemporary scene.

Difference between a Textual and an Expository Sermon

It is well at this point to understand clearly the difference between a textual and an expository sermon.

We have shown previously that a textual sermon is one in which the main divisions are derived from a text consisting of a brief portion of Scripture, usually a single verse or two, or sometimes even a part of a verse. In the case of an expository sermon, the text may be a more or less extended portion of Scripture, sometimes covering a whole chapter or even much more than that, with the divisions drawn from the passage. Again, in the textual form of address, the divisions which are derived from the text are used as a line of suggestion. That is to say, they indicate the trend of thought to be followed in the sermon, allowing the preacher to draw his subdivisions or ideas for the development of the outline from any other part of Scripture consonant with a logical development of the thoughts contained in the main divisions. The expository sermon, on the other hand, makes it necessary for the homilist to derive all the subdivisions, as well as the main divisions, from the same unit of Scripture which he proposes to expound. In this way, the entire sermon consists of an exposition of a certain portion of Scripture and the passage becomes the very warp and woof of the discourse. In other words, the body of thought is drawn directly from the text, and the sermon is definitely interpretative.

As we stated in Chapter 2, there are some texts which, though comprising only a single verse or two, are so detailed that we may derive not only the main divisions but also all the subdivisions from the same passage. When this is done, the textual sermon is thus treated expositorily, and the whole discourse becomes an exposition of the text.

Examples of Expository Sermon Outlines

For our first example of an expository sermon outline we use Ephesians 6:10-18. In order that the student may follow the procedure used in constructing the outline, we urge that he first read the passage repeatedly and study it carefully before observing the outline below. We suggest that he also do this in his approach to each of the other outlines in this chapter and in all the successive chapters in this volume.

Even a brief consideration of Ephesians 6:10-18 will bring us to the conclusion that Paul is dealing here with the spiritual warfare of the believer and seeking to acquaint him with various features related to that conflict so that he may become a successful warrior.

If we consider the passage with close attention we shall see that in verses 10 through 13 the Apostle is encouraging the believer to be courageous and firm in the face of overwhelming spiritual foes. In other words, Paul refers in these verses to the Christian's morale. Verses 14 through 17 have to do with the various pieces of armor which the Lord has provided for the saint in the face of superhuman enemies. We therefore conclude that this section may be described as the Christian's armor. But before the Apostle finishes his discussion of the features involved in this spiritual warfare, he adds verse 18. Here he tells the believer, clad with the armor of God, that he must also give himself to persistent prayer in the Spirit and to constant intercession for all saints. Obviously, then, the final feature which Paul discusses in connection with this spiritual conflict is the Christian's prayer life. We are now ready to set forth in outline form the three main features which the Apostle discusses in connection with the believer's spiritual warfare:

    I. The Christian's morale, vv. 10-13.
   II. The Christian's armor, vv. 14-17.
  III. The Christian's prayer life, v. 18.

As we examine verses 10 through 13 more closely, we see that there are at least two aspects of the Christian's morale which the great Apostle stresses. To begin with, he urges the believer in spiritual conflict to place his confidence in the Lord and, having done so, to "stand firm" (see verses 11, 13, and 14a), no matter how great and powerful the enemies may appear to be. In the development of the expository outline we thus discover two subdivisions under "The Christian's morale." First, the Christian's morale should be high, and second, the Christian's morale should be steadfast.

When we approach the second section of the expository unit, namely, verses 14 through 17, we observe that the various pieces of the Christian's armor may be grouped into two main parts, the first pieces of equipment being the defensive armor and the last item on the list, the sword of the spirit, the offensive armor. Incidentally, it is interesting to note that the armor provides no protection for the back for the obvious reason that the Lord does not intend that His soldiers should ever turn and run in the day of battle.

The final section, verse 18, can also be subdivided into two parts. Careful attention to the first portion of the verse reveals that the Christian's prayer life should be persistent, and the second half of the verse discloses that his prayer life should consist of prayer in behalf of others.

Having made these observations, we are now ready to present the outline in full, with all the subdivisions as well as the main divisions drawn from the same passage. In keeping with the portion of Scripture to be expounded, we also select as our title for the outline, "The Good Fight of Faith."

    Title: "The Good Fight of Faith"
    Subject: Features relating to the believer's spiritual warfare.

    I. The Christian's morale, vv. 10-14a.
       1. It should be high, v. 10.
       2. It should be steadfast, vv. 11-14a.
    II. The Christian's armor, vv. 14-17.
       1. It should be defensive in character, vv. 14-17a.
       2. It should also be offensive in character, v. 17b.
   III. The Christian's prayer life, v. 18.
       1. It should be persistent, v. 18a.
       2. It should be intercessory, v. 18b.

If the sermon is to be truly expository, the subdivisions as well as the main divisions of the outline must be interpreted or properly explained. In this way the preacher fulfills the purpose of exposition, which is to draw the bulk of the material for his sermon out of the passage and to expound its contents in relation to one main theme.

For a second example of an expository sermon we select Exodus 14:1-14. We cannot go into all the processes of exegesis for this passage here, but until this task is done we are not in a position to undertake the construction of an expository sermon.

However, once we have made the necessary careful examination of the text, we are ready to work on an outline of the passage. We choose as our main point of emphasis, lessons to be derived from "Wit's End Corner," for it is obvious that, like the people of Israel at the Red Sea, we also sometimes find ourselves in a predicament where there seems to be no way of escape or deliverance. With this idea in mind, we then draw several lessons or truths from the text, as follows:

    I. "Wit's End Corner" is the place to which God sometimes leads us, vv. 1-4a.
    II. "Wit's End Corner" is the place where God tests us, vv. 4b-9.
   III. "Wit's End Corner" is the place where we sometimes fail the Lord, vv. 10-12.
   IV. "Wit's End Corner" is the place where God undertakes for us, vv. 13-14.

If the reader is to learn how these truths have been derived from the text, he should turn to the passage once more, and observe the development of the outline point by point.

Exodus 14:1-14 not only yields four main lessons, but also furnishes all the subheads for the outline. The text thus provides the bulk of the material necessary for the sermon.

We now present the outline on Exodus 14:1-14, showing the subdivisions under their respective main divisions:

Title: "Wit's End Corner"
   I. "Wit's End Corner" is the place to which God some-
      times leads us, vv. 1-4a.
      1. By specific command, vv. 1-2.
      2. For His own purposes, vv. 3-4a.
  II. "Wit's End Corner" is the place where God tests us,
      vv. 4b-9.
      1. In the path of obedience, v. 4b.
      2. By allowing overwhelming circumstances to over-
      take us, vv. 5-9.
  III. "Wit's End Corner" is the place where we sometimes
      fail the Lord, vv. 10-12.
      1. By our unbelief, v. 10.
      2. By our complaints, vv. 11-12.
  IV. "Wit's End Corner" is the place where God under-
      takes for us, vv. 13-14.
      1. At the right moment, v. 13.
      2. By taking control, v. 14.

Once again, we advise the serious student to compare the outline above with the text, and see for himself how the subpoints, like the main divisions, have all been suggested from the passage at hand.

We base our third example of an expository sermon outline on Luke 19:1-10. Having first made an exegetical study of the passage, we approach these verses using the winning of Zacchaeus, the "lost" man, as our theme. What does this portion of Scripture say in connection with our subject? As we examine it carefully we discover the following main facts about the winning of Zacchaeus, the "lost" man, and these facts provide us with the analysis of the passage.

     I. The search for Zacchaeus, vv. 1-4.
    II. The befriending of Zacchaeus, vv. 5-7.
   III. The salvation of Zacchaeus, vv. 8-10.

We examine the passage more carefully now and consider what the text contains with respect to these main points. The result of our further study reveals, under the first main division, two features in connection with the search for Zacchaeus:

     1. The search for Zacchaeus which Jesus made was
      conducted in an unobtrusive manner.
     2. The visit by Christ to Jericho stirred Zacchaeus'
      interest to see Him.

Under the second main heading, we discern two other features:

    1. Jesus befriended Zacchaeus, the man who was friendless (see v. 7) by inviting Himself into his home!

    2. The self-invitation of Jesus to the home of Zacchaeus had a two-fold effect—a happy effect upon Zacchaeus, but an unpleasant one upon the people of Jericho.

Under the third main division, we find the following facts:

    1. The salvation of Zacchaeus is indicated by the extraordinary change which came over him immediately.

    2. The salvation of Zacchaeus is declared by Christ in unmistakable terms.

It is evident from the contents of the passage that Zacchaeus, the lost sinner, found a friend in Jesus or, better still, that Jesus found him! We therefore select for the title of the message, "Won by Love."

We are now ready to put our outline together:

Title: "Won by Love"
- I. The search for Zacchaeus, vv. 1-4.
  - 1. The manner of it, v. 1.
  - 2. The effect of it, vv. 2-4.
- II. The befriending of Zacchaeus, vv. 5-7.
  - 1. The manner of it, v. 5.
  - 2. The effects of it, vv. 6-7.
- III. The salvation of Zacchaeus, vv. 8-10.
  - 1. The evidence of it, v. 8.
  - 2. The declaration of it, vv. 9-10.

As we look at the outline we can see that there is a natural progression of ideas, all related to the winning of Zacchaeus, climaxed by the salvation of the chief of the publicans.

The Mechanical Layout of a Scripture Passage

Many Bible students find it helpful to prepare a mechanical layout of a Scripture passage in order to discover its structure. To construct a mechanical layout, we write down the main statements of the text in a way which will make the text most meaningful to us. We should distinguish between primary and subordinate clauses by indenting, placing series of words, phrases, or clauses in arrangements which will emphasize their relationships. We should also give prominence to main verbs, and important words or ideas, including significant connectives such as now, for, and, but, then, and therefore.

In accordance with this procedure, we have reproduced the text of Luke 19:1-10 below. Observe that this layout of the text assists us not only to analyze the passage and see its main parts but also to observe items in the passage which would otherwise escape our attention.

v. 1   Jesus entered Jericho
       and was passing through.

v. 2   A man was there   by the name of Zacchaeus;
                      he was a chief tax collector and
                        was wealthy.

v. 3   He wanted to see who Jesus was,
           but being a short man
           he could not,
             because of the crowd.

v. 4   So
     he ran ahead and
       climbed a sycamore-fig tree
      to see him,
           since Jesus was coming that way.

v. 5 When Jesus reached the spot,   "Zacchaeus,
        he looked up and   come down immediately.
          said to him,   I must stay at your house
                         today."

v. 6   So
     he came down at once and
       welcomed him gladly.

v. 7   All the people saw this and   "He has gone to be the guest
           began to mutter,   of a 'sinner.' "

v. 8   But
     Zacchaeus stood up   "Look, Lord!
          and   Here and now
          said to   I give half of my possessions
          the Lord,   to the poor, and
                         if I have cheated anybody
                           out of anything,
                     I will pay back
                        four times the amount."

v. 9 Jesus said to him,
  "Today salvation has come
     to this house,
     because
   this man, too, is a son of Abraham.
v. 10 For the Son of Man came to seek ⎤
      and to save   ⎦ what was lost."

Following is another mechanical layout, this one of 1 Thessalonians 4:13-18, which shows how we discovered the structure of the passage from the syntactical relationships between the main and subordinate sentences as well as from the relationships between clauses and phrases in the passage.

Subject: Our hope concerning the dead in Christ.

I. Counsel con- 13 Brothers,
 cerning our   we do not want you
 hope, v. 13.   to be ignorant about those who fall asleep,
         or
        to grieve like the rest of men,
             who have no hope.

II. Bases for our 14 We believe that Jesus died
 hope, vv. 14-15.   and
          rose again
          and so
 1. The death   we believe that God will bring with Jesus
  and resurrec-   those who have . . .
  tion of   . . . fallen asleep
  Christ.   in him.
 2. The word of 15 According to the Lord's own word,
  the Lord.   we tell you that
        we who are still alive,
         who are left till the coming of the Lord,
         will certainly not precede
            those who have . . .
            . . . fallen asleep.

III. Fulfillment of 16 For the Lord himself will come down from heaven,
 our hope,   with a loud command,
 vv. 16-17.   with the voice of the archangel
         and
 1. The coming   with the trumpet call of God,
  of the Lord.   and

```
  2. The raising         the dead in Christ will rise
     of the dead            first.
     in Christ.

  3. The snatch-  17 After that,
     ing up of the       we who are still alive
     living saints.         and
                                    are left
                                    will be caught up with them
                                                    in the clouds
                                                    to meet the Lord
                                                    in the air.
                            And so we will be with the Lord forever.
IV. Exhortation   18 Therefore
    relating to          encourage each other
    our hope, v.18.                    with these words.
```

Forms of Discourse Erroneously Regarded
as Expository Sermons

Because two types of sermons are sometimes mistakenly regarded as exposition, it may be well to mention them. As we define these forms of discourse it will be evident to the reader that they differ in one or more important respects from the expository sermon.

1. The Biblical homily.

The Biblical homily is a running commentary on a passage of Scripture, long or short, explained and applied verse by verse, or phrase by phrase. Usually the Biblical homily has no homiletical structure but consists of a series of disconnected remarks on the text, with no attempt to show the relationship of the parts of the text to each other or to the whole—that is, without structural unity or cohesion.

2. The exegetical lecture.

An exegetical lecture is a detailed commentary on the meaning of a text, with or without logical order or practical application. It is important that the homilist be able to make an exegetical study of the Word of God. However, what the congregation desires is not the process of study, but the results. Exegesis draws out the hidden meaning of a passage; exposition sets forth that meaning in an appropriate and effective order.

Some writers on homiletics are very caustic in their remarks concerning the use of the Biblical homily and the exegetical lecture. However, certain preachers seem to possess the gift of finding in the text such features as require emphasis or elucidation so that their messages, though consisting wholly of disjointed sermonettes, are a great blessing to the people of God.

Basic Principles for the Preparation of Expository Outlines

1. Any passage under consideration should be carefully studied to understand its meaning and to obtain the subject of the text.

The discovery of the theme in a passage is one of the first tasks in the development of an expository outline. Once this is obtained, it usually simplifies the development of the outline. In order to find the main topic in the passage, however, it is necessary to give diligent study to the text (see Chapter 9).

The importance of a thorough study of a passage cannot be overemphasized. It gives the preacher an insight into the Scriptures which he can obtain in no other way. Cursory, haphazard, or slipshod methods will never make a true expositor. The ministry of teaching the Bible requires that the man of God give his heart and soul to this work. It will mean that he will have to spend hours of prayerful and painstaking research in sustained concentration of thought to learn the intent of the sacred writer and the true meaning of the passage.

As a result of such study he will gain fresh, encouraging insight into the purpose of the passage. The whole text will often light up before him so that he may see truths of which he was formerly unaware.

In the process of his investigation of the text, he will sooner or later begin to observe the main subject which runs through the expository unit, and the natural parts into which the passage may be divided.

2. Significant words or phrases in the text may indicate or form the main divisions of the outline.

We have already pointed out that in many passages there is a special purpose for the repetition of various significant words or phrases, and it is evident that some of these words or phrases in a given passage occur where they are to suggest the writer's movement of thought as he passes from one important idea to another.

To show this we take one example from the Epistle to the Ephesians. Read Ephesians 1:3-14, and note the following:

> v. 6—"to the praise of his glorious grace"
> v. 12—"for the praise of his glory"
> v. 14—"to the praise of his glory"

The repetition of these phrases leads us to inquire if the Spirit of God intended that each of these was indicative of a division of thought. As we study Ephesians 1:3-14 with this in mind, we learn that the Apostle deals here with God's work in redemption. The first section which concludes with verse 6 describes the work of God the Father in our redemption; the second section which ends with verse 12 tells of the work of God the Son; and the third section which consists of verses 13 and 14 sets forth the work of God the Holy Spirit. Thus the work of redemption is ascribed to the three persons of the Trinity. No wonder the Apostle exclaims as he finishes each section, "to the praise of his glory"!

3. The outline may be drawn from the expository unit in an order different from that of the text.

Generally speaking it is well that the main divisions and subdivisions follow the precise order of the verses in the Bible, but this is not always necessary. There may be occasions, for the sake of logical or chronological order, when the main divisions or subdivisions should be placed in a sequence different from that in the text.

Note the following outline on Exodus 12:1-13, where the fourth and fifth main divisions do not follow the sequence of the verses in the expository unit:

> Title: "The Lamb of God"
> Subject: Features of the passover lamb which prefigure
>   Christ, the Passover Lamb.
>   I. It was a divinely-appointed lamb, 12:1-3.
>   II. It was a perfect lamb, 12:5.
>   III. It was a slain lamb, 12:6.
>   IV. It was a redeeming lamb, 12:7, 12-13.
>   V. It was a sustaining lamb, 12:8-11.

4. The important truths suggested by the passage may form the main divisions of the outline.

Outlines of this type will generally be drawn from historical and prophetical Scriptures, taking from the factual material the main spiritual truths or lessons which the facts seem to suggest or illustrate. These spiritual truths or principles then become the main divisions of the outline.

We use as an example the historical event of the flood (the references are to Genesis, chapters 6-7):

Title: "The God with Whom We Have to Do"
Subject: Truths about God in relation to His dealings with men.
    I. He is the moral governor of the universe, 6:1-7, 11-13.
       1. Who takes notice of the deeds of men, 6:1-6, 11-12.
       2. Who pronounces judgment upon men for their guilt, 6:7, 13.
    II. He is the God of grace, 6:3, 8-22.
       1. Who provides a means of escape from the judgment for sin, 6:8-22.
       2. Who extends His mercy toward the guilty, 6:3.
    III. He is the God of faithfulness, 7:1-24.
       1. Who fulfills His Word regarding judgment, 7:11-24.
       2. Who keeps His promises to His own, 7:1-10, 23.

Let us note a second example. This one is from the book of Obadiah, a book of only 21 verses which is a prophecy about the destruction of Edom. As we consider the text we discover that it contains a two-fold revelation of the character of God, as follows:

    I. He is a God of justice, vv. 1-16.
       1. Who judges men for their pride, vv. 1-9.
       2. Who judges men for their violence, vv. 10-16.
    II. He is a God of grace, vv. 17-21.
       1. Who brings deliverance to His people, vv. 17, 21.
       2. Who brings His own into their possessions, vv. 17-21.

5. Two or three more or less extended passages from various parts of Scripture may be put together to form the basis of an expository outline.

According to this principle the expository unit does not necessarily have to consist of a single passage where the verses run together consecutively, but when two or three passages—brief or extended—are definitely related to each other they may be treated as though they were one.

The fellowship offering, translated in the New American Standard Bible as "a sacrifice of peace offerings" and described in the book of Leviticus, is an example of this. The first description of it is in chapter 3:1-17, and we find further information about the peace offering in Chapter 7, verses 11-15 and 28-32. In order therefore to obtain a complete picture of the regulations for the peace offering we put the three passages together, and as a result we construct the following outline (to be applied by typology to Christ and the believer):

Title: "Peace with God"
Subject: Regulations relating to the reconciliation of a sinner with God.
   I. The manner in which reconciliation was obtained, 3:1-17.
     1. By a divinely-appointed sacrifice, 3:1, 6, 12.
     2. By the identification of the sinner with the victim, 3:2, 7-8, 12-13.
     3. By the death of the victim, 3:2, 7-8, 12-13.
   II. The method by which reconciliation could be enjoyed, 7:11-15, 28-32.
     1. By the participation in the feast by the offerer, 7:11-15.
     2. By the participation in the feast by the priests, 7:28-32.

Biographical sermons are often constructed along similar lines. Beginning with a somewhat extended Scripture passage which deals with a Bible character, we can check every other reference to that individual and thus obtain a composite picture for a biographical sermon outline.

We select Rahab for an example. The main description of Rahab's life is found in Joshua chapter 2 and Joshua 6:22-25, but with the help of a concordance we find that there are eight other references to Rahab, including Matthew 1:5. By further study we learn that three of these references, namely, Psalm 87:4, 89:10, and Isaiah 51:9, do not deal with the individual in whom we are interested. Instead, these three texts refer to a mythical sea monster spelled "Rahab" and the word is used in Scripture as an emblem of Egypt. We therefore give careful study to the other five occurrences of Rahab's name, as well as the two detailed accounts in Joshua. As a result of thorough observation, analysis, and classification of all these passages, we are able to prepare two biographical outlines on Rahab, based primarily on the accounts in the book of Joshua. The first of these outlines is analytical, and the second shows the truths or principles which can be learned from Rahab's "living faith":

Title: "From Sinner to Saint"
   I. Her tragic past, Joshua 2:1; Hebrews 11:31; James 2:25.
   II. Her faith in God, Hebrews 11:31.
   III. Her work of faith, Joshua 2:1-6; James 2:25.
   IV. Her blessed testimony, Joshua 2:9-13.
   V. Her wonderful influence, Joshua 2:18-19, 6:22-23, 25.
   VI. Her noble posterity, Matthew 1:5; cf. Ruth 4:21-22.

Title: "Living Faith"
   I. It is a faith which saves, Hebrews 11:31.
   II. It is a faith which works, Joshua 2:1-6; James 2:25.
   III. It is a faith which testifies, Joshua 2:9-13.
   IV. It is a faith which influences others, Joshua 2:18-19; 6:22-23, 25.
   V. It is a faith which results in abiding fruit, Matthew 1:5; cf. Ruth 4:21-22.

Another example for a biographical sermon is Lot, based on Genesis 13:2-13, 14:1-16, 19:1-38, and 2 Peter 2:6-8. By combining these passages we see a tragic example of a man who walked "in the counsel of the wicked," who stood "in the way of sinners," and who sat "in the seat of mockers."

Title: "The Cost of Worldliness"
   I. He chose his own way in life, Genesis 13:1-13.
   II. He persisted in his own choice, Genesis 14:1-16, 2 Peter 2:6-8.
   III. He suffered the consequences of his wrong choice, Genesis 19:1-38.

By applying the spiritual truths which we can derive from this biographical sketch, we come up with the following outline:

Title: "Gain or Loss: The Choice Is Ours"
   I. We may choose our own way in life.
      1. By making our own plans independently of God, as Lot did, Genesis 13:1-13.
      2. By disregarding the associations into which it may bring us, as Lot did, Genesis 13:12-13, 2 Peter 2:6-8.
   II. We may persist in our own way of life.
      1. By disregarding the voice of conscience, as Lot did, 2 Peter 2:6-8.

　　　　2. By disregarding the warnings God may graciously
　　　　　 give us, as Lot did after being rescued by
　　　　　 Abraham, Genesis 14:1-16.
　　III. We must suffer the consequences of our own evil
　　　　　 way.
　　　　1. By the possible loss of all we hold dear, as Lot
　　　　　 suffered, Genesis 19:15-16, 30-35.
　　　　2. By the loss of our own character, as Lot suffered,
　　　　　 Genesis 19:1, 6-8, 30-38.

Biographical sermons may proceed along other lines, and include items such as the individual's background, character, accomplishments, and influence.

A biographical sermon dealing with the character of an individual may sometimes contrast the positive and the negative aspects of the person's character. Drawing his facts from Mark 16:14-29 and Luke 23:6-12, Charles Haddon Spurgeon once preached a sermon of this kind in which he set forth the good and the bad traits of Herod the King.

　　I. Hopeful points in Herod's character.
　　　1. Although Herod did not possess justice, honesty,
　　　　 and purity, yet he had some respect for virtue,
　　　　 Mark 6:14-20.
　　　2. He protected John the Baptist because of his right-
　　　　 eousness and holiness, Mark 6:20.
　　　3. He enjoyed listening to John the Baptist, Mark
　　　　 6:20.
　　　4. His conscience was evidently greatly affected by
　　　　 what he heard from John the Baptist, Mark 6:20.
　　II. Flaws in Herod's character.
　　　1. Although he respected John the Baptist, he did not
　　　　 turn to John's Master, Mark 6:17-20.
　　　2. He did not love the message which came from
　　　　 John the Baptist, Mark 6:17-20.
　　　3. Although he "did many things" as a result of hear-
　　　　 ing John the Baptist, he remained under the sway
　　　　 of sin, Mark 6:21-26.
　　　4. He slew the man whom he respected, Mark
　　　　 6:26-27.
　　　5. He ended by mocking the Savior, Luke 23:6-12.

*6. By means of the method of multiple approach, we may treat a pas-
sage of Scripture in various ways and thus have two or more entirely different outlines on the same portion.*

We have already made reference to the method of multiple approach in connection with the treatment of textual sermons. What is true of the treatment of certain individual verses by means of this method is also true of the treatment of an expository unit.

Through the application of the method of multiple approach we may produce several outlines from the same passage, each different from the other. Each outline will be based upon one dominant idea which the Spirit of God may reveal to us to meet some special need or circumstance of the people to whom we minister, or to affect other conditions facing the church in the complex world in which we live.

If, however, we begin our sermon preparation by deciding on a purpose and then choosing a passage, we must never force ideas from the text to fit our aim. Instead, we should seek in the passage such concepts or truths as relate properly to our objective, and which are drawn naturally from the Scripture portion in support of our aim. Should we be unable to find in the passage that which may suit our objective, we will need to turn to some other text which will correspond with the aim of our discourse.

To demonstrate how a single expository unit may apply suitably to various situations, we show below four different outlines based on Matthew 14:14-21, which deals with the feeding of the five thousand. In seeking to discover the contents of the passage, we may consider the passage from the standpoint of each person or group of persons referred to in the text, including the persons of the Trinity. In so doing, we may ask ourselves questions such as the following: What does the passage reveal about them, and what does each person say, or do, or experience?

For our first illustration we shall take attributes of Jesus as the dominant thought of the expository unit:

> Title: "Our Peerless Lord"
> I. The compassion of Jesus, v. 14.
>   1. Shown in His interest in the multitude, v. 14.
>   2. Shown in His ministry to the multitude, v. 14.
> II. The gentleness of Jesus, vv. 15-18.
>   1. Shown in His gracious answer to His disciples, vv. 15-16.
>   2. Shown in His patient dealing with His disciples, vv. 17-18.
> III. The power of Jesus, vv. 19-21.
>   1. Manifested in the feeding of the multitude, vv. 19-21.
>   2. Exercised through the service of the disciples, vv. 14-21.

We now treat the same passage from the viewpoint of Christ as the supplier of our needs:

> Title: "Watch God Work"
>   I. Christ is concerned about our needs, vv. 14-16.
>   1. He has compassion upon us in our needs, vv. 14, 16.
>   2. He considers us in our needs when others do not care, vv. 15-16.
> II. Christ is not restricted by circumstances in the supplying of our needs, vv. 17-19.
>   1. He is not restricted by our lack of resources, vv. 17-18.
>   2. He is not restricted by any other lack, v. 19.
> III. Christ meets our needs, vv. 20-21.
>   1. He meets our needs abundantly, v. 20.
>   2. He provides much more than enough, vv. 20-21.

For our third outline, we regard the text from the standpoint of the problems we face:

> Title: "Solving Our Problems"
>   I. We are sometimes confronted with problems, vv. 14-15.
>   1. Of great proportions, vv. 14-15.
>   2. Of a pressing nature, v. 15.
>   3. Of impossible solution, humanly speaking, v. 15.
> II. Christ is abundantly able to solve our problems, vv. 16-22.
>   1. On condition that we yield our limited resources to Him, vv. 16-18.
>   2. On condition that we obey Him implicitly, vv. 19-22.

For our fourth illustration on this passage we shall base the outline on the idea of faith in connection with human need:

> Title: "Relating Faith to Human Need"
>   I. The challenge to faith, vv. 14-16.
>   1. The reason for the challenge, vv. 14-15.
>   2. The substance of the challenge, v. 16.
> II. The work of faith, vv. 17-19.
>   1. The first act of faith, vv. 17-18.
>   2. The second act of faith, v. 19.
> III. The reward of faith, vv. 20-21.
>   1. The blessedness of the reward, v. 20a.
>   2. The greatness of the reward, vv. 20b-21.

Thus we have noted four different ways in which Matthew 14:14-21 can be treated; each of these approaches may be used to fulfill a different aim or purpose.

7. *Note the context of the expository unit.*

We have learned in connection with the textual sermon that consideration of the context is essential to correct interpretation. This principle applies as much to the expository sermon as it does to the textual. A regard for the context, both immediate and remote, will assist us materially in the understanding of a passage and enable us to see the text in its proper light.

When the Apostle Paul reaches chapter 12 of his Epistle to the Romans he begins with the words, "Therefore, I urge you, brothers, in view of God's mercy." The word "therefore" throws us back to the preceding chapters and indicates that the practical exhortations which follow are based upon the vital doctrinal truths presented in the preceding section.

Lack of space forbids us to discuss this principle any further, but we wish to emphasize that the study of the context must always be carried out if we are to be faithful expositors of the Scriptures.

8. *Examine the historical and cultural background of the passage, wherever possible.*

Many portions of the Bible cannot be understood properly apart from their historical and cultural background. A sound interpretation of such passages will therefore be determined by an examination of the historical portions to which they are intimately related, and the cultural and geographical setting of the text.

This rule affects principally the major and minor prophets in their connection with the historical books of the Old Testament and the epistles of Paul in their relation to the Book of Acts. Take, for instance, the Book of Jonah. The message of this little book cannot be grasped without reference to 1 and 2 Kings, particularly chapter 14 of 2 Kings, from which we learn of the tragic condition of apostasy in the land of Israel in the days of Jonah. The Book of Jonah is then seen to be a call to the Northern Kingdom to repent, as Nineveh repented, and also to be a warning to God's people of terrible judgment to come upon them if they continued in their obstinate rebellion against God.

9. *The details of the text should be treated properly, but not exhaustively.*

We have already pointed out that in an expository sermon it is necessary to interpret the Scripture. This means that we must treat the details of the text in such a way as to unfold the meaning of the passage. It is this very feature which makes expository preaching distinctive as a means of communicating divine truth, for as the Word is explained, portion by portion, it enables the congregation to understand the meaning and purport which the text is intended to convey.

It is just at this point that the beginner needs to exercise special care. In an attempt to be thorough in his exposition, the young preacher often loses himself in such a mass of detail that his sermon becomes laden with exegetical material, but exegesis is not the ultimate purpose of a discourse. It is merely the means by which we discover the truths contained in a passage. The sermonizer should therefore keep in mind that while he must make the meaning of the passage clear to his people, an expository sermon has as its objective the presentation of only one main theme. Accordingly, the preacher ought to introduce into his message only such details as are relevant to that topic. Other material in the text, no matter how interesting or appealing, must be resolutely laid aside. The homilist should therefore realize that he can be true to his passage and his exposition can be positively Scriptural, even though many of the details are left out. Of course, the longer the passage chosen for exposition, the greater the need to discriminate as to the details to be omitted from the discourse.

We need to add, however, that sometimes details which at first sight seem to be insignificant may really be very important. It is not the big word, nor the peculiar term, that is always of chief value in exposition; in fact, the very gist of the truth which the homilist should express may be discovered in a tense, or a preposition, or some other seemingly insignificant part of speech.

10. The truths contained in the text must be related to the present day.

One of the criticisms which is commonly levelled at expository discourse is that the preacher who employs this method of address often fails to make the truths of Scripture pertinent to men in their present circumstances and environment. Only too often the sermonizer contents himself with a mere explanation of the text and does not show how the passage is applicable to current and vital issues. The fault does not lie with the Scriptures, for the Word of God is living and powerful and has constant and universal application to men in every age and in every walk of life. Rather, the blame must be laid at the door of the man who does not see the need or the importance of bringing divine truth to bear upon the problems and conditions which face men today. The homilist should therefore see to it that as he interprets the Scriptures he also draws therefrom the timeless truths suggested in the text for practical application to the congregation.

Because comparatively little has been written on the subject in texts on homiletics, we have devoted an entire chapter later in the book to a discussion of this important aspect of preaching, together with some suggestions to enable the student to make the truth relevant.

Common Errors on the Part of Would-be Expositors

It may take considerable time and much effort to acquire the ability to interpret the Scriptures properly and to learn what to include and what to exclude in the exposition of a passage. Because certain errors are commonly made by beginners in this connection, we draw special attention to these mistakes.

Some have difficulty in exposition because in the process of exegesis they become lost in a mass of detail and are unable to see the main message which emerges from the text. Each sermon then consists of so much detail that it becomes difficult for the listener to follow the message.

Others, forgetting the principle that interpretation is the basic feature in expository preaching, spend too much time in application instead of explanation, not realizing that the Holy Spirit will apply the Word of God to the hearts of men and women as the Scriptures are proclaimed with clarity and simplicity.

Another common mistake on the part of would-be expositors is that they allow themselves to become diverted from the passage to be expounded and wander off for some time on a tangent before turning to the text at hand.

Perhaps the most serious error is failing to interpret the passage correctly. This may sometimes be due to an inability to understand the text, but with so much excellent material available today there is hardly any excuse for the homilist to violate the principles of sound Bible hermeneutics.

Variety in Expository Preaching

It is probably obvious to the reader by this time that the method of expository discourse can cover a wide range. An expository unit may involve doctrine when the text deals with some of the fundamentals of the Christian faith. It may be devotional, containing teaching about a deeper walk with God. It might include ethics because much of the material in the Bible is ethical in character. On the other hand, it could be prophetic or distinctly typical in character, with the type being explained by its antitype. Again, it may be biographical or historical. Other expository units, primarily evangelistic in content, give special opportunity for the presentation of the claims of the Gospel.

Many chapters or portions of Scripture are so full and rich in the variety of material they contain that several of the features just mentioned can be included in one passage. Although the expository sermon must have one controlling idea, the development of the sermon may combine in one discourse such elements as the presentation of the Gospel, doctrinal teaching, and an exhortation or message of comfort to believers.

To give an idea of the variety of materials which can be touched upon in a discourse we present four illustrations of expository outlines. The first of these is based upon an historical portion of John's Gospel, namely, John 11:1-6, 19-44; the second is from the latter portion of Christ's parable on the prodigal son, but deals with the elder brother, Luke 15:25-32; the third is taken from Hebrew poetry, Psalm 23; and the fourth is derived from the epistles of Paul, Ephesians 4:30—5:2.

> Title: "The Best Friend"
> Text: John 11:1-6, 19-44.
> Subject: Jesus, the best friend we can have.
>   I. Jesus is a loving friend, vv. 3-5.
>   1. Who loves each one of us individually, vv. 3, 5.
>   2. Who nevertheless allows affliction to befall us, v. 3.
>   II. Jesus is an understanding friend, vv. 21-36.
>   1. Who understands our deepest woes, vv. 21-26, 32.
>   2. Who sympathizes in our deepest sorrows, vv. 33-36.
>   III. Jesus is a mighty friend, vv. 37-44.
>   1. Who can do miraculous things, v. 37.
>   2. Who performs His miracles when we meet His conditions, vv. 38-44.

Title: "The Pharisee: Yesterday and Today"
Text: Luke 15:25-32.
Subject: Features of pharisaism as seen in the elder brother's
         character.
    I. He was a self-righteous man, vv. 29-30.
      1. As indicated by his own claims of obedience,
        v. 29.
      2. As manifested by his attitude toward his brother,
        vv. 29-30.
   II. He was an unloving man, vv. 28-30.
      1. As indicated by his attitude toward his brother's
        return, v. 28.
      2. As indicated by his virtual disowning of his
        brother, v. 30.
  III. He was a fault-finding man, vv. 25-30.
      1. As indicated by the faults he found in his brother,
        v. 30.
      2. As shown by the faults he found in his father,
        vv. 27-30.
  IV. He was a stubborn man, vv. 28-32.
      1. As manifested by his refusal to go into the house,
        v. 28.
      2. As indicated by his persistent attitude, v. 29-32.

Note: Although the latter sermon outline appears to
lack any teaching of a positive, constructive nature,
quite the opposite is true in its development and conclusion.

Title: "The Psalm of Contentment"
Text: Psalm 23.
Subject: The bases for the contentment of the Lord's sheep.
    I. The sheep's Shepherd, v. 1.
      1. A divine Shepherd, v. 1.
      2. A personal Shepherd, v. 1.
   II. The sheep's provision, vv. 2-5.
      1. Rest, v. 2.
      2. Guidance, v. 3.
      3. Comfort, v. 4.
      4. Abundance, v. 5.
  III. The sheep's prospect, v. 6.
      1. A bright prospect for this life, v. 6.
      2. A blessed prospect for the hereafter, v. 6.

Title: "Walking in Love"
Text: Ephesians 4:31-5:2.
Subject: A true Christian disposition.
    I. It is marked by an absence of all ill-feeling, 4:31.
      1. Of every kind, v. 31.
      2. Of every degree, v. 31.
   II. It is marked by an attitude of forgiveness, 4:32.
      1. Toward one another, v. 32.

      2. In view of God's grace to us, v. 32.
   III. It is marked by an attitude of loving devotion, 5:1-2.
        1. In accordance with our sonship, v. 1.
        2. With a Christ-like love, v. 2.

Observe that in each of these outlines all the subdivisions are derived from the same passage of Scripture as their respective main divisions.

The student will recall that, according to its definition, the expository sermon is based on "a more or less extended portion of Scripture." The expository outlines presented so far are drawn from fairly brief passages, but variety in expository preaching may also be produced in sermons derived from more extensive portions. However, it is impossible for such a sermon to touch upon all the details contained in the text. Instead, the outline will have to deal only with some of the salient features of the passage. We show below an expository outline covering the First Epistle to the Thessalonians.

    Title: "The Church at Its Best"
    Text: 1 Thessalonians.
      I. Faith, 1:1-2:16.
        1. Which is based upon the Word of God, 1:2-5,
          9-10; 2:13.
        2. Which keeps the believers steadfast in the face of
          trial, 1:6; 2:14-16.
     II. Love, 2:17-4:12.
        1. Which believers show toward their elders in the
          faith, 3:6.
        2. Which believers show toward one another, 3:12;
          4:9-10.
   III. Hope, 4:13-5:28.
        1. Which is set upon the coming of the Lord for His
          own, 4:13-18; 5:9-10, 23.
        2. Which looks forward to the reunion with loved
          ones who have gone before, 4:13-18.

In John 12:41 we read that Isaiah "saw Jesus' glory and spoke about him." This statement in the Gospel of John directs our attention to the book of Isaiah, from which we derive the following basic outline:

    Title: "Beholding Christ's Glory"
    Subject: Predictions concerning Christ in the book of Isaiah.
      I. We behold Him in the mystery of His incarnation,
        7:14; 9:6.
     II. We behold Him in the wonder of His deity, 9:6.
   III. We behold Him in the lowliness of His servitude,
        42:1-7; 49:5-6; 50:4-10; 52:13; 53:12.
   IV. We behold Him in the agony of His vicarious sacri-

fice, 52:13-53:12.
V.   We behold Him in the glories of His coming king-
      dom, 11:1-16; 59:20-66:24.

Series of Expository Sermons

The expository method is admirably suited to the development of a series of expository messages. It is quite natural and normal for a preacher to continue for several weeks his expositions on an extended passage or to use expository units which are related to each other.

When a minister delivers a series of expository sermons skillfully, he accomplishes in the highest degree the ministry of teaching the Word of God to his people. He is thereby able to help his hearers observe the wholeness of a given book or of a large segment of Scripture, also the relationship of the parts to the whole, and the relationship of the parts of the book to one another. In addition to this, preaching of this kind gives continuity to a Bible-teaching ministry, and as passage after passage is unfolded successively to the congregation it enables them to progress in the knowledge of divine revelation.

There are various ways of developing a series of expository sermons. One of the most common is a series of expositions on a book of the Bible. The number of sermons in the course will depend upon the length of the book and also upon its contents. The purpose which the preacher aims to accomplish can also have a bearing upon how many messages will be in the series.

When it is desired to preach through a book, it is well to devote the first sermon to a panoramic view of the book. This will give the congregation a general idea of the scope and purpose of the book and enable them to follow with more understanding the various parts of the text as each section is unfolded from week to week.

However, the beginner should not attempt to deliver a series of messages on a Bible book until he has thoroughly mastered it and can think through its contents from the first to the last chapter.

The examples which follow will give the student an idea how a group of messages can be arranged on an entire book.

A series on the book of Jonah, beginning with a comprehensive message on the book as a whole, could contain titles such as the following:

"A Call to Repentance"—based on Jonah, chapters
        1-4.
"The Folly of Disobedience"—based on 1:1-16.
"Entombed in a Fish"—based on 1:17.
"Praying under Difficulties"—based on 2:1-10.
"When God Repented"—based on 3:1-10.
"Quarreling with God"—based on 4:1-11.

Robert R. Fritsch, once a professor of English Bible at Muhlenberg College, Allentown, Pennsylvania, also had a course of four connected titles on the book of Jonah which he arranged in alliterative style, based consecutively on its four chapters:

"The Prodigal Prophet."
"The Praying Prophet."
"The Preaching Prophet."
"The Pouting Prophet."

The book of Genesis, coupled with the list of men of faith in Hebrews 11, provides the substance for seven consecutive messages on "The Life of Faith." The progressive order in which these men of faith appear in the divine record is specially significant.

"Abel—The Sacrifice of Faith"
        (Genesis 4:1-5; Hebrews 11:4)
"Enoch—The Walk of Faith"
        (Genesis 5:21-24; Hebrews 11:5-6)
"Noah—The Work of Faith"
        (Genesis 6-7; Hebrews 11:7)
"Abraham—The Obedience of Faith"
        (Genesis 12-18; Hebrews 11:8-10)
"Isaac—The Vision of Faith"
        (Genesis 26-27; Hebrews 11:20)
"Jacob—The Discernment of Faith"
        (Genesis 27-35; Hebrews 11:21)
"Joseph—The Assurance of Faith"
        (Genesis 37-50; Hebrews 11:22)

The Epistle of Paul to the Philippians sets the stage for a series on "How to be Happy," based consecutively on its four chapters:

"Through Christ: Our Life."
"Through Christ: Our Example."
"Through Christ: Our Object."
"Through Christ: Our Satisfaction."

Besides a series of expository messages drawn from an entire book, a number of messages on a continuous topic can be developed by selecting a broad theme and using various passages related to that theme as the bases for the sermons in the group. "Miracles of Conversion" could be the title of a series in which each message describes the conversion of an individual. The list below refers to four such miracles of conversion.

> The woman of Samaria, or "Transformation
>   through Conversion" (John 4:1-44)
> The thief on the cross, or "Instantaneous
>   Conversion" (Luke 23:39-43)
> The Ethiopian eunuch, or "Divine Coincidence
>   in Conversion" (Acts 8:26-40)
> The Philippian jailer, or "Heavenly Joy
>   in Conversion" (Acts 16:22-40)

There is an abundance of material in the Bible which lends itself to various series of expository messages. Detached passages which bear a relationship to each other can be used for such groups of messages. The song of Moses and the children of Israel in Exodus 15:1-21; the song of Moses in Deuteronomy 31:30-32:44; the song of Deborah in Judges 5; and the song of David in 2 Samuel 22 could form a series of "Songs of Old Testament Saints." The prayers of the Apostle Paul found in his epistles provide another course of expository messages.

Some time or other during one's ministry, it would be well to deliver a course of sermons from the Psalms. We may present a succession of messages on the Coronation Psalms (Psalms 93-100), on the Hallelujah Psalms (Psalms 106, 111, 112, 113, 135, and especially Psalms 146-150), or on the Penitential Psalms (Psalms 6, 32, 38, 51, 102, 130, and 143). We should without doubt have a series such as "Christ in the Psalms," selecting some of the Messianic Psalms as the bases of our discourses. Psalm 8 depicts Christ as the Son of Man, Psalm 23 as the Good Shepherd of the sheep, Psalm 40 as the Divine Prophet, and Psalm 2 as the Coming King. We should also observe the remarkable connection between Psalms 22, 23, and 24 and give three successive messages with titles such as "The Good Shepherd in His Death" for Psalm 22, "The Great Shepherd in His Power" for Psalm 23, and "The Chief Shepherd in His Glory" for Psalm 24.

Adopting an entirely different approach to the Psalms, we could arrange a series of expositions on "Voices from the Psalms" with titles like the following:

> "The Voice of Penitence" (51st)
> "The Voice of Thanksgiving" (103rd)

"The Voice of Confidence" (27th)
"The Voice of Exultation" (18th)
"The Voice of Praise" (34th)

We may also use a section of a book as the basis of a series. The portion may consist of several chapters which run along the line of a certain theme, such as Exodus 25-40 on the tabernacle, or Genesis 37-50 on the life of Joseph, or Daniel 7-12 on the visions of Daniel. The messages to the seven churches in Asia in Revelation 2 and 3 give us the substance for a set of seven sermons with these titles:

"The Busy Church" (2:1-7)
"The Suffering Church" (2:8-11)
"The Compromising Church" (2:12-17)
"The Corrupt Church" (2:18-29)
"The Dead Church" (3:1-6)
"The Missionary Church" (3:7-13)
"The Indifferent Church" (3:14-22)

One other method of developing a series of expository sermons is to take a chapter, or a portion of a chapter, and through careful study of the text develop a number of related messages from the passage. We use as an illustration 1 Kings 10:1-13 concerning the visit of the Queen of Sheba to King Solomon. From this portion we find the following titles for a series of expositions on "Riches That Last":

"Finding Riches That Last" (vv. 1-5)
"Enjoying Riches That Last" (vv. 6-9)
"Possessing Riches That Last" (vv. 10-13)

A close observation of 2 Kings 5:1-15 will reveal several instruments which God used in bringing Naaman the leper to a knowledge of Himself. As a result, we may formulate a course on "Instruments God Uses for Blessing."

Isaiah 6:1-13 provides the basis for a course of messages on "Preparation for Service" with the following titles treating the successive steps in the preparation of a man of God for the Lord's service:

"A Vision of the Lord" (vv. 1-4)
"Confession to the Lord" (v. 5)
"Cleansing by the Lord" (vv. 6-7)
"Dedication to the Lord" (v. 8)
"Commissioning by the Lord" (vv. 9-13)

The first message in the series could be developed along the lines shown below:

> I. The man who is to serve the Lord effectively needs to have a vision of the Lord in His glory, vv. 1-2.
> II. The man who is to serve the Lord effectively needs also to have a vision of the Lord in His holiness, vv. 3-4.

The experienced expositor may take entire books of the Bible and present a plan of messages giving a synopsis of each book in the course. For example, "Four Men Who Foretold the Future" can be the general title for a series on the major prophets, stressing in each case a distinctive feature of the prophet.

> "Isaiah, the Messianic Prophet"
> "Jeremiah, the Weeping Prophet"
> "Ezekiel, the Silent Prophet"
> "Daniel, the Apocalyptic Prophet"

We leave this discussion on preaching series of expository sermons with a word of counsel. Although such a series makes possible the teaching of the Bible with a thoroughness which no other method of preaching is able to achieve, we need to be careful that the series is not too long. It is possible that, even with a congregation which is used to the expository method, the people may grow weary of hearing one major emphasis brought to their attention over a protracted period of time. The need for caution applies particularly to the less experienced expositor who may not be able to give sufficient variety or interest to the messages in a series when they follow one main theme or are derived from one book.

Conclusion

From all we have said in this chapter, we may be justified in claiming that the expository method is in one sense the simplest way to preach. This is because all the basic materials for the expository sermon are contained in the passage to be expounded, and as a general rule the preacher has only to follow the order of the text.

But there are other advantages in expository preaching. In contrast to other types of messages it insures a better knowledge of the Scriptures on the part of both the preacher and the hearers. Furthermore, as

Dr. James M. Gray has said, "Expository preaching makes it necessary for sermons to contain more of pure Scriptural truth and Scriptural modes of viewing things," and will lead the preacher to include in his messages many practical admonitions which might under other circumstances seem to be offensively personal to some of the hearers.

There is another important advantage. The student who becomes an able expositor of the Word of God will realize more and more in the course of his experience that expository preaching will give repeated occasion for remarking on passages in the Bible which otherwise might never enter into his ministry.

EXERCISES

1. Indicate by the verse numbers the expository units of Philippians 4, and state what you consider to be the main point of emphasis in each.

2. Prepare an expository outline on 1 Corinthians 3:1-8, giving the title, subject, and main divisions of the passage. Indicate the verses which relate to each main division.

3. Make a biographical sermon outline on Miriam, the sister of Moses (note all the Scripture references to her, including Exodus 2:1-10). Give the title, subject, and main divisions, and indicate the references which relate to each main division.

4. Formulate an outline from Numbers 21:4-9, utilizing some of the truths suggested by the passage for your main divisions. State the title and subject of the text.

5. Select two or three more or less extended related passages from various parts of Scripture and use them as the basis for an expository outline. Give the titles, subject, and main divisions, with the verses supporting each main division.

6. By use of the method of multiple approach, prepare an outline on Luke 19:1-10, selecting another point of emphasis than that used in this chapter. State the title, theme, and main divisions, and show the verses which belong to each main division.

7. Choose your own expository unit and prepare two different expository outlines on the same passage. Indicate the topic and main divisions of each.

8. Select five more or less extended passages related to one another and give titles to each for a series of five messages. Prepare an expository outline on the first.

9. List five titles on the life of Joseph, drawn from Genesis 37-50. Indicate the expository units for each title and formulate an expository outline on

one of these portions.

10. Carefully study the text of the Epistle of Jude and give at least three titles for a series of messages on the epistle. Develop the first into an expository outline, showing the subject and main divisions.

BIBLIOGRAPHY

Baumann, J. Daniel. *An Introduction to Contemporary Preaching*. Grand Rapids, Michigan: Baker Book House, 1972, pp. 102-103.

Blackwood, Andrew W. *Preaching from the Bible*. Nashville, Tennessee: Abingdon-Cokesbury Press, 1941.

Broadus, John A. *On the Preparation and Delivery of Sermons*. Revised by Jesse B. Weatherspoon. New York: Harper & Brothers, 1944, Part II, Chapter 3.

Caemmerer, Richard R. *Preaching for the Church*. St. Louis, Missouri: Concordia Publishing House, 1959, p. 70-71, Chapters 24, 25, and 27.

Etter, John W. *The Preacher and His Sermon*. Dayton, Ohio: United Brethren Publishing House , 1902, Chapter 7.

Evans, William. *How to Prepare Sermons and Gospel Addresses*. Chicago: The Bible Institute Colportage Assn., 1913, Chapter 11.

Faw, Chalmer E. *A Guide to Biblical Preaching*. Nashville, Tennessee: Broadman Press, 1962.

Holmes, George. *Toward an Effective Pulpit Ministry*. Springfield, Missouri: Gospel Publishing House, 1971, Chapters 9, 10, and 11.

Kaiser, Walter C., Jr. *Toward an Exegetical Theology, Biblical Exegesis for Preaching and Teaching*. Grand Rapids, Michigan: Baker Book House, 1981, Chapters 8-11.

Knott, Harold E. *How to Prepare an Expository Sermon*. Cincinnati: The Standard Publishing Company, 1930.

Koller, Charles W. *Expository Preaching without Notes*. Grand Rapids, Michigan: Baker Book House, 1962.

Lane, Denis. *Preach the Word*. Welwyn, Hartfordshire, England: Evanglical Press, 1979, Chapters 2-8.

Lloyd-Jones, D. Martyn. *Preaching & Preachers*. Grand Rapids, Michigan: Zondervan Publishing House, 1972, Chapter 10.

Meyer, F. B. *Expository Preaching: Plans and Methods*. New York: George H. Doran Company, 1912.

Montgomery, R. Amos. *Expository Preaching*. New York: Fleming H. Revell Company, 1939.

Pattison, T. Harwood. *The Making of the Sermon*. Philadelphia: The American Baptist Publication Society, 1898, Chapter 6.

Perry, Lloyd M. *A Manual for Biblical Preaching*. Grand Rapids, Michigan: Baker Book House, 1965, pp. 106-124, 126-145.

Ray, Jeff D. *Expository Preaching*. Grand Rapids, Michigan: Zondervan Publishing House, 1940.

Robinson, Haddon W. *Biblical Preaching*. Grand Rapids, Michigan: Baker Book House, 1980, pp. 15-30.

Stibbs, Alan M. *Expounding God's Word*. Grand Rapids, Michigan: The Eerdmans Publishing Company, 1961.

Unger, Merrill F. *Principles of Expository Preaching*. Grand Rapids, Michigan: Zondervan Publishing House, 1955.

White, Douglas M. *The Excellence of Exposition*. Neptune, New Jersey: Loizeaux Brothers, Inc., 1977.

Whitesell, Faris Daniel. *Evangelistic Preaching and the Old Testament*. Chicago: Moody Press, 1947, Chapters 9-10.

_____ . *Power in Expository Preaching*. New York: Fleming H. Revell Company, 1963.

PART II
The Mechanics
of
Sermon Construction

"Do your best to present yourself
to God
as one approved, a workman who does not need to be
ashamed
and who correctly handles the word of truth"
(2 Timothy 2:15).

4. HOMILETICAL STRUCTURE

The Importance of Homiletical Structure

D. Martyn Lloyd-Jones, the well-known pastor of Westminster Chapel of London, England, has pointed out in his work, *Studies in the Sermon on the Mount,* that a sermon is not an essay or a literary composition intended for publication to be read and re-read, but is a message which is intended to be heard and to have an immediate impact upon the listeners.

In order to secure this impact the sermon must be free from ambiguity and contain no extraneous material which is foreign to its main theme. On the other hand, it must have a distinct form or pattern, with the ideas in the sermon indicating continuity of thought and the whole discourse moving toward a definite goal or climax. In other words, the sermon must be so constructed that the hearers are able to grasp without difficulty the main thrust of the message, as well as the various features which make up the discourse. This is the reason for homiletical structure.

The chapters which follow will deal with the mechanics of sermon construction. There is no easy road to effective sermonizing. It calls for much laborious effort and patient study. After these principles have been learned, there must also be an assiduous application of these rules if the student is to attain to a mastery of homiletics.

However, the rewards of such diligence will be worth more than all the time and labor involved, for if the student has thoroughly grasped the principles of sermon construction he will be well on his way toward becoming a sermon builder. His messages may be so clearly presented from beginning to end that his hearers will be able to follow, point by point, the truths he seeks to unfold from the Word of God.

Format of a Sermon Outline

The preceding chapters have indicated some of the main features of a homiletical outline, but in order that the reader may obtain a complete picture of the proper format for a sermon outline, we present one below.

```
            Title _____
            Text _____
            Introduction
                1. _____
                2. _____
            Proposition _____
            Interrogative sentence _____
            Transitional sentence _____
             I.  First main division_____
                1.  First subdivision _____
                                Discussion
                2.  Second subdivision _____
                                Discussion
                Transition _____
            II.  Second main division_____
                1.  First subdivision _____
                                Discussion
                2.  Second subdivision _____
                                Discussion
                3.  Third subdivision _____
                                Discussion
                Transition _____
            Conclusion
                1. _____
                2. _____
                3. _____
```

Such a pattern is typical of the construction of most Biblical sermons, that is, the text precedes the introduction, which is followed by the proposition, interrogative, and transitional sentence in that order, then the main divisions, subdivisions, and conclusion. Transitions connect the main divisions with each other and with the conclusion. (For an explanation of the proposition, interrogative, and transitional sentence, see Chapter 7; for instruction on transitions, see Chapter 8.)

One of the purposes of a format is to make the outline obvious. A clear outline is an invaluable help to the speaker. When an outline is put in this form it serves as a visual aid, enabling the sermonizer to see the entire message at a glance. Heading the introduction and conclusion and numbering the points under them causes each item in the introduction and conclusion to stand out clearly so that progression of thought is easily discerned. Main divisions are placed to the left of the paper, and by the use of indentation the subheads are clearly seen to be subordinate to the main divisions. Note that the main divisions and subdivisions are spaced uniformly on the page so that their proper relationships are plainly evident.

The main points and subpoints are also listed by the use of Roman and Arabic numerals, respectively, rather than by the use of letters of the alphabet. The reason for this is that if in the course of delivery the preacher has to deal with a theme where he is obliged to enumerate the main divisions or subdivisions, it is easier for him to mention the items numerically than alphabetically. For instance, if the speaker wishes to speak of the terms used by the Apostle Paul to describe the Christian worker in 2 Timothy chapter 2, it is simpler to refer to the first, second, third, and fourth terms than to speak of "Term A," "Term B," "Term C," and so forth.

If it becomes desirable to list a number of items which are subordinate to the subdivisions, they can also be itemized by the use of Arabic numerals in parentheses—(1), (2), (3) and so forth.

Of course, the number of main divisions and subdivisions is not limited to the number contained in this format; the same is true of the number of items under the introduction and conclusion. The discussion of these matters will be found in later chapters.

Brevity in Outlining Sermons

An outline should be brief. The introduction and conclusion, as well as the main divisions, should be expressed in as few words as possible consonant with adequate comprehension. In like manner, the items contained in the discussion—which is simply an elaboration of each subdivision—must be stated concisely. In other words, we should strive to compress whole paragraphs into brief statements and to use abbreviations in place of complete words wherever possible (see the complete sermon outlines in Chapters 9 and 11).

Modification of the Principles of Homiletics

In spite of all the lessons he had taught on the preparation and delivery of sermons, Dr. James M. Gray once pointed out to his class that the Lord is not restricted to any rules of rhetoric or homiletics. Instead, we may have a message from the Word without any apparent plan or unity of thought. It is not necessary, therefore, that the preacher feel he is always bound to the principles of homiletics. "The Spirit gives life; the flesh counts for nothing," and with our hearts open to the Holy Spirit to fill and to use us, let us "hold out the word of life"!

But while the student is learning homiletics it would not be wise for him to exercise this liberty. On the contrary, the beginner should apply himself rigidly to the rules until he has mastered them thoroughly. There will come a time later in his ministry when, under the leading of the Spirit of God, he may disregard some of these principles. As he gains experience in preaching he may find it both advisable and necessary on certain occasions to modify the rules which he has learned, depending upon his own feelings and those of his hearers at the time of delivering the message, thus leaving room for impassioned appeal.

BIBLIOGRAPHY

Baird, John E. *Preparing for Platform and Pulpit*. Nashville, Tennessee: Abingdon Press, 1968, pp. 67-69.

Bowie, Walter Russell. *Preaching*. Nashville, Tennessee: Abingdon Press, 1954, Chapter 9.

Brack, Harold A. and Kenneth G. Hance. *Public Speaking and Discussion for Religious Leaders*. Englewood Cliffs, New Jersey: Prentice Hall, Inc., 1961, Chapter 1.

Broadus, John A. *On the Preparation and Delivery of Sermons*. Revised by Jesse B. Weatherspoon. New York: Harper & Brothers, 1944, Part II, Chapter 1.

Burrell, David James. *The Sermon, Its Construction and Delivery*. New York: Fleming H. Revell Company, 1913, Part II, Chapters 1-2.

DeWelt, Don. *If You Want to Preach*. Grand Rapids, Michigan: Baker Book House, 1957, Chapter 2.

Evans, William. *How to Prepare Sermons and Gospel Addresses*. Chicago: The Bible Institute Colportage Assn., 1913, Chapter 7.

Koller, Charles W. *Expository Preaching without Notes*. Grand Rapids, Michigan: Baker Book House, 1962, Chapters 5, 13.

Lockyer, Herbert. *The Art and Craft of Preaching*. Grand Rapids, Michigan: Baker Book House, 1975, pp. 28-40.

Perry, Lloyd M. *A Manual for Biblical Preaching*. Grand Rapids, Michigan: Baker Book House, 1965, pp. 1-4.

Reu, M. *Homiletics, A Manual of the Theory and Practice of Preaching*. Minneapolis: Augsburg Publishing House, 1950, Chapters 14-15.

Skinner, Craig. *The Teaching Ministry of the Pulpit*. Grand Rapids, Michigan: Baker Book House, 1979, pp. 162-163.

White, R. E. O. *A Guide to Preaching*. Grand Rapids, Michigan: William B. Eerdmans Publishing Co., 1973, Chapter 9.

Whitesell, Faris Daniel. *Evangelistic Preaching and the Old Testament*. Chicago: Moody Press, 1947, Chapter 1.

Whitesell, Faris Daniel and Lloyd M. Perry. *Variety in Your Preaching*. Westwood, New Jersey: Fleming H. Revell Company, 1954, Chapter 8.

5. THE TITLE

Definition of the Title

In the construction of a discourse the title is usually one of the last items to be prepared. The general procedure is to formulate the proposition and the main outline first, but to conform to the order of the format in Chapter 4 we shall discuss the title before considering the other steps in the making of a sermon.

We need at the outset to obtain a clear understanding of the meaning of the subject, topic, theme, and title. Some homiletical writers differentiate between subject, topic, and theme. They claim that the subject gives the general idea, whereas the theme or topic is a specific or particular aspect of the subject. However, Webster's Dictionary indicates that these terms are synonymous. In other words, a subject, topic, or theme is that which forms the basis for our discussion or study.

Thus, a subject may be broad, or it may be narrowed to a limited area for discussion. For example, there are so many aspects of the broad theme "grace," such as the meaning of grace, the source of grace, the manifestation of grace, the evidence of grace, the effects of grace, and so forth, that it is impossible to treat the subject adequately in one message. Hence, it is always best for the homilist to narrow his theme to a particular aspect to treat that one limited area properly.

The title, however, is an expression of the specific feature to be presented in the sermon, stated in a manner which may be suitable for advertising the sermon.

Thus the title is an embellishment of the subject. For example, if our topic or theme is, "conditions for growth in grace," our title, to be advertised in a church bulletin or newspaper, can be, "How to Grow in Grace" or "Maturing in Spiritual Stature." On the other hand, if we select the second half of Romans 5:17 as a text—"how much more will those who receive God's abundant provision of grace and of the gift of righteousness reign in life through the one man, Jesus Christ"—the general subject may be "victory," the specific subject, "prerequisites for victory," and the title, "The Secret of Successful Christian Living," or "Victorious Christian Living."

There may be times when the theme and the title are exactly the same, especially if the theme or topic is sufficiently interesting in itself to be suitable as the sermon title.

Proper titling of sermons calls for careful thought and skillful phrasing. This usually requires much effort on the part of the beginner, but his time and thought will be amply rewarded by the stimulation of interest on the part of those who read the titles of his sermons wherever they are advertised.

Principles for the Preparation of Sermon Titles

1. The title should be pertinent to the text or to the message.

It is obvious that the title must have definite connection with the text or with the discourse. For example, if the text is taken from Genesis 22:1-18 where we read of the sacrifice of Isaac by Abraham, the title should in some way bear a relationship to that passage. If the thought to be emphasized in the sermon is that of obedience, we may limit our title to, "The Cost of Obedience." If, on the other hand, our dominant idea is to be that of Abraham's fatherhood, we could entitle the sermon, "An Exemplary Father."

2. The title should be interesting.

The title should be worded to arouse attention or curiosity. It should be attractive, not by the use of mere novelty, but because it is of vital interest to the people.

To be interesting, the title must be in keeping with life situations and needs. Many varied circumstances, both from within and from without, will affect the corporate life and thinking of the church. Times of spiritual blessing, days of testing, conditions of prosperity or adversity, social or political upheavals, celebrations and anniversaries, occasions of rejoicing or of mourning—all of these, as well as the personal affairs of the individual members of the congregation, affect the people to whom the pastor ministers. The pastor ought to be alert to the needs of his people as they face such circumstances from time to time, and under the direction of the Lord his messages should be relevant to the times and conditions in which his people find themselves. The titles of his messages must likewise be suited to their circumstances and interests.

We should therefore avoid titles which have no special meaning or significance to the people. For example, a title on 1 Kings 17:1-6, such as, "Elijah by the Brook Cherith" or "The Famine in the Days of Elijah," would not be particularly meaningful to men and women today. Instead, "Tested to be Trusted" immediately carries significance to everyone in the congregation who is passing through a time of trial. Likewise, the heading, "At the Waters of Meribah," for a sermon dealing with the bitterness of God's people described in Exodus 15:22-26, will certainly not arouse interest, whereas such a title as, "Bitter Waters and Bitter Souls," will immediately create a response in the minds of those who may be harboring bitterness in their hearts over some adverse stroke of God's providence.

When the words of the title are set in an alliterative pattern, it often serves to arrest attention by the very uniqueness in which the words are placed side by side. The effectiveness of such patterns can be readily seen in the following examples by well known preachers of the past and present:

> "The Great Gain of Godliness" by Alexander
> Maclaren, based on 1 Kings 4:25-34.
> "The Defeat of Death" by A. T. Pierson,
> based on 1 Corinthians 15.
> "The Re-Action of Revenge" by Clarence E.
> Macartney, based on Esther 1-10.
> "Rest for the Restless" by Charles H. Spurgeon,
> based on Matthew 11:28-30.
> "The School of Sorrow" by W. H. Griffith Thomas,
> based on Genesis 35:8-29.
> "Barrenness or Blessedness" by Stephen F. Olford,
> based on Numbers 21:10-18.

Here are some other examples:

> "From Weeping to Witnessing" based on John
> 20:10-18.
> "Fact, Faith, or Feeling" based on John 20:19-29.
> "Prayer That Prevails" based on Acts 12:1-19.
> "Turning Opposition into Opportunity"
> based on Philippians 1:12-20.

> "The Sufficiency of the Savior" based on Hebrews
>   10:14.
> "Living Hope in a Hopeless World" based on
>   1 Peter 1:3-9.

It may take some time and thought for the beginner to phrase the title in a manner which stimulates interest. However, when the sermon heading is attractive, and particularly when it is published in advance of the time the sermon is preached, it could be the means of drawing people to the church and promoting new interest on the part of the congregation.

3. The title should be in keeping with the dignity of the pulpit.

In an effort to arouse attention, some preachers make the mistake of employing titles which are bizarre or sensational. Observe the following examples:

> "Snoopy or Mickey Mouse"
> "Wine, Women, and Song"
> "An Old Testament Style Show"
> "The Cat's Whiskers"
> "Should a Husband Beat His Wife?"
> "Smart Alec"
> "Astronauts and the Man in the Moon"
> "The Hot Place"
> "Hippies and Mini Skirts"
> "The Big Sissy"

Sermon headings such as these are either fantastic, coarse, crude, or irreverent, and entirely out of keeping with the sacred task of ministering the oracles of God to men.

While we seek to create interest by an attractive title, we must always maintain the dignity and reverence which is due the Word of God. We need not strive after cleverness and must at all costs avoid the sensational or that which is calculated to arouse undue attention or curiosity. Above all, we should never use a title which may border upon the frivolous or the vulgar.

4. The title should generally be brief.

A condensed or compact title is usually more effective than a lengthy statement, provided it is forcefully phrased. It is also far more apt to catch the reader's eye than a line of fifteen or twenty words.

Hence, the preacher should generally make the title short but not abrupt. However, we must not sacrifice clarity merely for the sake of brevity. A title consisting of only one word will generally be too abrupt and usually will not succeed in creating interest.

5. *The title may be stated in the form of either affirmation, interrogation, or exclamation.*

Although generally the title is briefly worded, there are times when it may be necessary to state it in a complete but concise sentence. That sentence may be either declaratory, interrogatory, or exclamatory. There are occasions when the title will be much more forceful if put in the form of an arresting question. Observe the difference between "Life Is Worth Living" and "Is Life Worth Living?"; also "We Should Be on the Lord's Side" and "Who Is on the Lord's Side?"

We show additional examples below.

> Interrogatory:
>> "Why Do the Godly Suffer?"
>> "What Is the Meaning of Faith?"
> Declaratory:
>> "God Can Handle Your Problems"
>> "What the Bible Says about Death"
> Exclamatory:
>> "For Better, Not for Worse!"
>> "Gaining by Losing!"

6. *The title may consist of a phrase followed by a question.*
Note the following titles:

> "Troubled Youth: What Is Our Responsibility to Them?"
> "The Perplexities of Life: How Do We Face Them?"

7. *The title may sometimes be stated in the form of a compound subject.*
Observe these examples:

> "The Christian and His Friends"
> "Discipleship: Its Challenge and Its Cost"
> "The Sign of the Times and the Second Coming of Christ"

8. *The title may consist of a brief quotation of a text of Scripture.*

Here are a few such quotations used as sermon titles:

"Prepare to Meet Your God"
"Who Is My Neighbor?"
"Teach Us to Pray"
"Thy Will Be Done"
"There We Saw the Giants"
"This One Thing I Do"
"Be Sure Your Sin Will Find You Out"

The last four items are quoted from the King James version.

Examples of Titles for Special Services

For a New Year's Day Service:
"New Horizons"
"The Threshold of Blessing"
"How Can My Life Count Most for God?"
"Taking Inventory of Ourselves"

For a Good Friday Service:
"The Meaning of the Cross"
"Sorrowful unto Death"
"The Place Called Calvary"
"The Price of Love"
"Smitten of God"
"The Sacrifice of Inestimable Worth"

For an Easter Service:
"The Triumphs of the Risen Christ"
"No Room for Doubt"
"The Power of Christ's Resurrection"
"The Comfort of the Living Christ"
"The Personal Knowledge of the Risen Lord"

For an Independence Day Service:
"Dimensions of Liberty"
"The Price of Freedom"
"Guarding Our Heritage"
"The Faith of Our Fathers"

For a Christmas Day Service:
"The Gift of Gifts"
"When God Became Man"
"Born to Die"
"The Wisdom of the Wise Men"

For a Missionary Service:
"The Marching Orders of the Church"
"The Imperative of Missions"
"A Man Sent from God"
"Life's Highest Priorities"
"Facing the Issues of Personal Commitment"
"Perspectives of Missions"
"Conscription or Constraint?"
"High Requirements for High Service"

EXERCISES

1. The following sermon titles appeared on the church pages of one of the newspapers in Portland, Oregon. Make a list of the numbers of those which do not meet the qualifications of a good sermon title and after each one state the reason for your decision.

    (1)   "God's Way is Simple and Strong"
    (2)   "Revival or Apostasy—Which?"
    (3)   "Return to Vital Religion"
    (4)   "Strength for Today"
    (5)   "What in the World is the U.C.C. Doing?"
    (6)   "The Tiptoe of Expectation"
    (7)   "Outside the Camp"
    (8)   "Come and Dine"
    (9)   "The Prince of Peace Predicts War"
  (10)   "Til the End"
  (11)   "Illusion and Reality"
  (12)   "The Door Was Shut"
  (13)   "Cater to the Rich"
  (14)   "Clearing the Way for God"
  (15)   "The Message of God's Prisoner"
  (16)   "Jesus is Lord"
  (17)   "From Fear to Faith"
  (18)   "Seven Women Shall Take Ahold of One Man"
  (19)   "The Tragedy of Religious Compromise"
  (20)   "Nebuchadnezzar's Dream Will Come True"
  (21)   "Go to Church? What For?"
  (22)   "My Greatest Necessity"
  (23)   "Joseph's Wagons"
  (24)   "Man and the Universe"

2. The list below contains twelve titles, each based on a separate passage of Scripture. Find those which need correction and indicate how you would improve them.

    (1)   "Rahab's Lie," based on Joshua 2.
    (2)   "The Beatitudes," based on Matthew 5:3-12.
    (3)   "Advice to a Young Man," based on 1 Timothy 4:12-16.
    (4)   "Vision," based on Genesis 13:14-17.
    (5)   "Paul's Burden for Israel," based on Romans 9:1-5.
    (6)   "A Prayer for Love," based on Ephesians 3:14-19.
    (7)   "The Man Who Is Blessed," based on Psalm 1.
    (8)   "Wrong Vision," based on Numbers 13:25-33.
    (9)   "The Smiting of Conscience," based on Matthew 14:1-12.
  (10)   "Concerning Spiritual Gifts," based on 1 Corinthians 12:1-31.
  (11)   "Christian Brotherhood," based on Philemon, vv. 4-21.
  (12)   "The City that Lies Foursquare," based on Revelation 21:10-27.

3. Prepare a suitable title for each of the following texts:

   (1) "We who are strong ought to bear with the failings of the weak and not to please ourselves" (Romans 15:1).
   (2) "But Daniel resolved not to defile himself with the royal food and wine" (Daniel 1:8a).
   (3) "I sat among them" (Ezekiel 3:15).
   (4) "Christ died for our sins according to the Scriptures" (1 Corinthians 15:3).
   (5) "I will not sacrifice to the LORD my God burnt offerings that cost me nothing" (2 Samuel 24:24).
   (6) "In everything he walked in the ways of his father Asa" (1 Kings 22:43).
   (7) "Stretch out your hand" (Luke 6:10).
   (8) "No good thing does he withhold from those whose walk is blameless" (Psalm 84:11).
   (9) "When your words came, I ate them; they were my joy and my heart's delight" (Jeremiah 15:16a).
   (10) "And they did not do as we expected, but they gave themselves first to the Lord and then to us in keeping with God's will" (2 Corinthians 8:5).
   (11) "And we have seen and testify that the Father has sent his Son to be the Savior of the world" (1 John 4:14).
   (12) "He (Moses) persevered because he saw him who is invisible" (Hebrews 11:27).

BIBLIOGRAPHY

Baird, John E. *Preparing for Platform and Pulpit*. Nashville, Tennessee: Abingdon Press, 1968, pp. 62-64.

Baumann, J. Daniel. *An Introduction to Contemporary Preaching*. Grand Rapids, Michigan: Baker Book House, 1972, pp. 128-131.

Blackwood, Andrew W. *The Preparation of Sermons*. Nashville, Tennessee: Abingdon-Cokesbury Press, 1948, Chapter 8.

Blocker, Simon. *The Secret of Pulpit Power through Thematic Christian Preaching*. Grand Rapids, Michigan: Wm. B. Eerdmans Publishing Company, 1951, Chapter 2.

Brastow, Lewis O. *The Word of the Preacher*. Boston: The Pilgrim Press, 1914, Chapter 2.

Broadus, John A. *On the Preparation and Delivery of Sermons*. Revised by Jesse B. Weatherspoon. New York: Harper & Brothers, 1944, Part I, Chapter 3.

Brown, H. C. Jr., H. Gordon Clinard, and Jesse J. Northcutt. *Steps to the Sermon*. Nashville, Tennessee: Broadman Press, 1963, pp. 95-105.

Davis, Henry Grady. *Design for Preaching*. Philadelphia, Pennsylvania: Fortress Press, 1958, Chapter 5.

Lloyd-Jones, D. Martyn. *Preaching and Preachers*. Grand Rapids, Michigan: Zondervan Publishing House, 1972, pp. 244-247.

Macpherson, Ian, *The Burden of the Lord*. Nashville, Tennessee: Abingdon Press, 1955, pp. 91-94.

Pattison, T. Harwood. *The Making of the Sermon*. Philadelphia: The American Baptist Publication Society, 1898, Chapters 7-9.

Perry, Lloyd M. *A Manual for Biblical Preaching*. Grand Rapids, Michigan: Baker Book House, 1965, pp. 65-66, 78-79.

Reu, M. *Homiletics, A Manual of the Theory and Practice of Preaching*. Minneapolis: Augsburg Publishing House, 1950, Chapter 16.

Whitesell, Faris Daniel and Lloyd M. Perry. *Variety in Your Preaching*. Westwood, New Jersey: Fleming H. Revell Company, 1954, Chapter 3.

6. THE INTRODUCTION

Definition of the Introduction

In actual practice the introduction, like the title, is usually one of the last parts of the sermon to be prepared. The reason for this is that after the main part of the sermon and the conclusion have been written, the sermonizer is better able to think of an introduction which is suited to the message and which is most likely to quicken and hold the interest of the people. But although the introduction is generally prepared later, we believe that it is well to consider it at this juncture and thus follow the order of the format outlined in Chapter 4.

Austin Phelps, in his excellent book, "The Theory of Preaching," points out that there is a difference between preliminaries in general and the introduction proper. In the former, general remarks may be made which have no definite connection with the sermon, but in the latter the homilist seeks to bring the minds of the congregation into such a relationship with his theme that they are willing to lend an ear to his discourse.

Thus, *the introduction is the process by which the preacher endeavors to prepare the minds and secure the interest of his hearers in the message he has to proclaim.*

The introduction is therefore a vital part of the sermon, and the success of the entire message often depends upon the ability of the minister to win the support of his hearers at the outset of the discourse. It is well that the utmost care be given to present the introduction in such a manner as to challenge the interest of the congregation from the very beginning.

Purpose of the Introduction

There are various purposes which the preacher may aim to accomplish in the introduction, but they can be summed up in two basic objectives.

1. To secure the good will of the hearers.

Although a minister may have a reasonable assurance that his congregation is favorably disposed toward him and his theme, this may not always be the case. In fact, in the average congregation it is very likely that there will be one or more individuals who, for one reason or another, are not in sympathy with either the preacher or the message he is to deliver. Sometimes the lack of rapport may be for superficial reasons and can be overcome without much difficulty, but there are times when certain unfavorable conditions or deep-seated resentments cause the hearers to be ill-disposed toward either the preacher or the sermon. The introduction then must be presented in such a way as to win the favorable attention of the entire congregation if at all possible.

However, the primary factor in securing the good will of the congregation is the person of the preacher himself. It is what we are that determines the acceptability of what we say, and this is never more true than when the minister stands before a congregation to deliver a message from the Word of God.

2. To arouse interest in the theme.

Besides a lack of sympathy with the theme on the part of certain individuals, other conditions may militate against proper attention to the message. One of these is the preoccupation of the minds of the people with other things. The hymns, prayer, and Scripture reading preceding the sermon may predispose a good proportion of the congregation to a receptive attitude when the preacher opens his message, but there will be many who, in spite of the most careful planning of the parts of the service before the sermon, will be preoccupied with their own joys or sorrows, hopes or fears, or with their own duties or cares. Another obstacle to attention is the indifference of some people to Biblical truth so that spiritual things do not particularly interest them. Other conditions, such as a poorly ventilated auditorium, insufficient lighting, a slamming door, or a cold building, also contribute to inattention.

The purpose of the introduction is to arouse the attention of the people and to challenge their thinking to such an extent that they will become actively interested in the subject. W. E. Sangster, minister of London's Westminster Hall and a writer of homiletics, says that as the preacher begins his sermon he must be sure the opening sentences have "grappling irons" to grip the minds of his hearers instantly.

Principles for the Preparation of the Introduction

1. It should generally be brief.

Since the objective in preaching is to bring the Word of God to men, it is well that we get into the main part of the message as early as possible. While it is true that we usually need to make a gradual approach to the subject, we must avoid any tendency to drag. We should eliminate all non-essentials, including unnecessary apologies, humorous anecdotes, or elaborate felicitations. There are occasions when cordial greetings may be proper, particularly when a minister is occupying the pulpit as a visiting preacher, but such greetings should not be extensive.

The following outline, drawn from the story of the prodigal son in Luke 15:11-24, exemplifies the manner in which the introduction should move rapidly and directly toward the theme:

Title: "Lost and Found"

Introduction: 1. At the World's Fair in Chicago, in order to assist parents to locate their children who had strayed on the grounds, the authorities established a "lost and found department" for children.
2. Luke 15 is the "Lost and Found Department" of the Bible. Here Jesus tells of three things that were lost and found—a sheep, a silver coin, and a son.
3. The story of the son who was lost and found illustrates the history of a repentant sinner who is "lost and found."

Subject: Steps in the history of a repentant sinner.
I. The sinner's guilt, vv. 11-13.
II. The sinner's misery, vv. 14-16.
III. The sinner's repentance, vv. 17-20a.
IV. The sinner's restoration, vv. 20b-24.

2. It should be interesting.

The first few minutes of the sermon are crucial. It is at this time that the minister will either gain or lose the attention of his congregation. If his opening remarks consist of dull, inane, or irrelevant trivia, he is likely to lose from the start the reception which his hearers may otherwise be willing to give to his message. If, on the other hand, he is able to begin his sermon with that which is of vital concern to the people, or which is appealing to them, he will gain their attention at the outset and prepare them for the message he is about to deliver. At this point the practical question will no doubt arise in the mind of the reader: How can we stimulate interest as we begin the sermon?

One method of arresting attention is to arouse curiosity. People are naturally curious, and this trait is often evident at the time when a sermon begins. For example, the preacher might commence his message with the description of a conversation he has had with an unbeliever. He may say, "As I began to talk with the man, the first question he asked was, 'Why doesn't the church leave me alone?' " The mention of this question raised by the unbeliever will immediately arouse the curiosity of the congregation to know just how the minister dealt with the man and if he was able to give a satisfactory answer to him.

A second method of creating interest is by means of variety. Do not begin each sermon in the same way, but employ different approaches from week to week. One sermon may open with an apt quotation, another with the stanza of a hymn, a third with a striking statement, and a fourth with a question, and yet another with a challenge as to the validity of the theme which the preacher is about to discuss. In other sermons we can refer to the historical background of the text, or the relationship of the text to its context.

Another means of arousing attention is to state the title of the sermon, or quote the text. We should then explain the reason for the choice of the title or text and proceed to show the relationship of either or both to the topic.

Yet another way of stirring interest is to relate the sermon to life situations, beginning with an allusion to a situation which is calculated to touch the lives and thinking of men and women in their day-to-day problems and needs. The description of an auto accident in which someone was injured, a child saved from drowning after having fallen into a well, a fire in a home, a young man's problem with his roommate at school, a man lost in the woods and never found, the success of a businessman, an unusual incident at a local parade—such stories will either appear in the newspapers or come to our attention in daily contact with people. It is the use of such features—the common experiences of men and current events—which will bring our preaching close to the lives of people and give relevance to our message. We should not tell anecdotes merely to entertain, however. Instead, we need to make sure that the incidents from life situations can be tied into the sermon itself.

We show below two examples of sermon introductions employing incidents from life situations.

If we speak on "Insensitive Christians," we can announce as our text, Jonah 1:4-5. "Then the LORD sent a great wind on the sea, and such a violent storm arose that the ship threatened to break up. All the sailors were afraid and each cried out to his own god. And they threw the cargo into the sea to lighten the ship. But Jonah had gone below deck, where he lay down and fell into a deep sleep." We may then begin by telling the following incident concerning a five-year-old child, Carol Lee Morgan, who lives near Astoria, along the coast of Oregon:

> Carol picked up the receiver and began to speak to the telephone operator. "My mother's sick. She won't talk to me." The young voice sounded serious. Sensing an emergency, Mrs. Madeline Markham, the operator, turned the call over immediately to the supervisor, Mrs. Marjorie Forness. The supervisor asked Carol for her full name, but the child could not remember the name of either her father, who was deceased, or her mother. Mrs. Forness read the names of the nine Morgans listed in the Astoria directory and Carol finally recognized her mother's name, "Mrs. Roberta Morgan." Mrs. Forness then asked Carol if she knew the names of any of her neighbors. After much probing Carol finally recalled the name of a Mrs. Bud Koppisch who lived across the street. The supervisor called Mrs. Koppisch who agreed to hurry over to the Morgan's residence. Later Mrs. Forness learned that when Mrs. Koppisch came to the home she found Mrs. Morgan in a near-comatose condition and arranged for her removal to the hospital. When Mrs. Morgan recovered and returned home she expressed her appreciation to the telephone operators who listened to her little daughter, and the two ladies in turn were happy that they had been able to find and send help in time.

> We would all commend Mrs. Markham and Mrs. Forness, the two telephone operators, for their presence of mind and sensitivity to a vital need. But while we applaud them, we ask ourselves, "Are we as alert to the serious spiritual plight of men today as were the two employees of the Pacific Northwest Bell Company to the need in the home of the Morgans?" While men are being tossed in seas of turmoil and despair, how many of us

have any real concern or sense of their spiritual need? Or are we much like Jonah? Though he was the one and only individual on the ship who knew the living and true God, yet in the hour of deepest need for the mariners, he was both oblivious and utterly insensitive to the desperation of those around him.

Suppose we were to give a devotional message on "The God We Can Trust." We may open the address with the following incident concerning the late V. Raymond Edman, former president of Wheaton College, Wheaton, Illinois:

> Dr. Edman describes a conversation he had on one occasion with the manager of the supermarket where he traded. After the manager had cashed a check for his predecessor at the register, Dr. Edman asked if he had ever cashed a bad check for a stranger. The manager answered thoughtfully, "No, because I don't look at the check, but at the man. If I can trust the man, then I have no hesitation in accepting his check." What a lesson this should be to us! We need but to look at the Promiser, and then we shall have no question regarding the validity of His promises.

Reference to up-to-date facts in almost every field of knowledge, if told accurately and interestingly, can also be used effectively in gaining attention. Note this example of an introduction for an address on "Communion with God," cited by Emory VanGerpen in the *Sudan Witness:*

> Hidden in an African cornfield near the city of Kano in Nigeria is an ordinary-looking building, enclosed by a fence about a block square. The building, filled with all kinds of electronic equipment, is a tracking station—one of eighteen around the world —to keep track of astronauts as they whirl through space. Intricate electronic devices constantly measure the astronauts' heart beat, blood pressure, breathing, temperature and many other items while the capsule hurtles through space. At the same time a huge tape recorder with tape an inch wide records all these details. While the tracking station is in communication with a man in orbit, the greatest care must be exercised that there is no interference from the earth because the signal from the capsule is so small. No automobiles are permitted within a radius of a half mile because of the possible interference created by their generators. Even the radar set at the airport at Kano several miles away is shut down.
> So it is with our communication with God. If we are to have

proper, uninterrupted fellowship with Him, we must cut ourselves off from every possible interference from the outside. Then as we sit in silence before the Lord, we shall be able to hear Him speak to us.

3. It should lead to the dominant idea or main thrust of the message.

The introduction should be aimed directly at the subject of the sermon. To accomplish this the statements contained in the introduction should consist of a series of progressive ideas culminating in the one main aim of the discourse. Any quotations, explanations, illustrations, or incidents that are told should have this one purpose in mind. Repetition and cumbersome expressions must be avoided, and the introduction made as simple and direct as possible, without giving the impression of abruptness or haste.

Consider the outline below in which the introduction consists of a series of progressive ideas leading to the theme of the sermon:

Title: "God's Secret Weapon"

Text: Genesis 18:17-33; 19:27-29.

Introduction:
1. The discovery of the secret of the atom and the power to destroy which men have obtained thereby.
2. The secret God has imparted to His children is a power greater than any nuclear bomb. Nuclear weapons are destructive, but the secret weapon God has placed in the hands of believers is constructive, capable of creative, blessed effects.

Subject: Truths about the secret weapon of intercessory prayer.
What does the text reveal to us in connection with this secret weapon? From the passage we may learn three important truths regarding the secret weapon of intercession which God has made available to believers.

I. God seeks men who will pray for others, 18:17-21.
II. God hears the prayers of those who intercede for others, 18:22-33.
III. God answers the prayers of those who pray for others, 18:23-32; 19:27-29.

4. It should be stated in the outline in a few brief sentences or phrases, with each successive idea on a different line.

Long complex sentences should be avoided. The expressions contained in the abbreviated introduction, although merely suggestive, must be clear enough to be read at a glance. As an example we give an introduction for the outline on "The Psalm of Contentment," drawn from Psalm 23, shown in Chapter 3. To enable the reader to see how the introduction is related to the sermon, we reproduce the entire outline here:

Title: "The Psalm of Contentment"
Introduction: 1. Sheepherder in Idaho with band of 1,200 sheep
—unable to give individual attention to sheep.
2. Contrast Shepherd of this Psalm—as though He has only one sheep for which to care.
3. Every child of God recognizes himself to be the sheep spoken of in this Psalm.
Subject: The bases for the contentment of the Lord's sheep.
   I. The sheep's Shepherd, v. 1.
      1. A divine Shepherd, v. 1.
      2. A personal Shepherd, v. 1.
  II. The sheep's provision, vv. 2-5.
      1. Rest, v. 2.
      2. Guidance, v. 3.
      3. Comfort, v. 4.
      4. Abundance, v. 5.
 III. The sheep's prospect, v. 6.
      1. A bright prospect for this life, v. 6.
      2. A blessed prospect for the hereafter, v. 6.

BIBLIOGRAPHY

Baird, John E. *Preparing for Platform and Pulpit*. Nashville, Tennessee: Abingdon Press, 1968, pp. 70-72.

Baumann, J. Daniel. *An Introduction to Contemporary Preaching*. Grand Rapids, Michigan: Baker Book House, 1972, pp. 135-142.

Breed, David Riddle. *Preparing to Preach*. New York: George H. Doran Company, 1911, Part I, Chapter 6.

Broadus, John A. *On the Preparation and Delivery of Sermons*. Revised by Jesse B. Weatherspoon. New York: Harper & Brothers, 1944, Part II, Chapter 2.

Brown, H. C. Jr., H. Gordon Clinard, and Jesse J. Northcutt. *Steps to the Sermon*. Nashville, Tennessee: Broadman Press, 1963, pp. 125-129.

Burrell, David James. *The Sermon, Its Construction and Delivery*. New York: Fleming H. Revell Company, 1913, Part III, Chapter 1.

Davis, Henry Grady. *Design for Preaching*. Philadelphia, Pennsylvania: Fortress Press, 1958, Chapter 11.

Demaray, Donald E. *An Introduction to Homiletics*. Grand Rapids, Michigan: Baker Book House, 1976, Chapter 4.

DeWelt, Don. *If You Want to Preach*. Grand Rapids, Michigan: Baker Book House, 1957, pp. 115-128.

Etter, John W. *The Preacher and His Sermon*. Dayton, Ohio: United Brethren Publishing House, 1902, Chapter 8.

Evans, William. *How to Prepare Sermons and Gospel Addresses*. Chicago: The Bible Institute Colportage Assn., 1913, Chapter 8.

Ford, D. W. Cleverley. *The Ministry of the Word*. Grand Rapids, Michigan: William B. Eerdmans Publishing Co., 1979, pp. 215-217.

Lane, Denis. *Preach the Word*. Welwyn, Hartfordshire, England: Evangelical Press, 1979, Chapter 9.

Macpherson, Ian. *The Burden of the Lord*. Nashville, Tennessee: Abingdon Press, 1955, pp. 97-104.

Pattison, T. Harwood. *The Making of the Sermon*. Philadelphia: The American Baptist Publication Society, 1898, Chapter 10.

Perry, Lloyd M. *A Manual for Biblical Preaching*. Grand Rapids, Michigan: Baker Book House, 1965, pp. 76-78.

Phelps, Austin. *The Theory of Preaching*. New York: Charles Scribner's Sons, 1892, Lectures 16-19.

Reu, M. *Homiletics, A Manual of the Theory and Practice of Preaching*. Minneapolis: Augsburg Publishing House, 1950, Chapter 18.

Robinson, Haddon W. *Biblical Preaching*. Grand Rapids, Michigan: Baker Book House, 1980, pp. 160-167.

Sangster, William Edwin. *The Craft of the Sermon*. Philadelphia: Westminster Press, n.d., Part I, Chapter 5.

Skinner, Craig. *The Teaching Ministry of the Pulpit*. Grand Rapids, Michigan: Baker Book House, 1979, pp. 171-173.

Sleeth, Ronald E. *Persuasive Preaching*. New York: Harper & Brothers, 1956, Chapter 3.

White, R. E. O. *A Guide to Preaching*. Grand Rapids, Michigan: William B. Eerdmans Publishing Co., 1973, Chapter 11.

Whitesell, Faris Daniel and Lloyd M. Perry. *Variety in Your Preaching*. Westwood, New Jersey: Fleming H. Revell Company, 1954, Chapter 10.

7. THE PROPOSITION

Definition of the Proposition

The proposition is a simple declaration of the subject which the preacher proposes to discuss, develop, prove, or explain in the discourse. In other words, it is a statement of the main spiritual lesson or timeless truth in the sermon reduced to one declarative sentence.

The proposition, also called the thesis, the big idea, the homiletical idea, or the subject sentence, is thus a principle: a rule which governs right conduct, or a fact or generalization which is accepted as true and basic. It consists of a clear declarative statement of a fundamental truth which abides through all time and which has universal application.

Observe the following examples of principles or timeless truths:

- Daily meditation in the Scriptures is vital for the Christian.
- The Lord desires worship that comes from the heart.
- The individual who has God possesses everything that is worth having.
- God uses chosen instruments to meet the needs of others.
- No one can escape the consequences of his own sin.
- Those who give God the first place will never be in want.
- Love for Christ will cause us to forget ourselves in the service of others.

The Bible is full of material from which we may derive theses or big ideas. Even a single verse of Scripture can be the source of a number of principles or timeless truths. Take, for example, Ephesians 2:8: "For it is by grace you have been saved, through faith—and this not from yourselves, it is the gift of God." From this brief text we draw the following principles:

- Every saved sinner is the product of God's unmerited favor.
- Although salvation is free, it becomes ours only by accepting
     it by faith.
- Salvation has its source in the grace of God.
- Faith receives that which God freely bestows.
- God's provision of salvation is entirely outside of man's doing.

The Importance of the Proposition

The importance of a correct proposition cannot be overestimated. It is, in fact, the most essential feature in the organization of a sermon. There are two main reasons for this.

1. The proposition is the foundation of the entire structure of the sermon.

The proposition is to the organization of the sermon what the foundation is to a building. Just as a house cannot be properly built without a solid foundation, so a sermon cannot be properly constructed without the right foundation for its thought structure. Therefore, every word of the proposition must be carefully stated to accurately express the main thought of the sermon.

When the proposition is formulated correctly it enables the preacher to organize his material around the dominant idea which he has planned. Many features may be introduced into the sermon, but everything, from start to finish, will bear upon the single and specific truth or principle revealed in the proposition. As the sermonizer follows this one main truth in his message it also helps him to recognize that which may be pertinent as well as that which should be excluded from the sermon. But when the proposition is not formulated correctly, the entire thought structure is thereby weakened or disorganized.

2. The proposition clearly indicates to the congregation the course of the sermon.

A correct proposition is not only beneficial to the preacher but also to the congregation. Almost instinctively the hearers will ask themselves as the minister begins his sermon, "What is he going to say about the subject?" If the message is without a clearly stated objective, it cannot be easily followed and will often make for inattention on the part of the audience. On the other hand, if at the outset the homilist can make perfectly clear the direction he proposes to take, he will enable his listeners to follow the message intelligently and with ease.

Note the outlines in the latter part of this chapter as well as in the successive chapters and observe how the thesis in each case sets the stage for understanding the message which follows it.

The Process of Developing the Proposition

The creation of the proposition is one of the beginner's most exacting tasks. But because the proper statement of the subject sentence is so important it is imperative that the homilist learn to do it accurately.

There are times when the big idea may flash into the preacher's mind early in the course of his sermon preparation, but as a general rule the discovery of the main truth of the passage and the formulation of the proposition are the result of the following steps in the construction of the sermon.

1. A thorough exegetical study of the passage.

We have already pointed out in Chapters 2 and 3 that a careful examination of the text is indispensable to an understanding of its proper meaning. In other words, a careful exegesis of the passage is a prerequisite to accurate and faithful exposition of any portion of the Word of God.

2. Statement of the exegetical idea of the passage.

After the work of exegesis has been completed, the next step is to discover the main idea of the passage. In our earlier chapters we have purposely tried to avoid reference to the proposition, and have limited ourselves to such terms as the topic, subject, dominant idea, or theme in connection with the construction of a sermon outline.

In a recent treatise on homiletics (*Biblical Preaching* by Haddon W. Robinson, copyright 1981 by Baker Book House), Haddon W. Robinson expands the idea of what we have previously called the subject or topic. He speaks of it as the exegetical idea. The exegetical concept consists of two parts, a subject and one or more complements. The subject is what you are going to talk about, while the complement consists of what you are going to say about the subject. The exegetical idea then combines the subject and complement or complements into a single comprehensive sentence.

Every unit of Scripture contains a subject and at least one complement. The task of the homilist is first to discover the subject and then to
find what the text says about it. Unless the student is able to accomplish this, he will probably have only a hazy notion of the contents of the
passage and will not be in a position to expound its contents clearly to
his people.

Application of the familiar interrogatives *who, what, why, how,
when,* and *where* to the contents of a passage will often help the homiletical craftsman to ascertain the subject.

Sometimes paraphrasing the entire expository unit will assist us to
discover both the subject and the complement. At other times making
a mechanical layout of a passage will enable us to analyze its contents
by setting forth the relationship of dependent and independent clauses
to one another (see the example in Chapter 3) and will provide clues to
what the text is about.

We shall now discuss four passages from which we propose to formulate exegetical ideas. It is beyond the scope of our textbook to do
the exegetical work on these texts. We shall therefore be obliged to
suppose that this necessary study has already been done.

Our first example is taken from Mark 16:1-4.

> When the Sabbath was over, Mary Magdalene, Mary the
> mother of James, and Salome bought spices so that they might
> go to anoint Jesus' body. Very early on the first day of the week,
> just after sunrise, they were on their way to the tomb and they
> asked each other, "Who will roll the stone away from the en-
> trance of the tomb?"
> But when they looked up, they saw that the stone, which was
> very large, had been rolled away.

In our search for the subject we ask ourselves, "What is the passage
all about, or who is it all about? Does it center upon the spices, or upon
the stone, or does it have to do with the problem which the women discussed?" Consideration of the passage will soon indicate to us that the
main idea gathers around the women, but we ask, "What women?" or,
"Who were these women?" Further reflection will indicate that the essential element in the narrative is "the women who came to the tomb to
anoint the body of Jesus." Thus we have the subject of the text.

We now address ourselves to a search for the complement. In other
words, we need to find out what the passage tells us about these

women. We soon gather several facts, such as the names of the women, the day that they went to the sepulchre, the spices they brought with them, the time of day they came, the conversation they had with each other, the problem which they discussed, and the way in which it was unexpectedly resolved. There are too many facts here to be listed in a comprehensive sentence and we therefore sum them up in two complements: first, "They were troubled in their own minds about the stone which was too big for them to remove from the tomb;" and second, "They found later that the stone had been removed before they ever reached the tomb."

Our next task is to state the basic idea of the passage, that is, the subject and the complement, in a single and complete sentence. Hence, we express the exegetical idea in the following comprehensive sentence: "The women who came to the empty tomb to anoint the body of Jesus worried about a problem which was too big for them but which was resolved before they ever had to face it."

We use Galatians 3:13 as our second example.

> Christ redeemed us from the curse of the law by becoming a curse for us, for it is written: "Cursed is everyone who is hung on a tree."

If we give special thought to the text, we shall see that the subject, or what the verse talks about, is our redemption from the curse of the law. The complement, or what Galatians 3:13 says about our redemption from the curse of the law, is that it was effected by Christ taking the curse for us when He hung on a tree. By uniting the subject and complement the exegetical idea may be stated thus: "Our redemption from the curse of the law was effected by Christ taking the curse for us."

Our third example is taken from Luke 15:1-2:

> Now the tax collectors and "sinners" were all gathering around to hear him. But the Pharisees and the teachers of the law muttered, "This man welcomes sinners and eats with them."

By considering these verses carefully we see that the subject is the complaining of the Pharisees and the teachers of the law against Jesus. The complement is what the text tells us about their complaint, namely, that Jesus welcomed and associated with sinners. We now combine the subject and the complement into this exegetical idea:

"The Pharisees and teachers of the law complained that Jesus welcomed and associated with sinners."

For our final example let us consider Philippians 1:9-11:

> And this is my prayer: that your love may abound more and more in knowledge and depth of insight, so that you may be able to discern what is best and may be pure and blameless until the day of Christ, filled with the fruit of righteousness that comes through Jesus Christ—to the glory and praise of God.

What is the subject of these verses? What are they all about? It is not difficult to see that they are a prayer which Paul offered on behalf of the believers of Philippi. As for the complement or complements, what does the text reveal to us about the prayer, or what petition or petitions does Paul make for the Christians for whom he prays? Verse 9 clearly reveals that the Apostle requests that the love of the believers might increase more and more; verses 10 and 11 indicate that as a result of a greater love these New Testament saints would become possessed with a spiritual discernment and with certain specific graces of Christian character which may redound to the glory of God. Hence, the subject is Paul's prayer for the believers at Philippi, and we list two complements: "It consisted of a request for an increase in their love, and it had as its two-fold object the possession by these saints of a spiritual discernment and the graces of Christian character which would bring praise to God."

The subject and complements which we have discovered thus evoke the following exegetical concept: "Paul prayed that the saints at Philippi might so increase in love that they would become possessed of such spiritual discernment and traits of Christian character as to bring glory to God."

Some portions of the Word are much more complex than the ones which we have considered, especially certain sections in the writings of the prophets and in the epistles. The ability to discern the subject and complement or complements in such cases will usually require special examination of the text in accordance with the principles of exegesis.

3. *The discovery of the one main truth which the passage seems to convey.*

The exegetical idea usually differs from the proposition or homiletical idea in that the former is a statement in a single sentence of what the text actually says, whereas the latter consists of the one main spiritual truth or abiding principle which the passage is intended to convey.

There are some instances where the exegetical idea and the timeless truth or thesis may correspond exactly with each other. For instance, the statement in Galatians 6:7, "a man reaps what he sows" is both a declaration of the contents of Galatians 6:7-8 as well as a universal principle which relates to all men everywhere.

However, when the exegetical idea does not consist of a foundational truth the man of God must ask himself, "What does the text say to me?" or "What is the vital and timeless truth which the passage is intended to teach?"

It is at this point that the exegete often senses how utterly dependent he must be upon the Spirit of God to illumine him concerning the one particular spiritual lesson which the Lord would have him present to His people out of the sacred text. It is also at this juncture that the exegetical idea provides a stepping stone to the statement of the proposition or subject sentence.

We shall illustrate this with the first exegetical idea we formulated earlier in the chapter from the account in Mark 16:1-4 of the women who purposed to anoint the body of Jesus. The exegetical idea was, "The women who came to the empty tomb to anoint the body of Jesus worried about a problem which was too big for them but which was resolved before they ever had to face it."

From this exegetical idea we are led to the following thesis or principle: "The Lord's people are sometimes confronted with problems which are too big for them." We could, of course, derive many other timeless truths from our exegetical idea; here are two: "We sometimes worry unnecessarily over problems which do not even exist," and "God is bigger than any problems we may face."

Let us now note a few examples of exegetical ideas derived from some of the passages we have discussed in earlier chapters and observe how they lead us to express the proposition.

We draw our first from Ezra 7:10: "Ezra set his heart to become a man whom God could use in Israel." The timeless truth may be stated: "God uses a man who puts first things first."

Our second is based on John 3:16: "Because of His love for the world, God gave His one and only Son that men may be saved through faith in Him." From this statement we may derive a timeless truth such as: "God's gift of His Son is the only means of salvation for men."

We take another example from Ephesians 6:10-18: "The believer is engaged in a spiritual warfare in which he is given direction and provision to be a successful warrior." Our homiletical idea thus follows: "In the spiritual warfare in which he is engaged, the Christian can count on being a successful warrior."

As a final example we state the exegetical idea we have drawn from an exegesis of Psalm 23:1-6: "The bases for the contentment of the Lord's sheep rest upon who his Shepherd is and what his Shepherd does for him, as well as what his Shepherd has in store for him in the future." This exegetical concept leads to the proposition: "Every individual who can claim the Lord as his own has adequate bases for contentment."

4. Statement of the proposition in the form of a succinct and forceful sentence.

As the proposition crystallizes in the homilist's thinking he may need to re-word it to express it as a succinct and vigorous sentence. At the same time he must make sure that his proposition faithfully reveals the concept of the Scripture passage.

The proposition may also require the preacher to rearrange or reconstruct his entire sermon plan to properly elaborate this one vital principle to his congregation.

Looking again at our proposition on Psalm 23, we may revise it to the following simple statement: "Contentment is the happy prerogative of every child of God."

Principles for the Formulation of the Proposition

1. The proposition should be a statement expressing in a complete sentence the one main or essential idea of the sermon.

As we have seen, the proposition is a statement of the one main truth which the preacher proposes to set forth in his sermon; when correctly formulated it promotes the organizational unity of the thought structure of the sermon. If more than one significant idea is introduced in the proposition, the unity of the entire structure is at once destroyed. An example of such a statement with two ideas is, "The Scriptures teach us how to live holy lives and to be faithful servants of Christ." Here we have two propositions, making it impossible to maintain singleness of thought in the sermon.

In order for the essential idea of the sermon to be expressed as a complete thought, however, it has to be stated in the form of a complete sentence. That is, the statement should consist of two main parts: a subject, or the thing about which we are to speak; and a predicate, or what we are to say about it. For example, we may select the second coming of Christ as the topic we are to talk about. If we were to leave this subject by itself we would have an incomplete idea because it does not indicate what we are going to say about our subject. We therefore need to add a predicate, which always includes a verb, to express precisely what we wish to say about the subject. Hence we add to our subject the phrase "is the hope of suffering believers." By placing subject and predicate together we now have a complete idea expressed in the form of a complete sentence: "The second coming of Christ is the hope of suffering believers."

2. *The proposition should be a declarative sentence.*

This means that the thesis or subject sentence must be an explicit and positive assertion, not a negative one. Such a statement as, "We honor the Lord when we praise Him for His benefits" is a declarative assertion. On the other hand, if we say, "We do not honor the Lord when we complain about our circumstances," we are making a negative statement.

Note the outline below and observe how the thesis or proposition is expressed in the form of a declarative sentence.

Title: "The Life of Dependence"
Proposition: The Christian life is a life of constant dependence.
  I. We are dependent upon Christ for salvation, Titus 3:5.
  II. We are dependent upon the Word of God for spiritual growth, 1 Peter 2:2.
  III. We are dependent upon prayer for spiritual power, James 5:15.
  IV. We are dependent upon fellowship for mutual encouragement, 1 John 1:3.

3. *The proposition should be a timeless truth generally stated in the present tense.*

The proposition is a principle or truth which is always valid and universal, and which is a standard for life and conduct. Hence, it must of necessity be scripturally sound; at the same time, it should usually be stated in the present tense.

But as we have indicated under the first rule, a truth cannot be fully expressed by a mere phrase or fragment of a sentence; it must be stated in a complete sentence with a subject and a predicate. For example, such an expression as, "The need of God's people in a time of trial," is not a declarative statement and does not contain a truth. It is merely a fragment of a sentence, and if a preacher were to attempt to use it as a proposition it would only lead to ambiguity and inanity in the development of the sermon. On the other hand, if we say, "God's people can always look to Him in a time of trial," we now have an assertion which is true for all time and universal in its scope.

It should also be obvious that a command is not a principle and hence does not express a timeless truth. A command is not a declarative sentence. Thus, it would be incorrect to express the proposition this way: Be diligent in your work.

In addition, an ageless truth will not include any geographical or historical references, nor make use of proper names except that of deity. So it would be incorrect to say, "As the Lord called Amos from Tekoa in the land of Judah to preach in the Northern Kingdom, so He calls some today to go to other lands to serve Him." Instead, we could say, "The Lord in His sovereignty calls believers to serve Him whereever He wills."

4. The proposition should be stated simply and clearly.

There should never be any vagueness or ambiguity in the statement of the subject sentence. For instance, if we were to express as a proposition the phrase, "Work is rewarding," the congregation may begin to ask themselves such questions as, "Whose work is rewarding?", "What type of work is rewarding?", "When is one's work rewarding?", or "What kind of rewards does a person receive for his work?"

But while it is necessary that the homiletical idea should be set forth clearly, it is not necessary to employ elegant or impressive language. Rather, the wording should be so simple and lucid that its meaning is immediately intelligible to the hearers. For instance, if we plan to speak about Christian witnessing, we can state the proposition in this way: "A radiant Christian makes an effective witness for Christ."

5. The proposition should be the assertion of a vital truth.

When a preacher delivers a message from the Scriptures, he is dealing with such human essentials as fear, guilt, frustration, grief, disappointment, heartache, love, joy, forgiveness, peace, grace, and hope, as well as a host of other emotions and aspirations. Accordingly, the thesis, which is the very heart of the sermon, must be expressed in terms which are significant to the lives of individuals.

Under these circumstances mere trivialities have no place in the thesis. For instance, sentences like, "Fish can swim upstream," or, "People have different tastes," are of no special significance; even though they may be universally true they have no particular bearing upon the vital issues of life.

The minister must therefore take pains to state his subject sentence in the form of what is rightfully called a big idea, a concept which expresses something vital or important. In other words, it should be a pregnant sentence, full of meaning or significance to his hearers.

6. *The proposition should be specific.*

The timeless truth to be expressed in the proposition must be limited or narrowed to a specific concept. If the big idea is stated in terms which are too general it will lack vigor and thus will not challenge the interest of the hearers. The following statements fall into this category:

> "There is great value in prayer."
> "Fathers are to discipline their children."
> "We should study the Word of God."
> "Christ loves the lost."

Contrast the next four statements and observe that in each case we have a declaration which by its limited scope becomes sharp and forceful.

> "A praying Christian exerts a mighty influence."
> "Fathers have to exercise wisdom in the disciplining of their children."
> "The study of the Word of God produces great benefits."
> "Christ's love reaches out to every individual sinner."

7. *The proposition should be stated as concisely as possible, consistent with perspicuity.*

An effective thesis must be stated in the briefest possible terms, provided that clarity is not sacrificed for brevity. Hence, in the formulation of the proposition it is necessary that lengthy, circuitous statements be avoided. In other words, the proposition should be a crisp, simple sentence. A good rule of thumb is to limit it to seventeen words or less. More words than this will reduce its effectiveness. Note the concise thesis in the outline below:

> Title: "Triumphant Living"
> Text: Philippians 1:12-21.
> Proposition: Christians can be gloriously triumphant in Christ.
>   I. In the face of adversity, as Paul was, vv. 12-14.
>   II. In the face of opposition, as Paul was, vv. 15-19.
>   III. In the face of death, as Paul was, vv. 20-21.

It should be pointed out that the thesis is not a formal statement of the main divisions. The purpose of the proposition is not to reveal the plan of the discourse, but rather to state in simple terms the main idea of the sermon in the form of a timeless truth. Each division of the sermon then grows out of this subject sentence and develops some aspect of it. Using the outline which we have just presented, it would therefore be incorrect to say in the proposition: Christians can be gloriously triumphant in the face of adversity, opposition, and death.

The Means of Relating the Proposition to the Main Divisions

The proposition is usually connected to the sermon outline by a question, followed by a transitional sentence.

Any one of five interrogative adverbs is commonly used to connect the proposition to the main points of the discourse. These interrogatives are: *why, how, what, when,* and *where*. For example, in the outline "The Life of Dependence " shown earlier in this chapter, the proposition reads, "The Christian life is a life of constant dependence." This proposition should now be followed by the question, "Why is the Christian life one of constant dependence?"

The interrogative sentence leads to the transitional sentence, which ties the proposition and the main points of the sermon together and provides a smooth passage from the proposition to the main divisions. At the same time the interrogative and transitional sentences indicate how the homiletical idea is going to be developed, elucidated, or explained in the body of the sermon. Note the examples of propositions in this chapter which are followed by interrogative and transitional sentences and observe that in each case the question which follows the proposition, and the transitional sentence which succeeds the interrogative sentence, clearly indicate how the sermon will develop the proposition.

The transitional sentence always contains a key word which classifies or delineates the character of the main headings of the outline. Using the same example on "The Life of Dependence," we may state the transitional sentence in the following manner: "There are several reasons why the Christian life may be said to be a life of constant dependence." Obviously the word *reasons* relates the proposition to the main points of the discourse, with each main division expressing one of the reasons why the Christian life is said to be a life of constant dependence.

So that the student may understand these instructions clearly we repeat the outline on "The Life of Dependence," with the homiletical idea, question, and transitional sentence in their proper order.

Title: "The Life of Dependence"
Proposition: The Christian life is a life of constant dependence.
Interrogative sentence: Why is the Christian life a life of constant dependence?
Transitional sentence: There are several reasons why the Christian life may be said to be a life of constant dependence.
 I. We are dependent upon Christ for salvation, Titus 3:5.
 II. We are constantly dependent upon the Word of God for spiritual growth, 1 Peter 2:2.
 III. We are constantly dependent upon prayer for spiritual power, James 5:16.
 IV. We are constantly dependent upon fellowship for mutual encouragement, 1 John 1:3.

The key word is a useful homiletical device which makes it possible to characterize or classify within the transitional sentence the main divisions of the outline. There must, of course, be structural unity in the outline. Without structural unity there cannot be a key word to connect the transitional sentence to each main division and the main divisions to each other. Therefore, a good test of structural unity in an outline is to see if the same key word can be applied to each of the main divisions.

In Chapter 3 we prepared the following expository outline on Luke 15:25-32:

> Title: "The Pharisee: Yesterday and Today"
> Subject: Features of pharisaism as seen in the character of the elder brother.
> I. He was a self-righteous man, vv. 29-30.
> II. He was an unloving man, vv. 28-30.
> III. He was a fault-finding man, vv. 25-30.
> IV. He was a stubborn man, vv. 28-32.

We now state the proposition, the interrogative sentence, and the transitional sentence as follows:

> Proposition: The Lord detests the spirit of pharisaism.
> Interrogative sentence: What are features of this spirit which He detests?
> Transitional sentence: The features of the elder brother as seen here in the description of his character manifest the spirit of pharisaism which the Lord detests.

The word "features" becomes the key word in the transitional sentence.

Let us purposely change the last main division to destroy the structural unity of the outline:

> I. He was a self-righteous man, vv. 29-30.
> II. He was an unloving man, vv. 28-30.
> III. He was a fault-finding man, vv. 25-30.
> IV. The father was concerned over the elder brother's attitude, vv. 28-32.

It is now impossible to connect the transitional sentence properly to this outline because the key word "features" can no longer be applied to all the main divisions.

To enable the student to understand more clearly the relationship of the thesis to the transitional sentence, we show below three outlines for which we set forth the subject sentence, the interrogative sentence, the transitional sentence, and the key word.

> Title: "Buying Up Opportunities"
> Proposition: An alert Christian discovers that unusual opportunities often rise to reach the lost.
> Interrogative sentence: When are such opportunities likely to occur?
> Transitional sentence: These opportunities are likely to arise on special occasions in the lives of individuals.
> Key word: Occasions.
> I. At the time when sorrow strikes a home.

II. At a time of danger which may threaten an individual.
III. At a time of illness.

Title: "An Exemplary Ministry"
Text: 1 Thessalonians 2:1-12.
Proposition: The servant of God has an exemplary pattern for his ministry.
Interrogative sentence: What are the characteristics of this pattern for the ministry?
Transitional sentence: According to 1 Thessalonians 2:1-12, Paul's ministry exemplifies four characteristics which should be true of the ministry of the servant of God today.
Key word: Characteristics.
I. It should be with holy boldness, vv. 1-2.
II. It should be in faithfulness to God, vv. 3-6.
III. It should be with gracious consideration, vv. 7-9.
IV. It should be in integrity of conduct, vv. 10-12.

Title: "The Mind of Christ"
Text: Philippians 2:5-8.
Proposition: A Christ-like Christian is an individual who possesses the mind of Christ.
Interrogative sentence: What aspects of Christ-likeness are implied by the mind of Christ?
Transitional sentence: In Philippians 2:5-8 we find that there are two aspects of Christ-likeness implied by the mind of Christ.
Key word: Aspects.
I. Christ-like self-denial, vv. 6-7.
II. Christ-like self-humiliation, v. 8.

Appropriate Key Words

A smooth transition from the homiletical idea to the main divisions is of special importance to the thought structure of a sermon. An awkward or faulty transition can be misleading and will weaken the effectiveness of a discourse. Because the key word is a vital part of the transitional sentence it is also necessary that great care be taken in the choice of the correct key word. The word "things" is too general a term to be employed as a key word. Instead, the student should aim to use the specific word which accurately characterizes the main divisions.

To aid the homilist in the discovery of the appropriate key word, we list some of the key words which are commonly used in transitional sentences.

actions	groups	parts
admonitions	guarantees	perils
advantages	habits	periods
affirmations	handicaps	points
aims	hindrances	practices
applications	hopes	problems
approaches	ideals	proofs
arguments	ideas	propositions
articles	illustrations	qualifications
attitudes	inferences	qualities
attributes	instances	questions
beliefs	issues	reasons
benefits	items	remarks
blessings	joys	responses
burdens	judgments	routes
causes	keys	rules
claims	kinds	safeguards
commands	laws	secrets
criteria	lessons	sins
dangers	limits	sources
deficiencies	lists	statements
demands	losses	steps
devices	manifestations	suggestions
differences	marks	teachings
distinctions	means	tendencies
doctrines	measures	thoughts
effects	methods	topics
elements	mistakes	truths
estimates	motives	undertakings
events	names	uses
evidences	necessities	values
expressions	needs	views
factors	objections	virtues
facts	objectives	warnings
features	observations	wishes
functions	obstacles	words
gains	occasions	wrongs
goals	paradoxes	

Alternate Forms of the Proposition

To avoid monotony in the presentation of the proposition, a few authorities on homiletics allow the substitution of an interrogative, hortatory, or exclamatory form in place of the timeless truth.

For the interrogative form the speaker simply omits the statement of the timeless truth altogether and uses the interrogative sentence in its place. Thus, if we use the outline shown above on "The Life of Dependence," the dominant idea of the sermon is presented by the interrogative, "Why is the Christian life a life of constant dependence?"

In the hortatory form the preacher aims to encourage or exhort his congregation to adopt a certain course of action. Observe how the hortatory form is used in the following outline.

Title: "The Wisest Student"
Alternate form: Let us study the Word of God diligently.
  I.   So that we may grow in the Christian life, 1 Peter 2:2.
  II. So that we may be approved of God as His workmen,
       2 Timothy 2:15.
  III. So that we may be fully equipped for Christian
       service, 2 Timothy 3:16-17.
  IV. So that we may be transformed into the likeness of
       Christ, 2 Corinthians 3:18 NASB

The exclamatory type is the form which the sermonizer uses when he desires to give special emphasis to his subject. For example, if he wishes to stress the blessings which the believer has in Christ as revealed in Ephesians 1:3-14, he may use an exclamation such as that shown in the outline below.

Title: "Supremely Blessed"
Alternate form: How wonderful are the blessings which we have
                in Christ!
  I.   We are chosen in Him, v. 4.
  II. We are redeemed in Him, v. 7.
  III. We are made heirs in Him, v. 11 (marginal note),
       v. 13.
  IV. We are sealed in Him, v. 13.

A few writers on pulpit address teach that a clearly defined statement of the objective of the discourse may sometimes constitute a legitimate and adequate alternative to a proposition. Many preachers in fact are able to communicate the truth effectively by developing an outline around a central thought or theme as the focus of the sermon without the use of a clearly defined proposition. If in a sermon of this kind a few timeless truths drawn from the passage are included in the discourse, especially at the close of the message, they enable the congregation to see how the Biblical text has relevance to the everyday world in which they live. Read Nehemiah 1:1 through 2:8 and note the following outline gathered around the subject, "Nehemiah, the man of prayer."

Title: "Power through Prayer"
  I. He realized the need of prayer, Nehemiah 1:1-3.
      1. In regard to the plight of his people, vv. 1-3.
      2. In regard to the conditions in Jerusalem, the place

of worship, vv. 1-3.
  3. In spite of his own comfortable circumstances, vv. 1-2, 11.
II. He prayed the right kind of prayer, Nehemiah 1:4-11.
  1. In earnestness of spirit, v. 4.
  2. In contriteness of heart, vv. 5-7.
  3. With faith in the promises of God, vv. 8-9.
  4. With specific requests, vv. 10-11.
III. He obtained glorious results through prayer, Nehemiah 2:1-8.
  1. In direct answers to his requests, vv. 1-8.
  2. By the gracious hand of God which was upon him, v. 8.

Either during the course of the sermon, or preferably at its conclusion, we could set forth and elaborate on the following timeless truths which are derived from the passage:

- The God of heaven delights to hear the prayers of His people on earth.
- We must meet the divinely prescribed conditions if we are to experience divine interventions on our behalf.
- The Lord has no substitute for confession—sin must be dealt with definitely, ruthlessly, and completely.
- God performs impossibilities for those who pray to Him.

A proper thesis for the above outline, containing a timeless truth as defined earlier in this chapter, could be stated like this: "The fervent prayer of a godly man has wonderful power." Our interrogative sentence might be, "How is this truth revealed in the passage before us?" The transitional sentence would then read, "By studying three main facts in this portion of Scripture concerning Nehemiah, the man of prayer, we shall see how this truth is exemplified." The sermon would naturally follow according to the lines shown above.

Even a narrative in the Bible can be more readily understood and remembered when we present it according to a simple plan. Note the effectiveness of this outline which David W. Fant once employed in connection with the story of the Good Samaritan in Luke 10:30-37:

I. The man who needed a friend, v. 30.
II. The two men who should have been friends, vv. 31-32.
III. The man who was a friend, vv. 33-37.

The narrative refers to four men, with the points leading to the Samaritan who proved to be a real friend. Hence, the obvious purpose of the story is to teach us our responsibility to an individual who is in need of a friend.

Although the alternate forms which we have discussed in this section may provide variety in the expression of the proposition, we recommend that the beginner avoid their use entirely until he has thoroughly mastered the technique of stating the proposition in accordance with the principles presented in this chapter.

We also urge that whenever one of these alternate forms is employed the preacher should remember to use the transitional elements leading to the body of the sermon. For example, in the outline in which the exclamation, "How wonderful are the blessings we have in Christ!" is used we may make the transition to the body of the sermon with a statement like the following: "Let us now consider these blessings one by one as we look into this portion of Paul's epistle to the Ephesians."

The Place of the Proposition in the Sermon Outline

The proposition should generally appear at the end of the introduction. The introduction leads up to the proposition which, together with its accompanying interrogative and transitional sentences, leads to the main body of the sermon. Observe how this is done in the outline below.

Title: "The Psalm of Contentment"
Text: Psalm 23.
Introduction: 1. Sheepherder in Idaho with band of 1,200 sheep —unable to give individual attention to sheep.
2. Contrast Shepherd of this Psalm—as though He has only one sheep for which to care.
3. Every child of God recognizes himself to be the sheep spoken of in this Psalm.
Proposition: Contentment is the happy prerogative of every child of God.
Interrogative sentence: Upon what is his contentment based?
Transitional sentence: The child of God learns from this Psalm that as the Lord's sheep his contentment is based on three facts in relation to the sheep.
I. The sheep's Shepherd, v. 1.
II. The sheep's provision, vv. 2-5.
III. The sheep's prospect, v. 6.

When we develop the sermon in this manner, stating the thesis before presenting the points which explain or prove it, we are using the deductive approach. This is the method which is most frequently employed in homiletical textbooks, and it is the one which we also have used for the most part.

There are occasions, however, when the preacher may desire to withhold the aim of his sermon until the very end, and use the main points to lead to the statement of the timeless truth. The following example shows how this is done.

Title: "Committing National Suicide"
Text: 2 Kings 17:7-23.
   I. A nation may sin wilfully against the Lord, as Israel did, vv. 7-12.
  II. A nation may harden herself against the Lord, as Israel did, vv. 13-14.
 III. A nation may reject the Word of God, as Israel did, vv. 15-16.
 IV. A nation may sell herself to do evil in the sight of the Lord, as Israel did, vv. 16-17.
Proposition: A nation cannot escape the divine judgment which results from her own guilt.
Conclusion: This was true of Israel, and the judgment which rests on her to this day is a constant reminder of God's retribution upon a nation's transgression.

By the use of four examples drawn from Israel's history of doing evil, we have set forth a principle with respect to a nation's self-destruction. This procedure, in which the points of the outline build up to the expression of the proposition, is called the inductive approach. Following is another example of the inductive approach.

Title: "How to be Saved"
   I. Can church membership save us?
  II. Can baptism save us?
 III. Can good works save us?
 IV. Can good intentions save us?
Proposition and conclusion: The work of Jesus Christ on the cross alone can save us from sin, Ephesians 2:8-9, Acts 4:12.

EXERCISES

1. Listed below are nine brief passages from which the student should have no difficulty in discovering the subject and comple-

ment. State the subject and complement or complements of each.
Genesis 15:1, Exodus 15:22-26, Joshua 5:13-15, Psalm 126:1-6,
Isaiah 1:18, Amos 7:10-17, 1 Corinthians 4:1-2, Ephesians 4:1-3,
and 1 Peter 3:7.

2. Based upon the subject and complement which you have discovered for the nine passages in Exercise 1, express a suitable exegetical idea in the form of a complete sentence for each one of them.

3. Which of the following statements meets the qualifications of
a proposition as set forth in this chapter?

(1) Have you praised God today?
(2) We should be faithfully serving Christ.
(3) God gives lavishly of His grace.
(4) The believer can depend upon the Lord's help in his
time of need.
(5) Children are often afraid of the dark.
(6) The gospel of the grace of God.
(7) The mystery of the ages: Christ in you.
(8) Daniel was not devoured by the lions because of his
faith in God.
(9) God's Word is both our guide and our strength.
(10) God is perfecting the saints.
(11) Don't be anxious about anything.
(12) A joyful Christian is a testimony to those around him.
(13) The Pharisees claimed that Christ cast out demons by
the power of Satan.
(14) If we are generous in our giving the Lord will bless us
abundantly.
(15) When we serve the Lord we are serving an excellent
Master.
(16) There is a time to be quiet before the Lord.
(17) Our Heavenly Father pays special attention to His
children.
(18) It is well for Christians to realize that God is always
right in what He does.
(19) The Ruler of this universe takes note of everything
that goes on in this world.
(20) God is no man's debtor and will reward us for everything we do for Him.

4. Read three sermons, each by a different preacher, and formulate a suitable subject sentence for each of them.

5. Prepare a suitable big idea for each of the following topical sermon outlines which appear in Chapter 1.

> "The Believer's Hope"
> "Knowing God's Word"
> "The Ability of God"

6. Formulate a correct proposition for each of the following textual sermon outlines which appear in Chapter 2:

> "Putting First Things First"
> "The Joy of Easter"
> "The Only Approach to God"

7. Write a thesis to fit each of the following expository sermon outlines which appear in Chapter 3:

> "The Good Fight of Faith"
> "Wit's End Corner"
> "From Sinner to Saint"

8. State what is wrong with the title and proposition in each of these outlines and show how you would correct them. Also add an interrogative sentence and a transitional sentence following each proposition wherever possible.

(1) Title: "Granting a Request"
    Text: 1 Samuel 1:4-28.
Proposition: These verses give five lessons on prayer which suit every believer.
    I. Hannah fretted over her barren condition, vv. 4-10a.
    II. Hannah prayed for a son, vv. 10b-11.
    III. Hannah was misunderstood by the priest, vv. 12-18.
    IV. Hannah received an answer to her prayer, vv. 19-20.
    V. Hannah presented Samuel to the Lord, vv. 24-28.

(2) Title: "Standards"
    Text: Romans 12:1-2
Proposition: The Christian life has high standards and we are able to live this life by the power of the Spirit of God.
    I. A dedicated life.
      1. Of sacrifice.
      2. Of service.
    II. An obedient life.
      1. Of non-conformity to the world.
      2. Of conformity to the will of God.

(3) Title: "The Victorious Daniel"
    Text: Daniel 1:1-21.
Proposition: The example of Daniel to every Christian of victory over sin.

I. The testing of Daniel, vv. 1-7.
II. The purpose of Daniel, v. 8.
III. The triumph of Daniel, vv. 9-21.

(4) Title: "Christ and the Christian's Privileges"
    Text: Ephesians 1-6.
Proposition: We shall seek to obtain a synthetic view of the Epistle
                to the Ephesians which deals with the position,
                walk, and warfare of the believer.
    I. The position of the believer, 1-3.
    II. The walk of the believer, 4-6:9.
    III. The warfare of the believer, 6:10-20.

(5) Title: "Have a Heart"
    Text: 1 Thessalonians 3:1-13.
Proposition: Have a heart like the Apostle Paul's.
    I. A sympathetic heart, vv. 1-4.
    II. A loving heart, vv. 5-9.
    III. A prayerful heart, vv. 10-13.

BIBLIOGRAPHY

Baird, John E. *Preparing for Platform and Pulpit*. Nashville, Tennessee: Abingdon Press, 1968, pp. 48-62.

Baumann, J. Daniel. *An Introduction to Contemporary Preaching*. Grand Rapids, Michigan: Baker Book House, 1972, pp. 76-79.

Brack, Harold A. and Kenneth G. Hance. *Public Speaking and Discussion for Religious Leaders*. Englewood Cliffs, New Jersey: Prentice Hall, Inc., 1961, Chapter 8.

Davis, Henry Grady. *Design for Preaching*. Philadelphia, Pennsylvania: Fortress Press, 1958, Chapters 1-4.

Davis, Ozora S. *Principles of Preaching*. Chicago: University of Chicago Press, 1924, Part II, Chapter 4.

Hogue, Wilson T. *Homiletics and Pastoral Theology*. Winona Lake, Indiana: Free Methodist Publishing House, 1949, Chapter 10.

Hoppin, James M. *Homiletics*. New York: Dodd, Mead and Company, 1881, Division 4, Section 16.

Koller, Charles W. *Expository Preaching Without Notes*. Grand Rapids, Michigan: Baker Book House, 1962, Chapters 7, 11.

Perry, Lloyd M. *A Manual for Biblical Preaching*. Grand Rapids, Michigan: Baker Book House, 1965, pp. 66-71.

Phelps, Austin. *The Theory of Preaching*. New York: Charles Scribner's Sons, 1892, Lectures 20-25.

Reu, M. *Homiletics, A Manual of the Theory and Practice of Preaching*. Minneapolis: Augsburg Publishing House, 1950, Chapter 16.

Robinson, Haddon W. *Biblical Preaching*. Grand Rapids, Michigan: Baker Book House, 1980, pp. 31-46, 66-68, 97-99, 115-127.

Skinner, Craig. *The Teaching Ministry of the Pulpit*. Grand Rapids, Michigan: Baker Book House, 1979, pp. 162-167.

Stibbs, Alan M. *Expounding God's Word*. Grand Rapids, Michigan: The Eerdmans Publishing Co., 1961, Chapter 4.

Vinet, A. *Homiletics or the Theory of Preaching*. New York: Ivison and Phinney, 1854, Part II, Chapter 4.

Whitesell, Faris Daniel and Lloyd M. Perry. *Variety in Your Preaching*. Westwood, New Jersey: Fleming H. Revell Company, 1954, Chapter 5.

8. THE DIVISIONS

Definition of the Divisions

The divisions are the main sections of an orderly discourse. Whether they are stated in delivery or not, a properly planned sermon will be divided into distinct parts with each component contributing to the unity of the address.

The numerous examples of sermon outlines in the preceding chapters should be sufficient to indicate the value of good arrangement in a discourse. Nevertheless, it may be well to discuss some specific reasons for the use of divisions in a sermon.

The Value of Divisions to the Preacher

1. Divisions promote clarity of thought.

If a sermon is to be properly constructed it cannot be built upon vague ideas or indefinite expressions. On the contrary, the thought structure must be so distinct and precise that the meaning of each point will be perfectly clear to the hearers at the moment each division is announced. Moreover, the discipline of arranging preaching material in an organized structure drives the preacher to state his thoughts distinctly and clearly. The message also becomes clear in the mind of the sermonizer when it has been arranged in proper order.

2. Divisions promote unity of thought.

We have said repeatedly that unity is essential to sermon construction. Outlining a sermon tends to unify it; for in the preacher's effort to classify his material under various headings he will be enabled to discern whether or not the sermon contains structural unity. Irrelevant items will soon be recognized as he endeavors to relate each division to the central idea of the discourse.

3. Divisions assist the preacher in the proper treatment of a subject.

As the minister organizes the material for his sermon he will be able to see the subject as a whole, the various aspects of the subject, and the relationship of one part to another. Some features will stand out as having special importance and therefore deserving of particular treatment or emphasis. Other features may then be seen as inconsequential or unimportant and may therefore be deleted from the sermon. Further consideration of the various parts of the subject will also indicate the order in which they should be taken up and thus lead to progression of thought in the development of the outline.

4. Divisions enable the preacher to remember the main points of his sermon.

A common error of the beginner in the pulpit is looking frequently at his notes instead of looking directly at his congregation and maintaining constant eye contact with the people. The preacher whose sermon is properly arranged will avoid this pitfall. His message is so clearly outlined that he can recall his main divisions without any difficulty and can move easily from one part of the sermon to the next with perhaps only a fleeting glance at his notes. His thoughts flow freely and uninterruptedly as he stands in the pulpit because, days before the delivery of the sermon, he has carefully constructed the divisions in an appropriate and effective order.

The Value of Divisions to the Congregation

A well-planned outline assists the hearer no less than it does the preacher. There are at least two important advantages to the congregation.

1. Divisions make the main points of the sermon clear.

It is much easier for the hearer to follow a spoken message when the main ideas are organized and clearly stated than when the ideas are unorganized and unrelated to one another. As the preacher announces his divisions and moves from one main point to the next, the listener is able to recognize the relationship of one part to the next and is also able to discern the evident progression in the discussion.

2. Divisions assist the memory in recalling the main features of the sermon.

How many times does an individual say after a church service that he has been blessed by the sermon, but if asked to recall what was said by the minister he has to admit that he has only a vague recollection of the sermon content. But, when a message is so delivered that the main headings are distinctly recognizable, the auditor will be able to think through the main ideas of the address, and each division will serve as a "peg" upon which he will be able to hang the truths he has heard.

Principles for the Preparation of the Main Divisions

1. The main divisions should grow out of the proposition, with each division contributing to the development or elaboration of the proposition.

Just as the proposition is the gist of the sermon, the main divisions are the unfolding or development of the proposition. Each main division must be derived from the thesis, serve as an explanation of the concept contained in it, or in some way be essential to its development. In other words, each division should be an expansion of the idea expressed in the proposition. Study the outlines in the last chapter and observe how the main divisions are derived from or develop and expand the proposition in each case.

With regard to the outline on Psalm 23 in Chapter 7, the proposition may not seem at first glance to be properly related to the main divisions until we note the analogy between the sheep and the child of God referred to both in the introduction and in the transitional sentence.

2. The main divisions should be entirely distinct from one another.

While each main division must be drawn from or be an elaboration of the proposition, each must be entirely distinct from the others. This means that there must be no overlapping of the divisions. Consider the outline below.

Title: "The Christian's Ideal"
Text: 1 Corinthians 13:1-13.
Proposition: Love is the ideal by which the Christian life is measured.
Interrogative sentence: What can we learn from this chapter about this ideal by which our lives are measured?

Transitional sentence: There are three main facts about love which
we may learn from 1 Corinthians 13.
   I. The pre-eminence of love, vv. 1-3.
   II. The characteristics of love, vv. 4-7.
   III. The permanence of love, vv. 8-13.

There is no overlapping of the divisions in this outline; each one of
the three divisions is wholly distinct from the other two. We shall now
purposely alter the outline by adding an extra division.

   I. The pre-eminence of love, vv. 1-3.
   II. The characteristics of love, vv. 4-7.
   III. The continuity of love, vv. 8-12.
   IV. The duration of love, vv. 13.

It is obvious that the third and fourth divisions overlap because duration of love is included in the idea of continuity. When the preacher
makes an error of this kind he will merely repeat himself in the sermon, expressing the same ideas while ignorantly assuming that he is
moving forward in the development of his discourse.

3. Main divisions should be arranged in some form of progression.
   While each main division is to contribute to the development of the
proposition, the divisions should also be arranged to indicate progression of thought. The order in which the divisions are organized will depend upon various factors, but some form of progression should exist.
   The preacher may wish to treat the items in the text according to
their time sequence or he may prefer to arrange the material in the
order of space or geographical location. On the other hand, the sermonizer may develop the divisions in a logical pattern, arranging them
according to the order of their importance, from cause to effect,
from effect to cause, or again in the order of comparison and contrast
or vice versa. When negative and positive items appear as divisions,
the negative divisions should usually be placed before the positive.
   In an expository outline it is usually best to follow the general arrangement of the passage, but this is not always necessary. Read Luke
15:25-32, and then note that the main points in the outline on "The
Pharisee: Yesterday and Today" in Chapter 7 do not follow the order
of the text, but are nevertheless arranged in an appropriate pattern.
   A sermon outline may also be arranged in such a manner that each
division begins with any of the following words: who, whose, whom,

what, which, how, why, when, where. The following outline illustrates this:

> Title: "The Abundant Life"
> Text: Romans 15:13.
> Proposition: An abundant life in Christ is available to every believer.
> Interrogative sentence: What does the text reveal about this abundant life?
> Transitional sentence: Several features are disclosed in Romans 15:13 concerning this abundant life which is available to every believer.
>> I. Where it comes from, "May the God of hope fill you."
>> II. What it consists of, "Fill you with all joy and peace."
>> III. How we may obtain it, "As you trust in him."
>> IV. Why we should possess it, "So that you may overflow with hope."
>> V. How we can live it, "By the power of the Holy Spirit."

A variation of this form of outline consists of the construction of a sermon in which each division poses a question. Using the same text, Romans 15:13, we can arrange the outline in the following manner:

> Title: "The Abundant Life"
> Text: Romans 15:13.
> Proposition: An abundant life in Christ is available to every believer.
> Interrogative sentence: What questions does this verse answer for the believer who is desirous of enjoying this life?
> Transitional sentence: There are five questions concerning the abundant life which can be answered from Romans 15:13.
>> I. Where does it come from?
>> II. What does it consist of?
>> III. How can we obtain it?
>> IV. Why should we possess it?
>> V. How we can live it?

The beginner often constructs outlines of this kind, but the reader will notice that we have not employed this type of sermon structure in any of the previous chapters. The reason for this is that we do not wish to encourage the frequent use of this form of sermon construction. Although its use is legitimate, the preacher who employs it too often may have difficulty in sustaining the interest of his congregation.

4. When the proposition consists of a statement which requires validation or proof, the main divisions should exhaust or defend adequately the stance taken in the thesis by the sermonizer.

In a sermon of this type where the proposition requires validation or proof, the hearers have the right to expect the preacher to give adequate reasons or support for its defense. Insufficient evidence or proof leaves the sermon unfinished and is likely to produce an unsatisfactory effect upon the auditors. Under these circumstances it is important that all the divisions necessary to the development of the homiletical idea be included in the discourse.

Observe the outline below.

Title: "The World-Wide Mission of the Church"
Proposition: The principal bases for world missions impose a solemn obligation upon the church.
Interrogative sentence: What are the principal Scriptural bases for world missions?
Transitional sentence: There are two principal Scriptural bases for world missions.
    I. All men have the same need of a Savior, Romans 5:12.
    II. God has provided salvation for all men, John 3:16.

If we omit the great commission which Christ gave to His disciples to proclaim the good news of salvation to all men, then we have failed to exhaust the proposition because the command of Christ to His servants to preach the Gospel to every creature is certainly one of the principal Scriptural bases for world missions. Therefore the transitional sentence should read: "There are three principal Scriptural bases for world missions," and a third main division should be added:

    III. God has commanded us to preach the Gospel to every creature, Mark 16:15.

5. Each main division should contain a single basic idea.

By limiting each main division to a single idea it is possible to treat each division as a unit in itself; thus, everything under the division will gather around its one basic concept. It would therefore be incorrect to deal in the same division with the meaning and the power of a truth because these are two distinct lines of thought which should be treated separately.

6. The main divisions should be stated clearly, with each division so related to the interrogative and transitional sentences as to express a complete idea.

Each main division should be stated so that its meaning is immediately intelligible to the hearers. In order to achieve this the minister should be sure that when he connects the interrogative and the transitional sentence to each respective main division, the latter is an expression of a complete idea.

In the outline which the preacher prepares in his study and which he may carry with him to the pulpit, he does not have to list the divisions in lengthy or complex sentences. On the contrary, a brief, clear statement or phrase is preferable to an extended sentence. Sometimes a single word may be sufficient to express the concept which the homilist has in mind to present to the congregation. For instance, in a topical outline on descriptive titles of the Word of God, the main divisions as they appear in the minister's notes may simply be the following:

I. Bread.
II. Lamp.
III. Hammer.
IV. Sword.

However, when the preacher delivers his address he must not sacrifice clarity for brevity. Instead, as he comes to each of the main headings he should state it in a complete sentence, using transitional sentences whenever necessary to accomplish this. Hence, in connection with the outline to which we have just referred, the preacher may state the first main division in words such as these: "One of the titles for the Word of God which we shall study today is that of Bread." As he comes to the second title he may say, "Another title for the Word of God which we find in the Scriptures is that of a Lamp," and so forth.

Joshua 1:1-9 provides material for an expository outline on "Essentials of Spiritual Leadership." Read the Scripture passage and then note the following outline:

Title: "Essentials of Spiritual Leadership"
Proposition: A man who is a spiritual leader must possess the proper qualifications.
Interrogative sentence: What are those qualifications?
Transitional sentence: A study of Joshua 1:1-9 reveals some of the essentials of spiritual leadership.

I. Confidence, vv. 1-2.
II. Appropriation, vv. 3-4.
III. Dependence, vv. 5-6, 9.
IV. Obedience, vv. 7-8.

If the reader is alert, he will see that these divisions do not express the ideas intended by the Scripture text in relation to the proposition. The text does not suggest that an essential of a spiritual leader is mere confidence. Confidence without qualification as expressed in the first division may be taken to mean any one of several things. It may be assumed to refer to Joshua's confidence in his own wisdom, confidence in his army, or confidence in something else.

Now observe the following outline which, when related to the transitional sentence, gives a proper expression of the truths contained in the text in connection with the essentials of a spiritual leader:

I. Confidence in the power of God, vv. 1-2.
II. Appropriation of the promises of God, vv. 3-4.
III. Dependence upon the presence of God, vv. 5, 6, 9.
IV. Obedience to the Word of God, vv. 7-8.

In the actual delivery of the message the minister will then link the idea contained in the transitional sentence with the statement of each main division. For instance, as the homilist deals with the first main point he may say, "As we begin our consideration of this passage which reveals certain qualifications for spiritual leadership, we learn from verses 1 and 2 that one of these essentials is confidence in the Word of God."

7. The main divisions should be as few as possible.

It has already been suggested that no division should be omitted which is necessary to the complete development of the proposition. On the other hand, the homilist must be careful not to introduce any unnecessary sections in the outline. As a general rule, he should aim to limit the divisions to the smallest number possible. It should be obvious, however, that there cannot be less than two divisions, for the simple reason that when something is separated it results in a minimum of two parts.

The number of divisions in an outline will depend upon the subject treated and the contents of the passage. Some subjects will require several divisions, while others may be treated properly with only two or three divisions. It is well that an outline be limited to a maximum of seven main divisions. Generally speaking, three, four, or five divisions will be sufficient to develop the proposition in relation to the Scripture text. Even an expository sermon based upon an extended passage of Scripture may be divided into two, three, or four main divisions, depending upon the contents of the passage.

8. *The sermon plan should be presented with variety from week to week.*

Although many sermons have just three main points, we should not employ the same plan from week to week. Instead, we should vary the number of divisions according to the content of the text or the subject treated.

In the course of delivery it is also wise to vary the manner of introducing the divisions. Reference to the numerical form of the divisions is a common method of calling attention to the movement from one division to the next. However, instead of using the numerical expressions "first," "second," "third," and so forth every time we state the divisions, we may introduce the divisions with words such as "to begin with," "again," "furthermore," "once again," and "finally." Other expressions similar to these will readily present themselves to the mind of the preacher as he makes the transition from the proposition to the first main division and from one main division to the next.

It is not always necessary to state the numerical order of the main divisions. Instead, we can refer to the proposition each time a new heading is presented. At other times recapitulating the previous main divisions before introducing the next one can make the divisions distinct in the minds of the people.

There are also certain conditions or circumstances in which it may be well to dispense with a formal declaration of the main divisions. No hard and fast rule can be given as to when the preacher should omit the statement of the divisions. Sometimes the general plan of the sermon may be so obvious that stating the structure of the outline would give the message a mechanical or stilted effect. An informal devotional message, a funeral address, or an occasion when the emotions of people are deeply stirred, are occasions when we should not leave the impression that we are delivering a formal discourse. Under such circumstances it would be wise to omit the expression of the divisions.

9. The main divisions should be in parallel structure.

Parallel structure is the arrangement of the outline in symmetrical form so that the divisions are properly balanced and matched with one another. By this means the main headings of the sermon follow a uniform pattern. For instance, if the first division is in the form of a phrase, the other divisions should also consist of phrases instead of sentences or single words; or if the first point is a question the other points should likewise be questions.

The same uniformity should be applied to words in positions of emphasis. For example, when the first division begins with a certain part of speech the other divisions should as a general rule begin with the same part of speech. Nouns should correspond with nouns, prepositions with prepositions, and verbs with verbs, in parallel form. Thus if the first point begins with a preposition, each successive point in the outline should begin with a preposition.

Two exceptions to this general rule should be noted. In one case, the article may or may not be used uniformly. In the other case, the proposition may allow a slight difference in the parallel structure. The outline below illustrates the application of these principles.

> Title: "When God Justifies a Sinner"
> Proposition: Justification produces blessed results in those who believe.
> Interrogative sentence: What results?
> Transitional sentence: These verses reveal several results of justification in those who believe.
> I. Peace with God, v. 1.
> II. Access to God, v. 2.
> III. Joy in God, v. 2.
> IV. Triumph in Christ, vv. 3-4.
> V. The witness of the Holy Spirit, v. 5.
> VI. Perfect security, vv. 6-11.

Since the proposition calls for a discussion of the *results* of justification and although the last two divisions are not in parallel structure with the rest of the outline, they are in harmony with the other divisions because they are also results of God's work in declaring men righteous.

Some men go to extremes in an effort to achieve symmetry in an outline. By the use of alliteration they will sometimes find a word to conform to the sound of words in other divisions, even though that word only misconstrues the thought of the sacred text.

Note the following alliterative outline on Psalm 23:

"The Seven Sweet P's of Psalm 23"
I. Possession—"The Lord is my shepherd."
II. Preparation—"He makes me lie down in green pastures."
III. Progress—"He guides me in paths of righteousness for his name's sake."
IV. Presence—"You are with me."
V. Provision—"You prepare a table before me in the presence of my enemies."
VI. Privilege—"You anoint my head with oil."
VII. Prospect—"I will dwell in the house of the Lord forever."

A careful study of Psalm 23 makes it clear that the words used in connection with the second and third main divisions are not in accordance with the thought of the sacred writer. The thought of the text under the second main division is not that of preparation but of rest, and the idea under the third main division is not that of progress but of guidance. Alliteration can serve as an excellent aid to the memory and may prove very useful in sermon structure, but the preacher should avoid its use if it strains the meaning of the text.

Transitions

Just as the transitional sentence is necessary to form a smooth connection between the proposition and the body of the sermon, carefully constructed transitions are also needed when moving from one main division of the sermon to the next. The hearer in a church service does not have the preacher's sermon before him in written form to help him follow the message as it is delivered; the only means he has of following the speaker's flow of thought is by listening to what the man is saying. Transitions aid this process.

It is easy for the auditor to lose the trend of the address from time to time, particularly when the homilist moves from one main section of the discourse to the next. At this point of transition, the mind of the average listener lingers behind that of the preacher. The transition offers the congregation a clue that the minister is ready to take up the next phase of his message. An effective transition should therefore make clear to the auditors each step in the progress of the sermon. It should also prepare their minds for and interest them in what is to follow.

A transition should be expressed in a manner which allows the easy movement of ideas from one part of the sermon to the next. Abrupt changes of thought tend to distract or confuse a congregation; a good transition smooths the way for the communication of successive units of thought.

Thus an effective transition may relate the division with the proposition or with the main transitional sentence; it may review one or more of the main divisions in the outline; it may create an interest on the part of the hearer in the next unit of thought; or it may refer to the previous main division and indicate the movement from the last unit of thought to the next. A transition should also link the last main division with the conclusion of the sermon.

One of the most helpful means of making transitions is by the use of the key word contained in the main transitional sentence (see Chapter 7). When the main transitional sentence is properly stated it always contains a key word which is applicable to each main division. Whenever the preacher comes to a main heading in his sermon, he should therefore be able to refer to the main transitional sentence with its key word. Thus, if he were using the outline shown above on Romans 5:1-11 with the following transitional sentence: "These verses reveal several results of justification in those who believe," the key word, *results,* or its equivalent, will apply to each of the main divisions as he speaks of one effect of justification after another.

Sometimes a transition will require a brief paragraph, but under ordinary circumstances it may be expressed by a sentence or two, or even by a single phrase.

The following outline provides an example of the use of transitions in a discourse.

Title: "The Best Friend"
Text: John 11:1-6, 19-44.
Introduction: 1. Wherever we go we find that people are lonely—looking for a true, real friend.
2. Proverbs 18:24 speaks of "a friend who sticks closer than a brother."
Proposition: Jesus is the best friend we can have.
Interrogative sentence: What characteristics does He possess which qualify Him to be the best friend we can have?
Transitional sentence: The passage before us reveals three characteristics of Jesus which qualify Him to be the best friend we can have.
I. Jesus is a loving friend, vv. 3-5.

            1. Who loves each one of us individually, vv. 3, 5.
            Discussion
            2. Who nevertheless allows affliction to befall us,
               v. 3.
            Discussion
            Transition: How wonderful to have a loving friend
               like Jesus, but He is more than that.
        II. Jesus is an understanding friend, vv. 21-36.
            1. Who understands our deepest woes, vv. 21-26,
               32.
            Discussion
            2. Who sympathizes in our deepest sorrows, vv.
               33-36.
            Discussion
            Transition: Jesus is indeed both a loving and an
               understanding friend, but there would be some-
               thing greatly lacking if these were the only
               characteristics Jesus possesses as a friend. What
               we need is a friend who is not only loving and
               understanding. As we shall now learn from vv.
               37-44, we see that
       III. Jesus is a mighty friend, vv. 37-44.
            1. Who can do miraculous things, v. 37.
            Discussion
            2. Who performs His miracles when we meet His
               conditions, vv. 38-44.
            Discussion
            Transition: We have seen that Jesus truly possesses
               the qualifications to be the best friend we can
               have, but an important question now faces us: Is
               He our friend?
Conclusion.

Additional examples of transitions in sermons may be found in the
expanded outlines at the end of Chapters 9 and 11.

Principles for the Preparation of the Subdivisions

The construction of the subdivisions closely follows the same principles governing that of the main divisions. There are some differences, however, in the application of these principles to the subpoints. It is well therefore that we give specific attention to certain distinctive principles for the formulation of the subdivisions.

1. The subdivisions are derived from their respective main divisions and should be a logical development of them.

The primary function of a subdivision is to develop the thought
contained in the main division. A subdivision therefore can only

achieve its purpose when the ideas expressed are directly related to and derived from the main division. It should be clear that subdivisions are not coordinate with the main divisions but are subordinate to them.

In one sense the main division is a topic, and each subdivision is a division of the topic. In this way, all the subheads must deal with the idea contained in the main point. As an illustration of this, we repeat the outline on Psalm 23 shown in Chapter 7:

Title: "The Psalm of Contentment"

Text: Psalm 23.

Introduction: 1. Sheepherder in Idaho with band of 1,200 sheep —unable to give individual attention to sheep.
2. Contrast Shepherd of this Psalm—as though He has only one sheep for which to care.
3. Every child of God recognizes himself to be the sheep spoken of in this Psalm.

Proposition: Contentment is the happy prerogative of every child of God.

Interrogative sentence: Upon what is his contentment based?

Transitional sentence: The child of God learns from this Psalm that as the Lord's sheep his contentment is based on three facts in relation to the sheep.

    I. The sheep's Shepherd, v. 1.
      1. A divine Shepherd, v. 1.
      2. A personal Shepherd, v. 1.
   II. The sheep's provision, vv. 2-5.
      1. Rest, v. 2.
      2. Guidance, v. 3.
      3. Comfort, v. 4.
      4. Abundance, v. 5.
  III. The sheep's prospect, v. 6.
      1. A bright prospect for this life, v. 6.
      2. A blessed prospect for the hereafter, v. 6.

With regard to the first main division which speaks of "the sheep's Shepherd," observe that each of the two subdivisions describes an aspect of the Shepherd. Let us now add a third subdivision to the first main division:

      1. A divine Shepherd, v. 1.
      2. A personal Shepherd, v. 1.
      3. A great assurance, v. 1.

It is evident that the third subdivision is not derived from the idea contained in the main division and therefore does not belong under that heading.

Consider the subdivisions under the second main division. Each of the four subdivisions deals with an aspect of the provision for the sheep. Likewise, the subheads belonging to the third main heading are directly related to it.

Another analytical treatment of Psalm 23 divides it into two main parts as follows:

     I. The shepherd in relation to his sheep, vv. 1-4.
    II. The host in relation to his guest, vv. 5-6.

Accordingly we submit the outline below.

Proposition: The believer has every reason to be content.
Interrogative sentence: Why does he have every reason to be content?
Transitional sentence: There are two reasons indicated in the Psalm as to why he has every reason to be content.
     I. Because of the kind of a Shepherd he has to care for him, vv. 1-4.
       1. A great Shepherd, v. 1.
       2. A personal Shepherd, vv. 1-4.
       3. A faithful Shepherd, vv. 2-4.
    II. Because of the kind of Host who entertains him, vv. 5-6.
       1. A powerful Host, v. 5.
       2. A munificent Host, v. 5.
       3. A faithful Host, v. 6

The following outline shows how the subdivisions are derived from their respective main divisions in a textual sermon:

Title: "Tested to be Trusted"
Text: Genesis 39:20-21.
Proposition: The Lord occasionally permits a believer to go through an experience which at the time may be difficult for him to understand.
Interrogative sentence: How may the believer regard such an experience?
Transitional sentence: Such an experience, as in the case of Joseph, may be regarded by the believer from two points of view:
     I. The human point of view, v. 20.
       1. Then it would seem to be one of tragic misfortune.
       2. Then it would seem to be one of utter hopelessness.
    II. The divine point of view, v. 21.
       1. Then it may be seen to be an experience of God's presence.
       2. Then it may be seen to be an experience of God's goodness.

3. Then it may be seen to be an experience of God's
power.

Dr. Richard S. Beal of Tucson, Arizona, once delivered a textual sermon drawn from John 19:17-18 in which he used the following main divisions:

Title: "The Place Called Calvary"
I. It was the place of crucifixion.
II. It was the place of separation.
III. It was the place of exaltation.

We have expanded this outline by inserting suitable subpoints under each respective main point:

I. It was the place of crucifixion.
1. Where Jesus was crucified for us, 1 Peter 2:24.
2. Where Jesus bore the curse for us, Galatians 3:13.
II. It was the place of separation.
1. Where Jesus was forsaken by His Father,
Matthew 27:46, Mark 15:34.
2. Where the repentant sinner was separated from
his sin, Luke 23:40-43.
3. Where the repentant sinner was separated from
the unrepentant sinner by the cross of Christ in the
center, Luke 23:39-43.
III. It was the place of exaltation.
1. Where Jesus was given the central place, John
19:18.
2. Where the Lord was exalted as the Savior of
men, John 12:32-33, 19:19, 1 Peter 3:18.

Subdivisions should be made not only for textual and expository outlines but also for topical sermons. Study the topical outline below and note how the subheadings are developed from their respective main heading.

Title: "Can We Know God's Will for Us?"
Proposition: It is possible for Christians to know the will of God
for their lives.
Interrogative sentence: How can we know the will of God for us?
Transitional sentence: There are at least three general principles
for ascertaining the will of God for our lives.
I. We discover the will of God for our lives through the
Word of God.
1. Which we must read, 2 Timothy 3:16-17, Psalm
19:7-8, 119:9, 11, 104, 105, 130.
2. Which we must obey, Joshua 1:8, Romans
12:1-2, Colossians 1:9-10.

    II. We learn the will of God for our lives through the inward conviction of the Holy Spirit.
        1. Who impresses upon our hearts that which God wants us to do, Romans 8:14, Galatians 5:16-18, 25.
        2. Who never urges us to do that which is contrary to the Scriptures, John 16:13-14, 17:17, Galatians 5:16-17.
        3. Who never leads us to do that which is contrary to plain duty, Romans 14:17-18, Ephesians 5:9-18.
    III. We ascertain the will of God for our lives through circumstances.
        1. Which may corroborate either or both of the previous principles, Acts 10:17-22, 11:4-15, 16:6-10.
        2. Which may open or close a door according to the Lord's purpose for us, Revelation 3:7-8, Philippians 1:22-26.

2. *The subdivisions should be in parallel structure.*

As in the case of the main divisions, the subdivisions should be symmetrical or properly balanced. The pattern set by the initial subdivision under the first main heading should be followed in all the subdivisions of the outline. Thus, in the outline shown below based on a passage which we considered in the last chapter, Mark 16:1-4, the initial subhead under the first main division begins with a preposition, and all the subordinate divisions follow the same pattern.

    Title: "Problems That Are Too Big for Us"
    Text: Mark 16:1-4.
  Proposition: The Lord's people are sometimes confronted with problems that are too big for them.
  Interrogative sentence: What do these verses teach us concerning such problems with which we may be confronted?
  Transitional sentences: From this passage we may learn two lessons in connection with such problems.

    I. Insurmountable problems may affect or confront even the Lord's most devoted people, v. 1-3.
        1. In their attempts to fulfill a loving service.
        2. In their attempts to fulfill a sacrificial service.
        3. In their attempts to fulfill a united service.
    II. Insurmountable problems are sometimes easily resolved, v. 4.
        1. At a time when the Lord's people may not anticipate.
        2. In ways which they may not expect.

Examine the other outlines in this chapter which contain subheads and observe the symmetry of the subdivisions in each of them.

3. The subdivisions should be limited in number.

The number of subdivisions under a main division depends upon the topic being discussed or the content of the text. For example, the outline on Psalm 23 would not be complete if we omitted one of the subdivisions beneath the second main division. Also, as a general rule there should be no more than three or four subheads under one main division. Exceptional circumstances may warrant more subdivisions, but in such a case it would be wise to limit the number of subdivisions under the other main divisions so that the outline is not bogged down with too many subordinate points.

It is generally unnecessary to have divisions of subdivisions, but there are some subjects or Scripture passages which require minute analysis. In such instances it may be necessary to make subordinate divisions of the subdivisions.

Read Psalm 1 and then note the example below.

Title: "Which Way Are You Going?"
Proposition: Every man has only two alternatives from which to choose the way he will go.
Interrogative sentence: What are these alternatives?
Transitional sentence: Psalm 1 describes these alternatives as the two ways of life.

    I. The way of the godly, vv. 1-3.
        1. It is marked by separation from evil, v. 1.
        2. It is marked by a devotion to the Word of God, v. 2.
        3. It is marked by the blessing of God, v. 3.
            (1) Stability, NASB.
            (2) Fruitfulness.
            (3) Vitality.
            (4) Success.
    II. The way of the ungodly, vv. 4-6.
        1. It is opposite in character to that of the righteous, v. 4.
        2. It ends in a manner that is opposite to that of the righteous, vv. 5-6.

Although the subdivisions should appear in the preacher's outline, they should not be formally stated in the course of delivering the address. To mention the subheads specifically would usually confuse in the minds of the auditors the subdivisions with the main divisions. The subdivisions should serve as a guide to the preacher in the development of his message, but it is best to make no reference to them in the sermon unless there are special reasons for doing so.

4. Like the main divisions, the subdivisions do not have to be in the order of the text.

In the case of an expository sermon it is generally best to follow the order of the text in the preparation of both the main divisions and subdivisions. However, for the sake of logical progression there may be occasions when it is desirable to use a different order in the outline than that of the Scripture passage. Read Exodus 16:4-36, and then note the following outline:

Title: "Bread from Heaven"
Introduction: 1. Israelites on pilgrimage from Egypt to Canaan; so believers on pilgrimage from earth to heaven.
2. The provision God made for Israelites on pilgrimage—manna; so spiritual food for God's people today—the Word of God.
3. There are at least three respects in which the manna pictures the spiritual food upon which God's people should feed.
I. In its provision, vv. 4, 15.
  1. From the Lord, v. 4.
  2. For the people of God, vv. 4, 15.
II. In the manner in which it had to be gathered, vv. 4-21.
  1. In accordance with the need of every man, vv. 16-18.
  2. At an early hour every day, vv. 4, 21.
III. In its purpose, vv. 4, 19-36.
  1. To sustain the people of God throughout their pilgrimage, vv. 32-35.
  2. To test the obedience of the people of God, vv. 4, 19-20, 23-29.
  The remarkable resemblance between the manna and the Word of God is to impress us with an important truth:
Proposition: We must feed regularly on the Word of God during our pilgrimage from earth to heaven.

It will be seen that the divisions of the above outline are arranged in logical order rather than in the order of the text.

EXERCISES

1. Point out all the errors you can find in the following topical outlines and correct them:

(1)   Title: "Wait upon the Lord"
Proposition: It is good to wait upon the Lord.

Interrogative sentence: Why is it good to wait upon the Lord?
Transitional sentence: Let us consider three essential aspects of waiting upon the Lord.

    I. The Lord listens to the cry of the believer, Psalm 40:1.
      1. God desires that men seek Him, Lamentations 3:25.
      2. My earnest desire for God, Psalm 42:1.
    II. God renews the believer's strength, Isaiah 40:31.
      1. Day by day, 2 Corinthians 4:16.
      2. Through knowledge, Colossians 3:10.
    III. Guidance is promised for the believer's pathway, Psalm 32:8.
      1. When we are yielded to Him, Psalm 25:4-5.
      2. Upright before Him, Proverbs 21;29.
      3. As we seek God's will, Proverbs 3:5-6.
      4. When we are bewildered, Romans 12:1-2.
      5. If we are meek, Psalm 25:9.

(2) Title: "God's Abundance"
Proposition: God is a God of abundance.
Interrogative sentence: How can we learn about God's abundance?
Transitional sentence: By noting the word "abundant" or "abundance" in the Bible in connection with God, we learn all about God's abundance.

    I. He is abundant in mercy, 1 Peter 1:3.
      1. The meaning of mercy.
      2. To all who believe.
    II. He is abundant in grace, Romans 5:17.
      1. Which means that grace is freely bestowed because all the demands of holiness have been satisfied.
      2. In Christ.
    III. He is abundant in comfort, 2 Corinthians 1:3-5.
      1. When we need it.
      2. To enable us to comfort others.
    IV. The abundance of God's power, Ephesians 3:20.
      1. Which is exceeding abundant.
      2. According to the power that works in us.

2. State what is wrong with the following textual outlines and show how you would correct them:

(1) Title: "The Peace of God because of Peace with God"
Text: Philippians 4:6-7.
Proposition: Fervent prayer and the peace of God go together.
Interrogative sentence: How can we obtain the peace of God?
Transitional sentence: These verses show the way to obtain peace with God.

    I. The command, "Do not be anxious about anything," v. 6.

       1. Because God is able to care for our needs.

       2. No matter how great or how small the problem is.

   II. The condition, "but in everything, by prayer and petition, with thanksgiving," v. 6.

       1. Fervent prayer.

       2. Continual thanksgiving.

   III. The effect, "and the peace of God . . . in Christ Jesus, v. 7.

       1. God's peace.

       2. Through Christ.

(2) Title: "God's Hand upon the Israelites"

      Text: "He led them safely," Psalm 78:53a (KJV).

Proposition: God's hand upon His people whom He brought out of Egypt.

Interrogative sentence: What evidences does this text reveal of God's hand upon His people?

Transitional sentence: From Psalm 78:53a we find a three-fold evidence of God's hand upon His people.

   I. Guidance, "He led them."

       1. Personal guidance.

       2. Sure guidance.

   II. Progression, "He led them on."

       1. Not going backwards.

       2. But forward.

   III. Securely, "He led them on safely."

       1. With a pillar of cloud by day.

       2. With a pillar of fire by night.

3. Indicate the errors in the following expository outlines and correct them:

(1) Title: "Purposeful Christianity"

      Text: 1 Corinthians 9:24-27.

Introduction: 1. 1964 World's Fair in New York, building with exhibit: "The Triumph of Man."

       2. What constitutes triumph or success in the Christian life?

Proposition: It is possible to find the goal of a Christian life and the guidelines so often missed.

Interrogative sentence: How can we find these things?

Transitional sentence: A consideration of the text will help us to discover the answers to our quest.

   I. We strive because of the prize, v. 24.

       1. Not all shall win.

       2. All must try.

   II. We strive because of the crown, v. 25.

       1. By being temperate.

       2. By seeking the incorruptible.

   III. We strive because of the certainty, vv. 20-27.

       1. Keep our goal in mind.

       2. Our bodies must be under subjection.

    (2) Title: "The Results of Faith"

        Text: Hebrews 11:1-8.

Introduction: 1. Hebrews 11 is God's honor roll of faith—a list of the heroes of faith.

             2. Four heroes of faith are referred to in our text.

Proposition: God honors faith.

Interrogative sentence: How does God honor faith?

Transitional sentence: The Apostle Paul discusses three results of faith in this text.

      I. By faith we understand, vv. 1-3.

          1. Things the natural eye has never seen, v. 1.

          2. How the worlds were made by the Word of God, v. 3.

     II. By faith we please God, vv. 4-6.

          1. As Abel obtained righteousness by the worship of faith, v. 4.

          2. As Enoch was translated by the walk of faith, v. 5.

    III. By faith we obey God, vv. 7-8.

          1. As Noah saved his house by the work of faith, v. 7.

          2. As Abraham received an inheritance by the waiting of faith, v. 8.

    (3) Title: "To Know the Love of Christ"

        Text: Ephesians 3:14-21.

Introduction: 1. The most important thing in the life of a Christian is love.

             2. Paul's great prayer for the Christians in Ephesus was that they might know the love of Christ.

Proposition: Every Christian should know the love of Christ and how to enjoy it.

Interrogative sentence: Why should Christians know the love of Christ?

Transitional sentence: There are three reasons why the Christian should know the love of Christ.

      I. To be strengthened spiritually, vv. 14-17.

          1. For a complete trust, v. 17.

          2. For a living faith, v. 17.

     II. To experience the magnitude of Christ's love, vv. 18-19.

          1. Personally, v. 18.

          2. Positively, v. 19.

    III. To be filled with God's fullness, vv. 20-21.

          1. Infinite power within us, v. 20.

          2. Salvation through Christ, v. 21.

4. Prepare a topical outline suitable for an Easter Sunday morning worship service, giving the title, introduction, proposition, interrogative sentence, transitional sentence, main divisions, transitions, and subdivisions.

5. Construct a textual outline on Isaiah 41:10, with the same features as called for under Exercise 4.

6. Prepare an expository outline on Acts 12:1-19, with the same features as required under Exercise 4.

BIBLIOGRAPHY

Baird, John E. *Preparing for Platform and Pulpit*. Nashville, Tennessee: Abingdon Press, 1968, pp. 72-81, 86-95.

Broadus, John A. *On the Preparation and Delivery of Sermons*. Revised by Jesse B. Weatherspoon. New York: Harper & Brothers, 1944, Part II, Chapter 3.

Brown, H. C. Jr., H. Gordon Clinard and Jesse J. Northcutt. *Steps to the Sermon*. Nashville: Broadman Press, 1963, pp. 103-118.

Davis, Henry Grady. *Design for Preaching*. Philadelphia, Pennsylvania: Fortress Press, 1958, Chapters 9 and 10.

Demaray, Donald E. *An Introduction to Homiletics*. Grand Rapids, Michigan: Baker Book House, 1976, pp. 82-89.

Hogue, Wilson T. *Homiletics and Pastoral Theology*. Winona Lake, Indiana: Free Methodist Publishing House, 1949, Chapters 11-13.

Hoppin, James M. *Homiletics*. New York: Dodd, Mead and Company, 1881, Division 4, Section 17.

Koller, Charles W. *Expository Preaching Without Notes*. Grand Rapids, Michigan: Baker Book House, 1962, Chapter 12.

Lloyd-Jones, D. Martyn. *Preaching and Preachers*. Grand Rapids, Michigan: Zondervan Publishing House, 1972, Chapters 4 and 11.

Pattison, T. Harwood. *The Making of the Sermon*. Philadelphia: The American Baptist Publication Society, 1898, Chapter 11.

Perry, Lloyd M. *A Manual for Biblical Preaching*. Grand Rapids, Michigan: Baker Book House, 1965, pp. 71-72.

_____ . *Biblical Sermon Guide*. Grand Rapids, Michigan: Baker Book House, 1970, Chapters 2 and 3.

Phelps, Austin. *The Theory of Preaching*. New York: Charles Scribner's Sons, 1892, Lectures 26-29.

Reu, M. *Homiletics, A Manual of the Theory and Practice of Preaching*. Minneapolis: Augsburg Publishing House, 1950, Chapter 17.

Robinson, Haddon W. *Biblical Preaching*. Grand Rapids, Michigan: Baker Book House, 1980, pp. 128-132.

Skinner, Craig. *The Teaching Ministry of the Pulpit*. Grand Rapids, Michigan: Baker Book House, 1979, pp. 168-171.

White, R. E. O. *A Guide to Preaching*. Grand Rapids, Michigan: William B. Eerdmans Publishing Co., 1973, Chapters 8 and 9.

Whitesell, Faris Daniel and Lloyd M. Perry. *Variety in Your Preaching*. Westwood, New Jersey: Fleming H. Revell Company, 1954, Chapter 8.

9. THE DISCUSSION

Definition of the Discussion

The main divisions and subdivisions are merely the skeleton of the sermon and indicate the lines of thought to be followed in the address. *The discussion is the proper unfolding of the ideas contained in the divisions.*

It is at this point in developing the sermon that the preacher needs to bring to the sermon all the knowledge and inventive genius at his command. He must somehow enlarge or expand his outline so that it will result in a well-rounded and vital message and accomplish the objective which he has in mind. In order to do this he must introduce, select, and arrange his materials so they will effectively develop each of the divisions.

Qualities of the Discussion

1. Unity

We have stated in the preceding chapter that the topic of each main division is a unit in itself. The subdivisions under each main division must be derived from and develop the topic of the main division. Everything discussed under the subdivisions should simply be an amplification or enlargement of the idea expressed in the main division. It follows that there should neither be any digressions nor the introduction of any irrelevant features. Instead, there should be a continual pressing toward an adequate discussion of the one idea in the division. Sometimes, however, material which may be irrelevant to one division may be necessary to complete the discussion in another part of the sermon.

2. Proportion

Experience will enable the preacher to recognize which parts of the sermon need more emphasis or more thorough treatment. Some divisions, because of their contents, may require more attention, while other divisions may not be as important insofar as the objective or purpose of the discourse is concerned. The profundity of the text, the importance of a certain truth, or the difficulty involved in that part of the sermon may also cause the preacher to consider an extended amplification of a division.

It is well for the sermonizer to remember that each main division must contribute to the whole discourse and, as a general rule, the main divisions should be wisely balanced in order to present a well-rounded sermon.

3. Progression

The ideas under each division should indicate a definite movement of thought. Every sentence should add something to the discussion. The arrangement should never be awkward or forced, but each idea should be an extension of the preceding one so as to compose a chain of ideas until the topic of the division has been amply developed or discussed. Every explanation, illustration, application, argument, or quotation should be in just that place which will make for orderly advance in the thought of the sermon. Progression will thus produce a cumulative impact on the hearers and help to create a vital interest in the message.

4. Brevity

One of the common faults of the man in the pulpit is verbosity. What can be spoken in twenty-five or thirty minutes often takes him forty or forty-five. The danger of such a practice is that the congregation wearies before the sermon is finished. The people may appear to be reverent and respectful in the pew, but it is doubtful that they will continue to be as attentive and interested as they were in the earlier part of the sermon.

As has been suggested, each division should be so developed as to give the subject matter its due force or expression. But if a man is to avoid the pitfall of an extended discourse he should train himself to speak concisely. Every word he says should count. Every idea he expresses should be pertinent. It may often be necessary or advisable to introduce an illustration, to offer an explanation, or to bring other material into the discussion in order to elucidate a point. Nevertheless, whatever the sermonizer brings into the development of a division must be directly related to the idea in that division and should be stated as briefly as possible.

It may take considerable discipline for the preacher to acquire the ability to condense his sermons, but the effort will be more than repaid in the advantages which accrue to himself and his congregation. Such a preacher will not waste time in the pulpit on empty platitudes, unnecessary repetitions or explanations. He will also avoid the habit of using needless illustrations or of telling so many anecdotes that his sermon is little more than a series of stories connected to one another by a quotation or text of Scripture.

5. Clarity

The primary purpose of the discussion is to unfold or to reveal more clearly the meaning of the ideas in the divisions. If the sermon is a biblical one, the divisions will naturally deal with some aspect of the text or of some truth in the text. It is therefore of vital importance that the material in the discussion illumine the truths of Scripture suggested under each division. Every means which can be utilized to achieve this end, consonant with unity and brevity, should be brought into play.

A common error of the beginner is to speak "over the heads" of the people. Forgetting that many individuals in the congregation may not have had the opportunity of higher academic training, he may address his people as though he were speaking to a group of postgraduate students of a college or seminary. The language of philosophy or theology may be necessary in the halls of higher learning, but in the pulpit it is of primary importance that the preacher make the Scriptures intelligible and clear. It may sometimes be necessary for him to use theological terms such as "existentialism," "antinomianism," "soteriology," and "justification"; but when he does so it would be well for him to define these in common, everyday language. The Lord Jesus Himself, though He spoke on the profoundest themes, presented the truth so simply that even "the common people heard him gladly."

6. Vitality

It is possible for a sermon outline to be structurally correct and for the discussion to be thoroughly orthodox and Scriptural while the message completely fails to challenge its hearers. This may happen because the discussion consists of dry and uninteresting facts, is made up of solid exegesis with little that is of personal interest and application to the congregation, or because it fails to progress from familiar facts and ideas to new insights into old truth.

In order for the discussion to quicken the interest of the hearers it must contain that which will cause the truth to be valid to them. The words of Scripture must be made meaningful to them in terms of their own life situations. The characters of the Bible must be set before the people in such a way that they may see their own circumstances, temptations, and failures portrayed in the experiences of the men and women in the Bible. The prophetic portions of Scripture must be interpreted to show their relevance to national as well as to personal problems and needs today. The didactic and hortatory sections should likewise be made to have a direct application to the contemporary scene. Only by thus relating the Scriptures to men and women in their present conditions can we expect the message we preach to have vital significance to them.

7. Variety

The preacher who seeks to infuse his sermons with perennial freshness and vigor must also see to it that the discussion contains variety. He will not draw all his quotations from Shakespeare or all his illustrations from his own children. On the contrary, he will take pains to gather the materials for the discussion from every available source, new and old, using them wherever they may be effectively applied.

Needless to say, while the homilist must aim for variety, he must at the same time make sure that the material he employs is of human interest. Anecdotes and factual material which are related to the things or circumstances in which men and women find themselves or which appeal to human emotions and sympathies are certain to arouse attention. But the preacher does not have to tell "sob stories" just to make people weep. Instead, the material brought into the discussion should display a vital touch with the hearts of individuals.

A word needs to be said concerning the use of humor. Some men are so full of wit that their sermons sparkle with good humor. But merely to get people to laugh for laughter's sake is out of keeping with the sacredness of the preacher's task. On the other hand, there is a place for sanctified humor in the pulpit. The preacher may lead his people in the message to the point where they become tense with emotion or interest. The introduction of a witticism that evokes laughter will often break the tension and condition the people to listen with even greater interest.

Sources of Material for the Discussion

The sermonizer may draw materials for the discussion from five principal sources.

1. The Bible

The Word of God is an inexhaustible source of material for the development or unfolding of the ideas contained in each division of the sermon. From the Bible we secure our main materials of exegesis.

It is of greatest importance therefore that the preacher observes what the text actually says. By the use of the little interrogatives *who, what, where, when, why,* and *how,* he must try to discover what the passage contains and record his significant finds.

In making observations on a portion of the Scriptures, the sermonizer will need to pay attention to important grammatical constructions. Sometimes significant verbs and their tenses will play a valuable part in his appreciation of the passage. Even a preposition or a conjunction may be the key to unlocking some vital feature in the text.

The minister must also take note of literary patterns which are to be found throughout the Bible. These include repetition, comparison, contrast, interchange, progression, and cruciality. For instance, Amos' repeated use of the cry, "For three sins, even for four, I will not turn back my wrath," in chapters 1 and 2 of the book of Amos powerfully drives home to the reader God's denunciation of Israel's evil neighbors and the impending judgment of Judah and Israel.

Sometimes a significant omission may indicate something very meaningful. For example, in Luke 10:30-35, when the Lord Jesus told the lawyer the story about the Good Samaritan and then asked him who had acted as a neighbor to the injured man, the expert in the law replied, "The one who had mercy on him." Observe that the lawyer did not say, "the Samaritan." Apparently this proud Jew, like his countrymen of that day, had an intense hatred for the Samaritans and could not bring himself to admit that the merciful stranger who had acted as a true neighbor belonged to a race which he utterly despised.

Inasmuch as the Bible explains itself, the student should constantly go to the Scriptures whenever he attempts to explain a text or passage. Parallel passages play an important part in this connection, and the preacher should not hesitate to quote the Scriptures, no matter how familiar the texts may be, if they relate to the text or passage being interpreted. Other points which at first sight seem to have no special importance, slight touches in the narrative, or minor links in the chain of thought, can also add greatly to the interest and vitality of the discourse.

In addition, the Bible contains illustrations suitable for almost any and every occasion. Familiarity with the historical portions of Scripture will furnish the preacher with a vast fund of vital and potent illustrations useful in illuminating other passages which at first sight may seem wholly unrelated.

When making observations on a passage of Scripture, the re-creation of the text in the form of a mechanical layout such as that which we have shown in Chapter 3 for Luke 19:1-10 often enables one to discover items which might otherwise go unnoticed. We suggest therefore that the reader turn back to the layout for the account of Zacchaeus and then note the following observations which we have made from this narrative.

vv. 1-4 No apparent reason why Jesus came to Jericho, but
          cf. v. 10, "Son of Man came to seek. . . ."
       Hence, the initiative was on Christ's part.
       Search of Zacchaeus for Jesus:
          Purposeful—not just to see Jesus, but to see who
          He was.
          Persistent—in spite of difficulties encountered.
          Resourceful—climbed tree from whence could
          obtain unobstructed view.
       Personality of Zacchaeus (vv. 2, 5, 7, 8)
          Dishonest, greedy, notoriously bad, unlovely,
          despised by others.

vv. 5-7 Jesus came where Zacchaeus was.
              looked up at Zacchaeus.
              addressed him by name.
              singled him out from everyone else.
              invited Himself to his house.
       Love of Jesus for Zacchaeus:
          Loved him in spite of his evil character.
          Befriended him when no one else cared for him.
       Response of Zacchaeus:
          Immediate, eager, joyful.

vv. 8-10   Statement by Zacchaeus:
             Called Jesus "Lord," hence, submitted to Him.
             Made open avowal to
               give half to poor, hence, become generous.
               make retribution wherever necessary, hence,
               become honest.
             Thus, Zacchaeus was a transformed man.
           Statement by Jesus:
             Declaration of salvation of Zacchaeus—His salva-
               tion was not to take place in the future, but had
               already taken place.
             Declaration of Christ's purpose—to seek, save the
               lost.
           Zacchaeus, the man who was lost, was saved.
           The self-righteous in Jericho (v. 7) remained lost!

There are many more notations which could be made on Luke 19:1-10. However, these are sufficient to indicate that as a result of prayerful meditation and careful observation it is possible to make many vital discoveries from a unit of Scripture. We suggest therefore that this may be a helpful procedure for the beginner who seeks to discover for himself, without the aid of extra-biblical sources, significant facts in a passage.

2. Other forms of literature

We include under this heading every other form of literature helpful in the development of the sermon.

Some types of literature will naturally be more helpful than others. Critical, expository, and devotional commentaries, devotional books, and hymnals will be particularly valuable. Christian biography will be another important source of material. Bible handbooks and Bible dictionaries, as well as books on archaeology and on the people and customs of Bible times and Bible lands, will provide insight into many portions of Scripture. The published sermons of great masters of the pulpit will also prove beneficial.

But the student does not have to confine himself to religious literature. The sources of material for unfolding his sermon outline may come from literature related to any and every field of knowledge. For instance, science and medicine are two areas from which the sermonizer may derive valuable materials, particularly when he is able to show how up-to-date discoveries in these fields relate to Scriptural facts and truths. In using any technical terms, however, it is well that the minister explain the expressions he employs. When he speaks concerning facts outside his own field of theology, it is also well that he be able to substantiate his statements by reference to authoritative sources.

Of course, the preacher will not neglect the daily newspaper and current magazines. These will keep him abreast of the times and be a continual source of material which he may weave into the discussion.

3. Experience

A minister's personal experience is another valuable means for the expansion of the sermon divisions. When the preacher can tell what he has lived through or undergone or seen himself, he is able to speak with unmistakable conviction and vividness. His words will leave the impression that he knows whereof he speaks.

Some pastors apologize for referring to themselves by such an expression as, "We trust that the following personal reference may be pardoned." It is usually unnecessary for the homilist to make such a remark. On the other hand, when the minister does relate an incident from his personal experience he must be careful that he does not draw undue attention to himself. His sole purpose should be to glorify the Lord and to give his people a clearer understanding of the text which he seeks to interpret. It need hardly be mentioned that under no circumstances should the preacher ever relate as a personal experience that which is not true.

The sermonizer should also be careful, as he tells of some happening, that names or references to individuals do not reveal their identity, particularly when the incident deals with something of a personal or adverse nature in relation to the individuals involved.

4. Observation of the world around us

Life abounds with things, some of them of a seemingly trivial character, which may add greatly to the interest of a sermon, if only the minister has eyes to see and a mind to perceive the relationship of the commonplace to spiritual truths contained in the Scriptures. The Lord Jesus used as object lessons the lilies of the field, the birds of the air, the seed on the ground, the fish in the sea, and even the hairs of men's heads. Likewise the preacher, whichever way he turns, may find in the everyday affairs of life abundant material, and by an effective and judicious use of the commonplace he can make his discourses alive with interest.

5. *Imagination*

It is possible for the homilist to conjure up mental images which may add greatly to the effectiveness of a discussion. Such ideas will create an element of originality and surprise and add a fresh approach to the treatment of a subject. The use of the imagination in a sermon can therefore become a valuable ally to the preacher.

There are certain restraints, however, which the minister must always exercise when he employs mental images. For one thing, he must be sure that he does not allow his imagination to go to extremes. For example, it is possible to draw a mental picture of a fire aboard a ship and of the terror of the passengers who are unable to find a way of escape. But to picture in detail the flames licking toward the victims and the suffering of the passengers would be an unwise use of the imaginative faculties. Again, the preacher must avoid the creation of mental pictures which are far-fetched or beyond all reason. Such a practice could be ludicrous. Once again, in connection with Biblical narratives, the homilist should not describe as true that which he only imagines or assumes to be true. For example, it would be wrong to say that the two young men whom Joshua sent to spy out Jericho were both strong and handsome and that they crossed the Jordan on a raft when, as a matter of fact, the Bible gives no such information concerning them. On the other hand, we may plainly indicate that we are speaking in the realm of the hypothetical. We might say: "Think of the two spies. We can picture them as agile and strong young men, eager to serve their God and their people Israel. They obeyed Joshua's command and went into the hostile city without hesitation."

From what we have stated, it should be clear that the exercise of the imagination can play a vital role in the discussion and give to the sermon a touch of freshness and interest which can be obtained in no other way. Two basic rules must always be applied, however, in its use; first, it must be exercised in moderation, and second, it should always be used with good taste; that is to say, we must avoid that which may be coarse or unrefined.

Rhetorical Processes in the Development of the Sermon Outline

There are several rhetorical processes which are used in the expansion or development of the sermon outline; namely, explanation, argumentation, quotation, illustration, and application. Not all of these devices may be employed in any one sermon, but their use will be determined by the manner in which the sermon is developed.

The order in which these rhetorical processes are used will depend upon various circumstances and conditions. Sometimes application may be made before quotation or argumentation; at other times an illustration might be given before explanation; on other occasions a quotation may come before explanation. The unity of the sermon and the proper progression of the message will indicate the order in which these rhetorical processes are introduced.

Because both illustration and application are of special significance in a discourse we shall devote a whole chapter to each of them. We shall now consider in detail the other three rhetorical processes.

1. Explanation

We have previously stated that one of the most important features in a sermon is the explanation of the text. This is true not only of the textual and expository sermon, but also of the topical sermon which is constructed upon Biblical truth. In other words, whenever a message is based upon the Scriptures, the portion or portions of the sacred text used should be explained clearly and properly. It is this feature in sermonizing which makes for true Biblical preaching and invests the message with authority. The Word of God then becomes the warp and woof of the sermon, and every important part of the discourse is built upon the solid foundation of Scripture.

But the careful student of the Scriptures soon realizes that the divine library of sixty-six books was written in many diverse literary styles. A considerable portion of the Bible was written in prose. This prose takes many forms—history, prophecy, epistles, apocalyptic literature, and parables. At the same time, a large portion of the Old Testament appears in the style of Hebrew poetry with its distinctive parallelisms. Included are such literary patterns as repetition, contrast, and amplification of thought, as well as the frequent use of images and figures of speech.

It is therefore evident that when a man embarks upon the interpretation of any portion of Scripture he must first recognize the type of literature in the Bible with which he is dealing and then observe the laws of hermeneutics which govern its interpretation.

a. Processes Involved in the Explanation of the Text

Generally speaking, the processes involved in the explanation of the text fall into certain clearly defined categories.

(1) The context

One of the processes in exegesis is the study of the context—both the immediate and the remote. Observing the context often helps the hearer, as well as the preacher, to recognize the limitations in the meaning of a word or statement and prevents misconstruing the proper sense of the text.

Suppose, for example, that the preacher is speaking on the second part of Philippians 2:12 which reads: "Continue to work out your salvation with fear and trembling." The immediate context shows that the Apostle did not have reference to any effort on the part of the Philippian believers to obtain salvation by works; but as the first part of the text shows, Paul had reference to the obedience of the Philippians not only when he was present with them but also in his absence.

(2) Cross references

A proper exegesis will also include the correlation of the text with other Scriptures. The minister should make frequent use of parallel passages, comparing or contrasting the text he seeks to explain with other portions of Scripture. This is especially true of many portions of the gospels where an examination of the parallel writings of the evangelists will sometimes throw much light on the text and enable the hearer to see more clearly the meaning of an isolated passage. The sermonizer should also be able to quote parallel passages from memory, but whenever he is unable to quote a text freely, it would be better for him to turn to the Scriptures and read the text from the Bible.

(3) Application of the laws of language

Sound interpretation of Scripture also depends upon an application of the laws of language. Drawing attention to some significant grammatical arrangement, the nuances or subtle variations in the meaning of certain words in the original, a figure of speech, some special form of expression such as an occurrence of metonymy or synecdoche, or the etymology of a word, can go a long way toward clarifying a text which may appear ambiguous to the average individual in the congregation.

To assist in the interpretation of a passage it is often helpful to quote from other translations or versions. Care must be exercised in the quotation from a paraphrase of Scripture, for it must be remembered that while a translation is an attempt to put into another tongue an accurate representation of the original text, the paraphrase is a means of representing the original more freely in the vernacular.

The writings of many learned and devout scholars are the results of Biblical research and contain spiritual treasures helpful in the preparation of sermons. The minister should therefore make use of standard exegetical, expository, and devotional commentaries in his study. Should he find a statement which is particularly applicable, he may quote it verbatim in the delivery of his sermon.

(4) Historical and cultural background

The historical and cultural background of the text, and geographical data mentioned in the passage, may also have an important bearing in ascertaining the meaning of the text in its ancient setting. The use of a good Bible encyclopedia, Bible introduction, or Bible handbook will be of great assistance in obtaining information concerning the historical and cultural background of a text, and reference to a Bible atlas will often provide significant geographical information, but the homilist should make a thorough examination of the Scriptures themselves in order to discover the setting of the passage.

We have discussed at some length the interpretation of the text because it is the preacher's solemn obligation to explain the Scriptures faithfully and clearly. In order to do this he should make a thorough investigation of the text to arrive at the meaning which he honestly and assuredly believes to be correct. He is bound in all honesty to tell his congregation not what he wishes the text would mean, nor what his church prefers him to say it means, but what he conscientiously believes it to mean.

In seeking to explain the text, the minister should avoid quoting Hebrew and Greek words and phrases but should rather mention how these may be understood today. Similarly, he should avoid referring to grammatical features which are meaningless to the average auditor. For example, to tell the congregation that a certain verb is in the aorist tense, subjunctive mood, active voice, would be of no particular value to most hearers. In fact, frequent reference to the grammar of a text in the original languages tends to confuse or distract the people and leaves the impression that the preacher is seeking to display his knowledge of Greek and Hebrew.

b. Handling of a problem passage

The occasion will no doubt arise when the sermonizer will have to deal with a difficult passage. Rather than make any dogmatic assertions of his own concerning the meaning of the text, it would be well for him to respect the interpretations of devout scholars, particularly if their interpretations have received wide acceptance by Christians in the past. On the other hand, if after diligent study the minister is unable to come to a satisfactory conclusion regarding the correct interpretation of an obscure text, he should be careful that he does not make the text more obscure to his congregation by a poor attempt at explaining it. Whenever the preacher's own research for a solution proves inconclusive and he is unable to make the meaning clear, it may be best for him merely to admit the difficulty and pass on to deal with such truths as he is able adequately to explain.

The homilist must make the meaning of the passage clear to his people, but as a general rule the congregation will grow weary if interpretation is extended for any great length of time. As we have previously indicated, the people do not need the process of the minister's exegetical study, but the results.

Before leaving the subject of explanation we should draw attention, as we did in Chapter 3, to a peculiar danger which faces the young preacher.

c. Treatment of details

Having studied the details of the text thoroughly and having become interested in them, the homilist is often tempted to remark upon a greater number of points than the limits of his sermon will permit. Thus, the discourse becomes so crowded that his hearers follow with difficulty and few of the numerous points presented have time to impress themselves upon their minds. The sermonizer must determine resolutely to omit many of the details and aim to choose only that which especially requires explanation and which will, at the same time, yield important and interesting matter. In other words, he must deal only with those salient features in the text which contribute toward the main impression the sermon is intended to convey.

Incidentally, when the preacher finds it necessary to discard certain points and facts of value in the text which are not pertinent to the sermon in hand, such material could be of great use to him at a future time. As he continues his study of the Scriptures he will gradually acquire more and more knowledge of the Word of God and will learn that the details he lays aside for one sermon might fit perfectly in developing or amplifying another.

The diligent student of the Bible will also find that by examining the details or the significant words in a passage he may discover the principles or truths suggested by the text. These principles or truths, in turn, might indicate the theme or dominant idea for the sermon. In other words, instead of attempting at the outset to formulate the thesis or proposition and thence to construct the outline and then examine the details of the passage, he may reverse the order of procedure.

2. *Argumentation*
a. Value of argumentation

Argumentation is given an important place in Scripture, and inasmuch as it often carries much weight in a sermon, the homilist should not hesitate to use it. Argumentation is also a forceful means of expanding a sermon outline, and in some discourses the production of valid evidence is essential. Methodical reasoning meets the demands of the human intellect for sound bases of belief, and a statement which can be corroborated by positive proofs is thereby rendered authoritative.

Furthermore, the times in which we live make it necessary for the minister of the Gospel to give clear and adequate assurance to believers for the reasonableness of their faith. Some young people in the church may be buffeted by doubts or assailed at school by critics of the Word of God; some may raise objections to Christian standards; others may be puzzled over the findings of archaeology and other modern scholarship in relation to the Bible. It is therefore highly important that the sermon should frequently contain well-documented evidence which will instill into the minds of people valid assurance that the fundamentals of the Christian faith rest upon a solid foundation of supernaturally revealed truth, and that the ethical principles of the divine revelation are valid in producing true Christian character and righteous conduct.

b. Methods of argumentation

There are various ways in which the servant of the Lord may verify the truth in the minds of his congregation.

(1) Use of Scripture

The first and foremost method is the use of Scripture. When the preacher can show in his sermon that "thus saith the Lord," he is speaking with an authority which demands the confidence of his hearers. People recognize instinctively that the minister is not expressing his own ideas or opinions, but that he is declaring divine proclamations which they have no right to contradict or deny. But in his efforts to persuade, the minister should employ the holy oracles intelligently and appropriately. Proof texts should not be wrested out of context, and interpretation should always be consonant with the meaning intended by the sacred writers.

(2) Logical reasoning

Another method of argumentation is reasoning; that is, the use of logical processes to arrive at a conclusion or to bring men to a decision. Argument from analogy, from cause to effect, from effect to cause, or from cumulative evidence, as well as from induction and deduction, are various forms of persuasive rhetoric.

The Bible contains numerous examples of logical reasoning, but for our purpose it will be sufficient to mention just a few instances of Biblical polemics. Joshua's final appeal to the elders and people of Israel contains proof after proof of the Lord's goodness to them in order to challenge them to loyal service for God. Peter's message at Pentecost establishes the validity of the resurrection of Christ on the basis of Old Testament Scriptures, the personal witness by Christ's followers of His resurrection, and the outpouring of the Holy Spirit upon believers. Stephen's address before the Jewish council contains a series of evidences of the reprehensible attitude of Israel toward the Lord, so as to lead to their condemnation for the slaying of their own Messiah. To a large extent Paul's Epistle to the Romans is a treatise on the reasonableness of the doctrine of justification by faith.

Christ Himself also employed argumentation. Witness His logic as He bade His followers to rest in the assurance of their Heavenly Father's care. Using the illustration of the flowers and the grass, He reasoned, "If that is how God clothes the grass of the field, which is here today and tomorrow is thrown into the fire, will he not much more clothe you, O you of little faith?" (Matthew 6:30). The Lord Jesus also argued when He was challenged by His foes. For example, when the Pharisees asserted that He cast out demons by the power of Beelzebub, He countered their wicked accusation by arguing that a house divided against itself cannot stand and if Satan were divided against himself his kingdom also could not stand.

(3) Testimony

A third type of argumentation is by means of testimony. This method may be properly classified under logical reasoning because proof can only be established by evidence. However, we prefer to treat testimony separately because of its special importance. The value of testimony depends upon its validity. Since this is the case, we should note the factors which are involved in establishing the veracity of a testimony. One of these is the number of witnesses. The greater the number the stronger will be the evidence, provided of course, that the facts are substantiated by their testimony. Another factor is the character of the witnesses. The knowledge, honesty, and sincerity of the witnesses all contribute toward establishing the credibility and veracity of their statements. Finally, the nature of the facts which the witnesses attest also tends to the acceptance of their evidence.

One form of testimony consists in the use of statistical data or facts. When the preacher is able to marshal together significant figures or facts as a means of argument, he thereby girds himself with strong evidence to support his case. But when he draws upon such materials he must be sure that his information is accurate, and in order to impress the people with its validity he may need upon certain occasions to quote the sources from which he derives his data. Incorrect data drawn from questionable sources could give the impression that the minister is naive or that he has sought to misguide his congregation by false statements.

(4) Logical sequence in a sermon outline

The orderly arrangement of a sermon outline in logical sequence may also be a means of persuasion, particularly when the outline is of such a nature as to prove a point. If, for example, we take as our thesis, "The Word of God can operate in wonderful ways in the life of an individual," we can proceed to give evidence from Scripture of its power.

We set forth the outline as follows:

> Title: "The Power of God's Word"
> I. It has power to quicken to spiritual life, 1 Peter 1:23.
> II. It has power to cleanse, John 15:3.
> III. It has power to sanctify, John 17:17.
> IV. It has power to produce spiritual growth, 1 Peter 2:2.

c. Cautions in the use of argument

We conclude this section on argumentation with some words of counsel. Some preachers in their zeal for the truth seem to be obsessed with the idea that they are called to be defenders of the faith and therefore fill their sermons with disputations or virulent tirades against all who differ with them. Charles Haddon Spurgeon in his *Lectures to My Students* speaks of a man like this who goes about with a "theological revolver" ready to shoot at anyone who may appear to be heterodox or who does not agree with his doctrinal views. Such a pugnacious attitude is wholly out of keeping with the Christian spirit and is apt to produce many harmful effects. While it is true that we should "earnestly contend for the faith," it is not necessary for us to be contentious.

The man of God must not only avoid a censorious or belligerent attitude in his preaching, but he should also be careful not to provoke the hostility of his hearers by ridicule or bitter sarcasm. Biblical polemics may sometimes demand what William Ward Ayer describes as "a sanctified sarcasm," like that of Elijah when he ridiculed the four hundred prophets of Baal at Mount Carmel, but as a general rule it is best for the homilist to adhere to sound and logical but trenchant argument.

Another word of caution should be spoken regarding the use of argument. When a sermon consists of a great deal of argumentation it is likely to become heavy and dull. Statistics and other detailed data quoted as evidence for a given case can also be dry and uninteresting. Therefore, the speaker should develop an ability to state his arguments and evidences so skillfully that they are graphic and interesting to his hearers. For instance, instead of saying that there are approximately one billion people in China, how much more meaningful it would be to declare that out of every four men in the world, one is a Chinese man; out of every four women in the world, one is a Chinese woman; out of every four boys in the world, one is a Chinese boy; and out of every four girls in the world, one is a Chinese girl.

3. *Quotations*

Quotations can add greatly to the development of the sermon outline. To quote a suitable saying at an appropriate time gives force and pungency to a message. The preacher should by all means make use of quotations, but he must be on guard not to employ them too extensively.

We draw attention to four types of quotations which may be used in a discourse.

a. Scripture texts

We have already made reference to the quotation of the Bible in a sermon, but it bears repetition that nothing invests a minister's sermon with authority like the apt quotation of Scripture. Even though the message may be an exposition of a passage, the citation of a parallel passage serves to drive the truth home to the hearers. But even in the quotation of Scripture, the preacher must be careful to see that the texts are both appropriate and pertinent.

b. Brief pithy sayings

These sayings may sometimes be in the form of proverbs such as "A friend in need is a friend indeed," "A stitch in time saves nine," and "A bird in the hand is worth two in the bush." Proverbs from other nations or civilizations may also be used to advantage. The Chinese have an adage, "He who stands still in the mud sticks in it"; other maxims from China are, "The highest towers begin from the ground"; "A wise man sees an opportunity in a difficulty; a fool sees a difficulty in an opportunity"; "The way man wishes to go, thither his feet will carry him"; "One thing acquired with pain is better than a hundred with ease."

A second type of pithy saying consists of specific spiritual truths stated in concise terms. Here are a few examples of these sayings:

> "Serving Christ is not overwork but overflow."
> "Outside the will of God there is no such thing as success; inside the will of God there is no such thing as failure."
> "Our great matters are little to His power; our little matters are great to His love."
> "Little is much when God is in it."
> "I have a great need for Christ; I have a great Christ for my need."

> "God is no respecter of persons, but He is a respecter
> of His promises."
>
> "The highest place we can reach in this life is to be
> bowed low at the feet of Jesus."
>
> "To be little with God is to be little for God."

The homilist should collect and organize such sententious sayings that they may be readily accessible to him when he needs them. If the citation of an aphorism is to be effective, it should be made from memory, but the sermonizer must be sure that it does not contain a mere half truth, an exaggeration, or a distortion of the truth.

c. Statements from authoritative sources

Significant statements from authoritative sources constitute another type of quotation profitable in sermon development. It is not necessary that the statements be entirely along theological lines. Instead, they should be pertinent to the message.

If, for example, the preacher is speaking on spiritual warfare and seeking to emphasize the necessity of enduring hardness as a good soldier of Jesus Christ, he may quote the following statement concerning the discipline of an American soldier to show the parallel in the training of the Christian soldier for the Lord's service. This statement was made by Brigadier General John H. Hay, Commander of the Berlin Brigade of the United States Army, and appeared in the *Billings Gazette* of Billings, Montana, on July 13, 1965.

> Soldiers must be proud of themselves. If they are not proud,
> if they are not well-disciplined, you have wasted your time. This
> is the first priority. The soldier must stand tall.

For another example of the use of a significant statement, we quote an article from *The Oregonian* of Thursday, May 25, 1967. The article consists of an address by Larry Dotson, an ex-convict, before a class of forty boys and girls in a junior high school in Portland, Oregon, describing life in a penitentiary.

> When the darkness and the silence of the late night envelop a
> big prison, each convict has the specter of his misspent life as a
> cellmate.
>
> And late at night when the men think everybody else is
> asleep, that's when you can hear the crying—the 35 and 40 year

old men crying. That's when you know it's misery and miser-
able, all of it.

There is a singular fitness in this description with the picture given
in the Word of God of the prison where men are to be reserved for the
blackness of darkness forever "where there shall be weeping and
gnashing of teeth."

In the course of delivering the message it is well for the minister to
mention the author of the quotation and, under special circumstances,
the source from which it was derived. He should particularly state the
name of an author when he is dealing with a matter of controversy if
the very mention of the author's name may lend support to his statement.

There are several other principles to note in connection with the
quotation of statements. The preacher should always be certain that
quotations are accurate and true. If it is necessary for him to use a quotation which does not represent his convictions, he should make it
clear that the citation is not in accord with his own views. Any quotation or statement which may be derogatory of a person's name or character, even though it may be corroborated by published evidence,
should be strictly avoided. To make remarks of this nature concerning
an individual or institution may lay the preacher open to the charge of
libel in court. Finally, the preacher should not resort to lengthy quotation.

d. Poetry

The quotation of poetry has a fitting place in a sermon. Hymns
which contain lofty expressions of worship or which speak of the fervent longings of the soul are a valuable source of quotations for messages of a devotional character. Hymns which deal with comfort under
trial can be used in sermons on suffering and testing. Other types of sacred songs can be quoted in connection with various forms of discourse. Secular poetry, when aptly quoted, can also be used to advantage in the expansion of the sermon outline.

In the use of poetry the sermonizer must be sure that the selections
are not too long. When quoting from a hymn, one or two stanzas will
generally be sufficient. Sometimes the quotation of even two lines
may be more effective than the use of an entire stanza.

The familiarity of the congregation with a hymn does not mitigate
against its value as a source of quotation; in fact, the very acquaintance

of the people with the hymn may often add to their interest when they hear a portion of it being cited in the sermon.

But the quotation of poetry, no matter how apt or expressive, must not be overdone. Like the use of other forms of quotations, the preacher must avoid using poetry too frequently.

The Method of Recording the Rhetorical Processes in the Notes of the Sermon

When writing out the notes of his sermon, the preacher should so prepare them that he can tell at a glance what he is to say. Every statement in the expansion of the sermon outline should be as concise as possible, consonant with readability. Instead of using complete sentences, the minister should use brief phrases whenever possible. Lengthy words can often be abbreviated into a few letters.

For the sake of clarity, every new idea should be stated on a separate line, and the material under each main division and subdivision should be indented so that the notes under each section of the outline are obvious at a glance.

The development of the outline on "Won by Love," drawn from Luke 19:1-10, is given below as an example of an expanded sermon outline. Observe the brevity of the statements and the use of indentation.

We have purposely worded all transitions in full so that the student may see how properly expressed transitions smooth the passage of ideas from one main section of the discourse to the next.

Introduction: 1. Bible describes conversion of several "hopeless cases," e.g., Mary Magdalene, demoniac of Gadara, woman of Samaria.
2. Prob. reason for description—to encourage us concerning salvation of "hopeless cases."
3. Z. another "hopeless case."

Proposition: The Lord delights in winning an individual who to us seems like a "hopeless case."

Interrogative sentence: How can we learn from the narrative about Z. that this is true?

Transitional sentence: Consideration of the three main facts in this passage in connection with Z. will reveal how the Lord delights in winning someone who seems like a "hopeless case."

I. The search for Z., vv. 1-4.
1. The manner of it, v. 1.
Quiet and unobtrusive, but cf. v. 1 w/v. 10

—Christ's one purpose in coming to Jericho
—seek Z., chief of publicans (KJV).
Publicans—tax collectors in Palestine under
employ of Roman govt., notorious for extortion,
corruption. cf. v. 8—Z. rich, prob. as result of
avarice, fraud.

2. The effect of it, vv. 2-4.
Christ's coming created consuming desire on part
of Z. to see J. "Sought," lit., "kept trying" but
could not—little of stature. So hated (v. 7) that
prob. no one would give opportunity to see J.,
hence climbed tree.
Commentators: Reason for Z's desire—curiosity, but cf. previous refs. in Luke to Christ's
interest in publicans (e.g., Luke 15:1-2; 18:9-14).
Z. prob. heard from other publicans: Christ's
kindly attitude toward men like himself, hence
"sought to see J." But long before Z. sought J., J.
sought him. Z. would not have sought J., if J. had
not first sought him. Like shepherd, leaving 90
and 9 to seek lost sheep, Christ came to Jericho
to seek this one lost sinner.

"Jesus my Saviour to Bethlehem came
Born in a manger to sorrow and shame,
O it was wonderful, blest be His name,
Seeking for me, for me."

Illus. Lady Huntington of England, fervent
Christian, called on unsaved dying man—Man
cried in agony: "I am dying and I am lost!"
Huntington: "Thank God for that." Dying man
surprised: "How can you thank God for that?"
Huntington: "Because Son of man came to seek,
save lost."
But if lost are to be won we, like Christ, must go
after them, one by one.

Transition: We have seen that because the Lord
delights in winning a "hopeless case" He searched
for Zacchaeus. But the narrative about Zacchaeus
leads us to observe another significant fact in connection with this man, namely,

II. The befriending of Z., vv. 5-7.
1. The manner of it, v. 5.
Christ addressed Z. by name; invited Himself to
his home.
Reason: Z. no friends; whole city regarded him as
man of ill repute—cf. v. 7.
Greek writer, Lucian, ranked tax collectors "with
adulterers, panderers, flatterers and sycophants."
Thus, Christ says in effect, "Though all hate you,
I want to be your friend."
"Make haste" suggests Christ's eagerness to be-
come his friend.

2. The effects of it, vv. 6-7.
Hearing own name, Z. prob. realized that though

Christ knew all about him, yet desired to be his
friend, hence made haste, rec'd Him joyfully
—overjoyed had found friend.
Thus, love found way into heart of Z.
Lost can be won when we, like Christ, love the
unlovely, reach them by kindness, win by being
winsome.
Illus. Salvation of sergeant through kindness of
Christian private.

Transition: We have now considered two important
facts in these verses in relation to the winning of
this "hopeless man." Let us now proceed to note a
third, and that is,

III. The salvation of Z., vv. 8-10.
    1. The manifestation of it, v. 8.
        (1) A changed attitude—"Look, *Lord*."
            Prior to this, Z. lived for self, now put self
            under mastery of Christ.
        (2) A changed life.
            From selfish, wicked fraud to generous,
            loving man. Love of J. had so entered heart,
            produced love:
            a. In giving to others—"I give half . . . to
               poor."
               Z's standard of giving—not one tenth, but
               one half.
               Note: "I give"—present tense—to be
               continual standard.
            b. Purpose to make restitution—"I will pay
               back four times the amount."
               O.T. law—when man confessed crime of
               stealing, had to return stolen goods, add
               one-fifth (Num. 5:7), but obligation Z.
               imposed self—4-fold.
            Christ also able today to transform hopeless
            cases. 2 Cor. 5:17—"If anyone is in Christ,
            he is a new creation." If no real change in
            lives, may question if we are truly saved.

                  "Nature forms us,
                  Sin deforms us,
                  School informs us,
                  Only Christ transforms us."

    2. The declaration of it, vv. 9-10.
        "Salvation"—lit. deliverance (from sin).
        "Son of Abraham"—cf. Gen. 15:6 and Gal. 3:7
        —As Abraham believed God and was counted
        righteous, so Z. believed in Christ and became
        spiritual descendant of Abraham.
        Acts 10:43—"Everyone who believes in him
        receives forgiveness of sins through his name."

Transition: How clearly this narrative about the
befriending and the salvation of Zacchaeus reveals

that the Lord delights to win an individual who may seem to us to be a "hopeless case." Surely this should bring assurance to us concerning the salvation of those whom we may regard as "hopeless cases."

Conclusion:

1. Christ can save and transform the hopeless cases for whose salvation we have longed.
2. Christ wants to use us as instruments to win hopeless cases by the manifestation of His love through us.

Note that besides the timeless truth contained in the proposition in the above expanded outline, we have stated three other principles in the course of the message. Under the first main division we have the following statement: If the lost are to be won we, like Christ, must go after them, one by one. Under the second main division we have expressed the next abiding truth: The lost can be won when we, like Christ, love the unlovely. Under the third main division, before reaching the second subpoint, we find the last timeless truth: Christ is able today to transform hopeless cases.

Another way to treat Luke 19:1-10 is to seek in the passage principles or truths which the text suggests. We may begin with the following thesis: "There is no such thing to Jesus as a hopeless case." Using this as our proposition, we now seek certain principles related to the thesis. As we consider these verses we discover three reasons why we can be assured that to Jesus there is no such thing as a hopeless case, and we now set them forth in the form of an outline.

Title: "Hope for the Hopeless"
I. Because Jesus seeks hopeless cases, vv. 1-4.
II. Because Jesus is gracious to hopeless cases, vv. 5-7.
III. Because Jesus saves hopeless cases, vv. 8-10.

A third approach to the passage is to make a biographical sketch of the character of Zacchaeus showing what he was before he met the Lord Jesus and the transformation which took place after the Lord addressed him when he was up in the tree. A fitting title for such a message could then be: "Transformed by Grace."

As an additional example of an expanded outline we present the following on "The Crown of Thorns," based on John 19:1-5 and Genesis 3:14-18. We can never plumb the depths of our blessed Savior's woes at the cross and reduce to mere human analysis His unspeakable agonies when God the Father made "his soul an offering for sin," but we present the outline as a pattern of a topical sermon.

Title: "The Crown of Thorns"
Introduction: 1. Annual Rose Festival in Portland, Ore., climaxed by coronation of queen w/glittering diadem, amidst pomp, ceremony.
2. Contrast coronation of Christ—ideal man, King of Grace, went about doing good. If any worthy of honor, He was, yet given, not glittering diadem, but crown of thorns.

Proposition: A devoted Christian takes delight in honoring his Savior.

Interrogatives entence: Why does he take delight in doing so?

Transitionals entence: Among the reasons why a devoted Christian takes delight in honoring his Savior is the three-fold significance which he sees in the crown of thorns which Jesus bore on the cross. He sees from the passages in the New Testament on the crown of thorns—Matt. 27:28, Mark 15:17, John 19:2, 5—that

I. It was a crown of suffering.
1. Indicative of the physical sufferings which He underwent.
What suffering Christ must have endured when crown placed on head, thorns pierced brow; and when soldiers smote Him on head with reed (Mk. 15:19).
Gen. 3:17-18—thorns came as result of sin, because Christ was made sin for us, also bore result of sin—the suffering which accompanied sin.
2. Expressive of the curse Christ bore for us.
Cf. Gen. 3:17-18—because man sinned even ground was cursed, thorns were expressive of that curse.
Thorns on Christ's brow likewise expressive of curse He endured for us—"by becoming a curse for us, for it is written; 'Cursed is everyone who is hung on a tree' " (Gal. 3:13). We cannot conceive how great His agony when cursed for us, but something of depth of His suffering indicated in cry, "My God, my God, why have you forsaken me?" (Matt. 27:46).
Transition: But as the devoted believer considers what the Scriptures say regarding the crown of thorns, he learns that it was not only a crown of suffering, but also that

II. It was a crown of derision.
1. Indicative of the derision which the soldiers heaped upon Him.
Soldiers no doubt heard trial of Christ under Pilate when His kingship discussed. In their blindness,

soldiers prob. thought it absurd anyone
apparently so helpless could claim to be king, so
put crown of thorns on head, as if to say: "He is
only a self-deceived, false king!"
What treatment for Christ, King of Grace mocked
w/ crown of thorns!

2. Expressive of the attitude which men had toward
Him.
Note the ridicule Christ underwent as hung on
cross, Matt. 27:39-44.
Isa. 53:3—"He was despised and rejected by
men."
Consider condescension of Christ to allow
wicked, heartless men treat Him, King of Glory,
with such contempt, shame.
Reason Christ endured this—Heb. 12:2—"Who
for the joy set before Him"—to lift us out of sin,
shame, bring us to glory.

"Bearing shame and scoffing rude,
In my place condemned He stood;
Sealed my pardon with His blood:
Hallelujah! what a Saviour!"

Transition: As we consider the passages in the New
Testament relating to the crown of thorns we find
that while wicked men meant for it to be an instrument of agony and shame for our blessed Savior,
yet in His sovereign power God saw to it that

III.   It was a crown of victory.
1. Indicative of the triumph He won over His foes.
"Crown" in each reference to crown of thorns is
wreath of victory given to winner in Olympic
games. Thus, though soldiers intended crown of
thorns to be symbol of ignominy, they by this act
crowned Him w/wreath of victory.
Note inscription on cross: "JESUS OF
NAZARETH, THE KING OF THE JEWS"
(John 19:19). Appeal by Jews for alteration of inscription, and Pilate's rejection of request, John
19:21-22.
Pilate was correct, for although Jews rejected
Christ as king, He was indeed still king, ruling
and over-ruling everything to accomplishment of
His own purposes.
What fitting crown for Christ to wear, for when
Satan did his worst, Christ did His best; when
suffering on cross, was accomplishing our
redemption; when died for us, brought life to us;
when seemed to go down into defeat, won greatest
victory.

2. Expressive of the triumph He has accomplished
for us.
Do we know anything about thorns—things
which prick, wound?
Because Christ won victory over sin, death, hell,

can make us triumphant in Him and turn thorns
into blessing, 1 Cor. 15:57.
Condition: we must submit to Him, 2 Cor. 2:14.
Illus. Paul's triumph in prison, Phil. 1:12-14.
Transition: We truly have every reason to honor our
Savior for wearing such a crown for us upon His
sacred head

Conclusion: 1. Blessed result of coronation of Christ w/ crown of
thorns—now crown for us—N.T. speaks of
various crowns for Christian—crown of rejoicing,
righteousness, life, incorruptible, glory that fadeth
not away.
But when we see Him, shall wish to cast crowns
before Him, saying: "Worthy is the Lamb, who
was slain, to receive power and wealth and
wisdom and strength and honor and glory and
praise." (Rev. 5:12).
2. Because of what Christ has endured for us,
should we not crown Him King today? Let us
respond in words of hymn:
"In all my heart and will, O Jesus,
Be altogether King.
Make me a loyal subject, Jesus
To Thee in everything."

EXERCISES

1. Make a list of ten proverbs and state under what circumstances you
would use them in a sermon.

2. Collect thirty pithy sayings and place them under appropriate classifi-
cations. Put the aphorisms under each classification on a separate sheet of
paper.

3. Find twelve significant and authoritative statements and show how you
would make use of each in a sermon. Cite the author and source of each of
these statements.

4. Re-create the text of Psalm 23 in a manner similar to the layout shown
in Chapter 3 on Luke 19:1-10. Without the aid of any books of reference, list
on a separate sheet of paper, verse by verse or section by section whatever you
discover in the Psalm which is worthy of note.

5. Prepare a topical outline suitable for the communion service, giving the
title, introduction, proposition, interrogative sentence, transitional sentence,
main divisions, subdivisions, and transitions between main divisions. Expand
the outline by use of the rhetorical devices discussed in this chapter; namely,
interpretation, argumentation, and quotation. Write your sermon notes as
briefly as possible.

6. Select your own text and construct a textual outline drawn from that text
for a message which would be appropriate for the first Sunday of the New

Year. Follow the same directions as for Exercise 5 in the construction and development of the outline.

7. Select a more or less extended passage on the subject of prayer and prepare an expository sermon which may serve as a challenge to prayer. Follow the same procedure as required under Exercise 5 in the construction and development of the sermon.

BIBLIOGRAPHY

Berkhof, L. *Principles of Biblical Interpretation*. Grand Rapids, Michigan: Baker Book House, 1960.

Blackwood, Andrew W. *Preaching from the Bible*. Nashville, Tennessee. Abingdon-Cokesbury Press, 1941, Chapter 12.

_____. *The Fine Art of Preaching*. New York: The Macmillan Company, 1937, Chapter 4.

Broadus, John A. *On the Preparation and Delivery of Sermons*. Revised by Jesse B. Weatherspoon. New York: Harper & Brothers, 1944, Part III, Chapters 1, 2, 4.

Burrell, David James. *The Sermon, Its Construction and Delivery*. New York: Fleming H. Revell Company, 1913, Part III, Chapter 2.

Davis, Henry Grady. *Design for Preaching*. Philadelphia, Pennsylvania: Fortress Press, 1958, Chapters 6, 9, and 14.

Davis, Ozora S. *Principles of Preaching*. Chicago: University of Chicago Press, 1924, Part II, Chapter 8.

Etter, John W. *The Preacher and His Sermon*. Dayton, Ohio: United Brethren Publishing House, 1902, Chapter 9.

Kaiser, Walter C., Jr. *Toward an Exegetical Theology, Biblical Exegesis for Preaching and Teaching*. Grand Rapids, Michigan: Baker Book House, 1981, Chapters 1-8.

Lane, Denis. *Preach the Word*. Welwyn, Hartfordshire, England: Evangelical Press, 1979, Chapters 4-8.

Lloyd-Jones, D. Martyn. *Preaching and Preachers*. Grand Rapids, Michigan: Zondervan Publishing House, 1972, pp. 220-223.

Macpherson, Ian. *The Burden of the Lord*. Nashville, Tennessee: Abingdon Press, 1955, pp. 111-114.

Mickelson, A. Berkeley. *Interpreting the Bible*. Grand Rapids, Michigan: Eerdmans, 1963.

Pattison, T. Harwood. *The Making of the Sermon*. Philadelphia: The American Baptist Publication Society, 1898, Chapters 13-16.

Perry, Lloyd M. *A Manual for Biblical Preaching*. Grand Rapids, Michigan: Baker Book House, 1965, pp. 7-64, 72-76.

_____. *Biblical Sermon Guide*. Grand Rapids, Michigan: Baker Book House, 1970, Chapter 1.

Phelps, Austin. *The Theory of Preaching*. New York: Charles Scribner's Sons, 1892, Lectures 11-14, 30-31.

Ramm, Bernard. *Protestant Biblical Interpretation*. Revised Edition. Boston: W. A. Wilde Co., 1956.

Robinson, Haddon W. *Biblical Preaching*. Grand Rapids, Michigan: Baker Book House, 1980, pp. 53-65, 79-96, and 137-148.

Stibbs, Alan M. *Understanding God's Word*. Chicago: Inter-Varsity Press, 1959.

Terry, Milton. *Biblical Hermeneutics*. Grand Rapids, Michigan: Zondervan Publishing House, n.d.

Unger, Merrill F. *Principles of Expository Preaching*. Grand Rapids, Michigan: Zondervan Publishing House, 1955, Chapters 13-18.

White, R. E. O. *A Guide to Preaching*. Grand Rapids, Michigan: William B. Eerdmans Publishing Co., 1973, Chapters 3, 4, 7, and 14.

Whitesell, Faris Daniel. *Power in Expository Preaching*. Westwood, New Jersey: Fleming H. Revell Company, 1963, Chapters 3, 5, and 8.

Whitesell, Faris Daniel and Lloyd M. Perry. *Variety in Your Preaching*. Westwood, New Jersey: Fleming H. Revell Company, 1954, Chapter 6.

10. THE ILLUSTRATIONS

Definition of Illustration

An illustration has often been said to be to the sermon what a window is to a building. Just as a window admits light into a building, so a good illustration elucidates a message.

But the very meaning of the word "illustrate" is to make clear by means of an example or examples. Thus *an illustration is a means of throwing light upon a sermon by the use of an example*. It is a word picture of a scene, or a description of an individual or incident used for the sake of lighting up the contents of a discourse so that it becomes easier for the hearer to grasp the truths proclaimed by the preacher.

An illustration may take any one of several forms. It may consist of a parable, an analogy, an allegory, a story (including an anecdote or fable), an account of a personal experience, an event in history, or an incident from biography. As we have mentioned in the last chapter, an illustration may also be invented or constructed out of a person's own imagination.

The Value of Illustrations

It needs to be stated emphatically that the most important factor in a sermon is not the illustration, but the explanation of the text. The interpretation, which must carry with it the burden of the preacher's message, is all-important; illustrations, no matter how vivid or interesting, are only of secondary importance. But the man with a God-given message and a yearning desire to make that message clear to his people will do all in his power to find and use illustrations which will make his sermon interesting and winsome. It is well, therefore, to point out some of the values of good illustrations.

1. They give clarity to the sermon.

Truth is sometimes so profound or abstruse that regardless how the preacher labors to explain a text, his people may be unable to grasp its meaning until he has put it into the form of a word picture. This is precisely in accordance with the definition of an illustration which, as we have noted, is to make clear by an example. The Lord Jesus Himself, in order to explain the blessed but profound truth of our union with Him, used the simple analogy of the vine and the branches.

2. They make the sermon interesting.

The fault of many sermons is not in their doctrinal content but in the heaviness or dullness with which the truth is presented. The message may be so dry and uninteresting that it is difficult for the hearer to maintain proper interest. The pulpiteer should bear in mind that the average individual is able to give sustained attention for only a limited time, and unless he introduces into the message that which is both interesting and challenging, the mind of the average listener will soon begin to wander. Relevant illustrations relax the mind, serve to arouse flagging attention, enliven the message, and prepare the hearer to listen thoughtfully to what follows.

Therefore the preacher should use such interesting illustrations that any tendency to listlessness on the part of the audience will be immediately dispelled. Appealing and interesting illustrations may be obtained from every conceivable source, and the sermonizer needs to be constantly on the alert to discover examples, new and old, which may make his sermons attractive.

The following illustration which comes from the past century has a fitting application for the present:

> A well known preacher was riding beside a cab driver who had once been a professional man but had lost all through drink. During the ride he appealed to the minister for help. After conversing for a while with the cab driver about his problem, the good man asked, "Friend, if your team of horses were running away with you, even after you had used every possible means to hold them, what would you do if you suddenly discovered that there was a person sitting next to you who knew exactly how to control your team and save you from disaster?" Without a moment's hesitation the driver replied, "I'd hand over the reins to him." And then the preacher told him that the Lord Jesus was willing to take control of his life if he would turn over the reins to Him.

Among the types of illustrations calculated to hold attention are stories about children, because the innocent and sometimes humorous sayings of little folks are often full of human interest. How intriguing is this story sent by a missionary couple in Guatemala concerning their two little boys:

> "One night Brent was telling us about the huge cockroach that he and his brother Mark found in their bedroom while we were gone. With his fingers he measured it to be about ten inches long. Then he added, 'And it had big whispers!' "

We may draw vital lessons from the actions or statements of young folks and find many occasions for their use as sermon illustrations. The experience of a teacher with her class of girls is just one evidence of this:

> With dramatic skill a Sunday school teacher was telling the story of Abraham and his obedient preparation to sacrifice his son, Isaac. As she neared the climax she described the details so vividly that one child pleaded nervously, "Oh, please don't go on! This story is too terrible!" Just then another little girl sitting across from her exclaimed, "Don't be silly, Mary, this is one of God's stories, and God's stories always come out right!" What truth was expressed by her statement, for God always sees to it that everything works out right in the end for those who belong to Him, for "we know that in all things God works for the good of those who love him."

Surprise is another factor which makes for an interesting illustration. The following incident in the life of Mr. D. L. Moody will serve as an example:

> After Mr. Moody had concluded an evangelistic service, someone inquired about the meeting. He answered that two and a half people had been converted that night. The inquirer was surprised at his reply and asked what he meant. Mr. Moody said: "Two children were saved and one adult," and then he explained the reason for his answer. Each of the two children now had a full life to give to Christ, whereas the adult had already spent half his life and had only the other half in which to serve the Lord.

3. They give vividness to truth.

The only thing that some people remember after a sermon is

preached is an illustration, the reason being that truth is often made vivid through illustrations. Good illustrations impress the mind by the forcefulness of the examples which they portray, whereby the abstruse becomes plain, and dull, abstract facts are transformed into living truth, so that people can see by word pictures what they otherwise might not fully understand. For example, a man may speak on the evils of dishonesty, but when he illustrates this by the story of Achan in Joshua 7, the lesson can be made vivid by an account of Achan's deception and the terrible consequences of his transgression. How significant it is to note that Achan means "trouble" and, as his very name implies, he brought trouble upon himself, upon his whole family, and upon the entire congregation of Israel through his secret sin.

Instead of a Biblical narrative, the preacher may relate a story such as this one:

> It is said of an Eastern monarch that he once called one of his friends, a builder, and said to him, "Friend, build me a house. Whatever you might need—men, money, materials, time, tools —all you require, I will provide for you. Go, build me a house." Did ever a man have an opportunity like this? No limit had been placed as to cost or time. The builder was free to do just as he pleased. He could have used the best of materials and could have used the finest workmanship. Before very long what appeared to be a magnificent house was under construction. But the man often did work that was poor and shoddy; he skimped here and there, using materials which were cheap and inferior. He failed to give of his best to the house which he was constructing for the king. At last the building was completed. Anything that marred or scarred it in any way, anywhere, was all carefully concealed. The great day came when with great pomp and ceremony the king was shown his new house. The inspection tour over, the king turned to his friend, the builder, and said, "See this house? I give it to you, and here is the key to this house which is now to be your own."

4. They give emphasis to truth.

There are many occasions when the preacher finds it necessary to show the importance of a truth. He may do so by simply stating its significance, by expressing it in vigorous terms, or by repeating it in one way or another. The use of a good illustration is yet another means of emphasizing a truth. By means of a specific example the illustration brings home to the hearers the lesson which the preacher seeks to teach. In fact, the more apt the word picture, the greater will be the emphasis.

For instance, if the minister is seeking to impress his people with the importance of assembling together in church on Sunday evenings as well as on Sunday mornings, this story by a junior boy would no doubt carry more weight than many words of exhortation or remonstrance by the pastor:

> "Last Sunday night I thought I would go to church. My buddy went to the movies and asked me to go along, but I didn't think I ought to, so I went to church. I looked for my Sunday school teacher but he wasn't there. I thought I would see two of the deacons I've always respected, but they weren't there. I looked also for my mother's Sunday school teacher who called at our house one day, but she too wasn't there. I suppose they don't think church on Sunday night is really important."

The following incident, if told in a message on temperance, is also far more effective than a thousand words of admonition or warning on the evils of drink:

> Four young people were killed in an automobile accident after they had been drinking. The tragic news that his daughter had died in an accident was brought to the father of one of the victims. In an outrage the grief-stricken father exclaimed, "I'll kill the tavern keeper who sold the liquor to them." But when he went to his own cupboard to take a drink, the father found a note written in his own daughter's handwriting: "Dad, we took some of your liquor. We are sure that you won't care."

Principles to be Observed in the Use of Illustrations

1. Use apt illustrations.

According to the etymology of the term, an illustration must elucidate or make clear. If it does not lead to a better understanding of the point which is being discussed or if the illustration itself is not obvious, it would be better to omit it. Otherwise, the illustration will tend to turn the attention of the congregation away from the thought of the sermon. But an appropriate illustration, introduced at the right time and told in the right way, is a most effective means of illuminating a text or truth and creating interest. If, for example, the preacher is dealing with the sufficiency of God's grace in the forgiveness of sins, he may quote verses such as 2 Corinthians 5:20-21 and Ephesians 1:7. How suitable then to bring in an illustration like the following:

> An unbeliever, scoffing at a minister who had called on a dying man who was notoriously bad, said to him, "Can one hour of repentance atone for a whole life of sin?" "No," said the man of God, "but the blood of Jesus Christ can."

2. *Be sure that the illustrations are clear.*

As we have learned, the basic meaning of the word "illustrate" is to make clear or obvious. A story or incident which is told in the sermon with the object of enhancing the apprehension of some truth defeats its own purpose if it fails to explain or clarify. Under such circumstances an illustration which may otherwise seem important or interesting had better be omitted entirely. But a clear, well-chosen example or illustration which contributes to the comprehension of a truth can add greatly to the value of the discourse.

> On January 25, 1981, a brief item appeared in newspapers across the nation. It stated simply that the Summer Institute of Linguistics had rejected the demands of certain Colombian terrorists who were threatening to kill kidnaped missionary Chester Bitterman if the institute did not shut down its Colombian operation by February 19. Shortly after this statement appeared in the newspaper, Bernie May, United States Director of Wycliffe Bible Translators, sent out a call to prayer which read in part:
> "Wycliffe has a corporation policy that we pay no ransom. It is part of the risk (which is just another word for faith) that we all take. We simply trust God to work all things together for good. . . .
> Chet knew when he joined Wycliffe that it was risky business. But following Christ is always that—for all of us. The man who wholly follows the Lord will invariably come under the shadow of the cross. It is inescapable. But the promise of a harvest of righteousness is just as invariable. So I ask you to join me in prayer for the Bittermans. I also ask you to reassess your own commitment to Christ. It is mandatory as we move from Gethsemane towards Calvary that we know who we are and where we stand when the torches light the garden at midnight."
> A few weeks after Bernie May circulated this appeal to the Christian world, Chester Bitterman was shot to death by his abductors.

If one of the aims of our message is to challenge   people to dedication to Christ surely an incident like the above will be a clear call to commitment to our Lord.

3. Use illustrations that are credible.

Illustrations which are far-fetched only discredit the ministry and suggest to the congregation that the preacher is wont to exaggerate or is gullible enough to believe that which is unworthy of credence. Even if the narrative or event is true but for some reason does not sound credible, the preacher should studiously avoid its employment in the sermon. If an illustration is to be suitable for use, it must be true to life. It must bear all the earmarks of truth and reality.

Sometimes a seemingly incredible fact may be used fittingly as an illustration, particularly when it is drawn from the realm of science or natural history and when the preacher is able to provide adequate proof of the accuracy of his statements.

4. State the facts of the illustration accurately.

An illustration which is worth telling is worth telling well. As a general rule, it should not be read. Like the sermon, an illustration which is read from the pulpit loses its impact. Therefore when a man uses an illustration, he should make sure that he knows the details well enough to state them accurately. If he forgets or omits one or two of the essential parts, he may ruin the illustration.

There are some cases, however, where an illustration may contain so much detail that it is not possible for the speaker to recall all the points. Note this example by Dr. M. R. De Haan who gave up his practice as a physician to go into the ministry.

> What potentialities dwell in these bodies. If you are a person of average size, you perform in **each day of 24 hours** the following functions: Your heart beats 103,689 times; your blood travels 168,000,000 miles. You breathe 23,040 times; you inhale 438 cubic feet of air. You eat between 3 and 4 pounds of food, and drink 3 quarts of liquid, and perspire about 2 pints through your skin; your body maintains a steady temperature of 98.6 degrees under all weather conditions. You generate 450 foot tons

> of energy; you speak 4800 words (men only), move and use over 700 muscles, use 7,000,000 brain cells, and walk 7 miles (women only in the home—not men, they ride). And this body belongs to God. With all this activity, how much of it is dedicated to the Creator? Surely this wonderfully made body should be dedicated to its wonderful Creator. Make it a present to God today.

Accuracy also demands that an illustration must be told truthfully. Honesty is an absolute essential. No statements should ever be made which are not true (with the sole exception explained in Chapter 9 under "Imagination"). Facts must not be distorted or exaggerated. A preacher who makes false declarations will soon ruin his ministry, and his congregation will rightfully distrust him.

5. As a general rule, use illustrations which are fairly brief.

An illustration should not be so prominent that it robs the message of its importance. After all, the main purpose of an illustration is only to clarify. Therefore, as a general rule illustrations should not be lengthy. In fact, some word pictures are more effective when they are told concisely. But if it is necessary to use an illustration of some length in one part of the sermon, it would be wise to keep other illustrations in the same message to a minimum.

6. Use discrimination in the selection of illustrations.

Illustrations should not be employed indiscriminately in a sermon. The bizarre, the coarse, and the grotesque have no place in preaching. Their use by the preacher may lay him open to the charge of frivolity, vulgarity, or irreverence—faults which must never be laid at the door of a minister of the Gospel.

Care must be exercised not only as to the character of illustrations, but also as to the number employed in any one sermon. The minister who uses too many illustrations may find himself classified as a "story-teller." But if a preacher's main objective is to preach the Word, he will introduce illustrations only when he believes that they will make the text more intelligible and give his people a better appreciation of the truth.

As to the proportion of illustrations employed in the body of the sermon, it is safe to suggest that usually one illustration under each main division may be sufficient. At times it may be satisfactory to use more than one example under one of the main headings, but if all the illustrations in a sermon of three or four main divisions were concentrated, say, under the first main division, that would obviously be a disproportion in their use.

If the preacher is selective in the use of illustrations, he will also make certain that they are employed with variety. As was suggested in a previous chapter, there must be diversity both in the types and sources of illustrations if a man is to avoid monotony and if his illustrations are to be effective.

The Accumulation of Illustrations

A good minister knows that it is unwise for him to repeat his illustrations to the same audience, except under rare circumstances. In order to avoid repetition of illustrations, it is necessary for him to produce new ones constantly. But appropriate and interesting illustrations are not always easy to find. Rather than search through his books for an illustration when he needs it, it is better for him to accumulate material whenever he comes across that which is of value and which might be put to use in future discourses. For example, the following story was found on the back page of a church bulletin.

> A man traveling through a foreign country discovered that his destination lay at the end of a rugged mountain trail. The journey was dangerous, and he would need a qualified guide to make it safely.
>
> One guide offered to make the journey with the man. Before hiring him, the traveler asked, "Have you ever been to the village to which I am going?"
>
> The guide answered, "No, but I have been halfway, and I have heard many of my friends describe the rest of the way."
>
> "Well," replied the traveler, "you will not do as a guide."
>
> The traveler interviewed another guide. Again he asked, "Have you ever been to the village to which I wish to go?"
>
> This guide answered, "No, but I have seen the village from the top of the mountain."
>
> "You will not do for a guide, either," the man replied.
>
> A third guide offered his services to the traveler. The traveler asked him the same question he had asked the other two guides.
>
> "Sir," replied the third guide, "that village is my home."
>
> Jesus said, "I am the way and the truth and the life. No one comes to the Father except through me."

Sometimes in a moment of illumination a striking idea comes to the preacher's mind. If he does not jot it down at once, that thought may be lost forever. The minister's reading, his daily round of calling and contacts with men, as well as his own study of the Scriptures, will also suggest numerous ideas which he can develop into effective illustrations. In the course of time the man will find himself acquiring such an alertness that ideas pregnant with meaning fairly leap at him from every corner. If he then preserves all this material in a methodical manner he will possess a fund of valuable material from which to draw whenever he needs an appropriate illustration.

In order that this accumulation of material may be readily available, the homilist should have a simple but adequate filing system. A practical and effective method of filing requires two sets of Manila folders, 8½″ x 11″. One set should be a textual file, consisting of a series of folders arranged according to the order of the books of the Bible—one folder for each book. The other set should be a topical file, consisting of a series of topical folders—one folder for each topic. The following is a list of suggested topics for the student's file:

Abortion	Conversion
Adolescence	Cults
Adventism, Seventh Day	Death
Apologetics	Dedications
Archaeology	Denominations
Assurance—Eternal Security	Easter
Atonement	Education
Baptism	Ethics, Christian
Bible—The Word of God	Evangelism
Children	Evolution
Christ—Blood of	Existentialism
Christ—Miracles	Faith—Trust—Belief
Christ—Person of	Fellowship
Christ—Resurrection & Ascension	Forgiveness
Christ—Second Coming	Funerals
Christ—Sinlessness	Geography, Bible
Christ—Suffering & Death	God
Christ—Virgin Birth	Grace
Christian Evidences	Heaven
Christian Graces	Hell
Christmas	Holy Spirit
Church—Believers	Home
Church History	Homiletics
Church Supervision	Humanism
Comfort	Humility
Communism	Hymnody
Comparative Religions	Israel & the Jews
Consecration	Jehovah's Witnesses

Law
Lord's Supper
Love
Marriage & Weddings
Missions
Modernism
Mormonism
Neo-orthodoxy
New Year
Praise
Prayer
Prophecy
Psychology
Public Speaking

Redemption
Revival
Roman Catholicism
Salvation
Sanctification
Satan
Sin
Stewardship—Tithing
Sunday
Sunday School
Temperance
Worldliness
Worship
Youth

EXERCISES

1. State how you would illustrate each of the following texts:

    (1) "The wages of sin is death" (Romans 6:23).
    (2) "He must become greater; I must become less" (John 3:30).
    (3) "He guides me in paths of righteousness for his name's sake" (Psalm 23:3).
    (4) "Bless those who persecute you" (Romans 12:14).
    (5) "I am your shield, your very great reward" (Genesis 15:1).
    (6) "Blessed are the pure in heart, for they will see God" (Matthew 5:8).
    (7) "Seek the Lord while he may be found" (Isaiah 55:6).

2. Use your imagination to invent an illustration for each of the following subjects:

    (1) A vessel unto honor.
    (2) An obedient son.
    (3) An idolatrous service.
    (4) Diligence in study.
    (5) A slave before his master.
    (6) Disappointment.
    (7) Persistent pleading.

3. Find two Scriptural examples or incidents to illustrate each of the following:

    (1) A manifestation of meekness.
    (2) A hasty action.
    (3) Joy in the midst of trial.
    (4) A hateful attitude.
    (5) A faithful servant.

   (6) A woman diligent in the service of others.
   (7) An expression of kindness.
   (8) A selfish attitude.
   (9) A forgiving spirit.
  (10) A wrong promise.
  (11) The love of money.
  (12) Resistance to temptation.
  (13) A cowardly act.
  (14) The folly of worldliness.

4. Henry Wadsworth Longfellow wrote, "The mills of God grind slowly, yet they grind exceeding small." Give two illustrations from the Bible and two from secular sources to corroborate this.

5. Give four illustrations—two biblical and two secular—for each of the following occasions:

   (1) A communion service.
   (2) An Easter service.
   (3) A Christmas service.
   (4) A missionary meeting.
   (5) An evangelistic service.

6. Select three of the topical outlines in Chapter 1 and provide two illustrations suitable for each of them.

7. If you do not possess a filing cabinet, secure a portable filing cabinet with which to begin a filing system. Prepare two sets of files—a topical and a textual file—as suggested in this chapter, and begin to accumulate material for future use.

8. The following stories were culled out of the newspapers. Show how you would make use of them as illustrative material.

> The *Milwaukee Journal* of Milwaukee, Wisconsin, on August 10, 1965, reported the arrest of eleven boys between the ages of 12 and 17 who were in a burglary ring accused of taking about $10,000 worth of loot from homes and garages on the northwest side of Milwaukee. All but one of the boys were said to have come from "good homes," and at least two of them were newspaper carriers. Their victims were people who were on summer vacations, and they broke into the homes in the early hours of the morning. According to the police the boys stripped the houses of everything that was not nailed or screwed down. Included in the loot was a coin collection worth $1,200, but by the time the boys were apprehended some of the valuable coins had been spent on candy.

In the *Milwaukee Sentinel* of August 13, 1965, there was an article concerning the Titan 2 missile silo disaster at Searcy, Arkansas, where about 50 men lost their lives when an explosion and fire took place in the underground silo. The article stated that the Air Force Secretary informed the President of the United States that some of the victims may have lost their lives because the escape ladder was blocked in a most unusual manner. It seems that in a desperate attempt to escape after the explosion, two men became jammed together in a restricted area on the ladder as they attempted to escape simultaneously, thus blocking the only means of escape for others who tried to follow them.

9. Read your local daily newspaper for five successive days and cull out from each paper two articles suitable as illustrative material. Place these articles in the appropriate folders in your file.

BIBLIOGRAPHY

Baumann, J. Daniel. *An Introduction to Contemporary Preaching*. Grand Rapids, Michigan: Baker Book House, 1972, Chapter 11.

Blackwood, Andrew W. *The Preparation of Sermons*. Nashville, Tennessee: Abingdon-Cokesbury Press, 1948, Chapter 13.

Brack, Harold A. and Kenneth G. Hance. *Public Speaking and Discussion for Religious Leaders*. Englewood Cliffs, New Jersey: Prentice Hall, Inc., 1961, Chapter 6.

Breed, David Riddle. *Preparing to Preach*. New York: George H. Doran Company, 1911, Chapter 14.

Broadus, John A. *On the Preparation and Delivery of Sermons*. Revised by Jesse B. Weatherspoon. New York: Harper & Brothers, 1944, Part III, Chapter 3.

Bryan, Dawson C. *The Art of Illustrating Sermons*. Nashville, Tennessee: Cokesbury Press, 1938.

Davis, Henry Grady. *Design for Preaching*. Philadelphia, Pennsylvania: Fortress Press, 1958, pp. 254-258.

Demaray, Donald E. *An Introduction to Homiletics*. Grand Rapids, Michigan: Baker Book House, 1976, pp. 42-64, and Chapter 7.

DeWelt, Don. *If You Want to Preach*. Grand Rapids, Michigan: Baker Book House, 1957, pp. 161-165.

Ford, D. W. Cleverley. *The Ministry of the Word*. Grand Rapids, Michigan: William B. Eerdmans Publishing Co., 1979, pp. 203-205.

Gowan, Joseph. *Homiletics or the Theory of Preaching*. London: E. Stock, 1922, Chapter 10.

Holmes, George. *Toward an Effective Pulpit Ministry*. Springfield, Missouri: Gospel Publishing House, 1971, Chapters 6 and 7.

Lane, Denis. *Preach the Word*. Welwyn, Hartfordshire, England: Evangelical Press, 1979, Chapter 10.

Lehman, Louis P. *Put a Door on It—The "How" and "Why" of Sermon Illustration*. Grand Rapids, Michigan: Kregel Publications, 1975, entire book.

Lloyd-Jones, D. Martyn. *Preaching and Preachers*. Grand Rapids, Michigan: Zondervan Publishing House, 1972, pp. 236-239.

Lockyer, Herbert. *The Art and Craft of Preaching*. Grand Rapids, Michigan: Baker Book House, 1975, pp. 43-52.

Macpherson, Ian. *The Burden of the Lord*. Nashville, Tennessee: Abingdon Press, 1955, pp. 105-111.

Pattison, T. Harwood. *The Making of the Sermon*. Philadelphia: The American Baptist Publication Society, 1898, Chapters 17-18.

Perry, Lloyd M. *A Manual for Biblical Preaching*. Grand Rapids, Michigan: Baker Book House, 1965, pp. 81-83.

Robinson, Haddon W. *Biblical Preaching*. Grand Rapids, Michigan: Baker Book House, 1980, pp. 149-155.

Sangster, William Edwin. *The Craft of the Sermon*. Philadelphia: Westminster Press, n.d., Part II.

Sleeth, Ronald E. *Persuasive Preaching*. New York: Harper & Brothers, 1956, Chapter 6.

White, R. E. O. *A Guide to Preaching*. Grand Rapids, Michigan: William B. Eerdmans Publishing Co., 1973, Chapter 15.

Whitesell, Faris Daniel and Lloyd M. Perry. *Variety in Your Preaching*. Westwood, New Jersey: Fleming H. Revell Company, 1954, Chapter 7.

11. THE APPLICATION

Definition of Application

Application is one of the most important elements of the sermon. By this rhetorical process the claims of the Word of God are focused upon the individual in order that he may respond favorably to the message. When properly employed, application shows the relevancy of Scripture to a person's everyday life. It makes the teachings of the Christian revelation pertinent to him. The kind of response which may be desired of the individual, however, will differ with the purpose of the message. In one case, the desired response may be a change of attitude, in another a decision to act, and in yet another a simple acquiescence in the truth which the preacher proclaims.

Application is often described in textbooks on homiletics as the process by which the sermonizer seeks to persuade his hearers to react favorably to divinely revealed truth. There is a subtle danger in this definition. The man who assumes to apply the truths of his sermon entirely to his congregation may sometimes appear to place himself upon a pedestal, admonishing his people without recognizing that the very words he speaks may be just as applicable to himself. Such an attitude may also give the hearers the impression that the minister is preaching *at* them, and once the people come to this conclusion it will prejudice them against him.

It would be far better for the preacher to apply the truths of his message to himself as well as to his people. He should let the congregation know that he, as well as they, may need admonition, rebuke, or exhortation. This will cause them to realize that the minister places himself on their level, and that he also has spiritual needs, human frailties, and like passions.

We therefore define application as the rhetorical process by which truth is brought to bear directly and personally upon individuals in order to persuade them to respond properly to it. This definition thus embraces both the speaker and the hearers.

The Time for the Application to Be Made

The time when application is made must be determined by the contents of the message. As a general rule, application is made in connection with each spiritual truth discussed. This means that the appeal is interwoven with the entire fabric of the sermon, and the truths are applied as the discussion progresses.

There are times, however, when it would be well to make the application at the close of each subdivision or at the end of each main division. On the other hand, there are occasions when application may precede most of the other rhetorical processes, namely, argumentation, quotation, or illustration, but it should rarely come before explanation.

There are some sermons where it might be best to omit the appeal entirely from the body of the sermon and to reserve the personal impact of the message until the end of the discourse. This is especially true of sustained argument where each part of the discourse is incomplete until the whole is presented. To insert some form of application any sooner would impair the discussion and weaken the force of the conclusion as the argument reaches its climax. Sermons of an evangelistic character often come under this category.

In the case of the expository sermon which necessarily involves a considerable amount of exegesis, if the truths expounded are not applied as the sermon progresses there would be a tendency for the discourse to become heavy and difficult for the average listener to follow. For the expository form of address, it would seem best therefore to apply the truths as the sermon develops, point by point.

The amount of time given in the sermon to application is another factor which deserves consideration. As we have mentioned previously, the beginner is often tempted to devote too much time to the enforcement of the truth upon his hearers, forgetting that his main responsibility is to interpret the Word of God so clearly that all may be able to understand it. Sometimes the lessons drawn from Scripture are so obvious that formal application is wholly unnecessary. There is a happy medium which the preacher must strive to reach between too much and too little application, but where practical application is necessary, he should not fail to make it.

Prerequisites to Effective Application

Although a minister clearly elucidates the text and gives his congregation a clear understanding of its meaning, yet some may never sense the need of relating the truth to themselves personally. It is the pastor's task so to link the Scriptures to the people that they realize its truths are applicable to them. But if the homilist is to take the truths of divine revelation and relate them to the needs, the sins, and the problems of his people, he himself must possess certain prerequisites.

Let us then consider six main prerequisites to effective application.

1. It is of vital importance that the preacher be a man who lives clos⌣ to God.

Preaching which warms the heart and stirs the conscience is noᴖ born in the cold atmosphere of intellectualism but in intimate and continual fellowship with the Lord. Like the Apostle John, the preacher must get close to the heart of Jesus until the glow of His great heart fills his being and radiates through his personality.

However, in this busy, demanding age when the pastor is constantly pressured with multitudinous obligations, it is one of the most difficult things for him to find the time to nurture his own soul. We therefore need to give heed to the counsel given by the saintly Handley C. G. Moule to his younger brethren in the ministry: "Take care that no pre-occupation with things pastoral allows you to forget the supreme need of drawing out of Christ's fulness and out of the treasures of His Word for your own soul and life, as if that were the one solitary soul and life in existence."

It is in the quietness of the preacher's trysting place with God that the Lord will fashion and mold him, gradually transforming his character into the image of his Master. As the Apostle Paul wrote, "And we, who with unveiled faces all reflect the Lord's glory, are being transformed into his likeness with ever-increasing glory, which comes from the Lord, who is the Spirit" (2 Corinthians 3:18). Close fellowship with Christ will also develop in the preacher a gentle, gracious, and wholesome attitude toward his people. The object of his ministry will not be to drive them like a herd of animals, but to lead and to edify them "until we all reach unity in the faith and in the knowledge of the Son of God and become mature, attaining to the whole measure of the fullness of Christ" (Ephesians 4:13).

There is no substitute for a godly life and character. To preach the truth but fail to live it will never impress anyone; but a holy life, with a loving concern for others, is the best sermon that a minister can preach. It is for this reason that Paul admonished Timothy, "Don't let anyone look down on you because you are young, but set an example for the believers in speech, in life, in love, in faith and in purity" (1 Timothy 4:12). Such an exemplary life is not the result of wishful thinking or even of fervent desire, neither is it produced in a week, or a month, or a year. Saintly life and character come only through a long process of assiduous application of the laws of spiritual growth, and diligent cultivation of daily fellowship alone with Christ. Whatever the cost, the minister who relates the Scriptures to the needs of the hour must discipline himself to take the time for this holy exercise. Only thus will he be able to speak from and in and for his Lord, and be able to minister effectively to the spiritual needs of men.

2. *In order to be successful in relating the Bible to the present, the man of God must be well educated.*

It is essential that the pastor should have a broad academic training, with an intelligent knowledge both of the Scriptures and of human affairs. He should have a solid foundation of general knowledge and also a thorough grasp and understanding of the Scriptures and of doctrine. He must not only be well trained in the schools, but must also keep abreast of the times. He will have to read widely. His reading will include the writings of men in the secular as well as the religious field. He should also keep in touch with contemporary theological trends and other movements which affect the life and service of his congregation. In addition, he must give constant attention to the thinking of the man on the street as it is expressed or reflected in current periodicals and in the newspapers.

If a minister is to apply the truth effectively to his congregation he must also be a diligent student of the Word of God. Next to his own devotional life, nothing is more important to the minister than that he be a constant and earnest Bible student. It is not sufficient for the man to have a devout faith, a sound academic and Biblical training, and a knowledge of homiletics. If the messenger of God depends on these alone, he cannot maintain an adequate and effective ministry in the pulpit. It is one of his primary functions to know the Scriptures better and better so as to explain its contents to his people. This he can accomplish only by concentrated effort, prolonged meditation, and hard application throughout the years of his ministry. Like Ezra of old, he must set himself to know the sacred oracles and allow nothing to take precedence over the hours which he should spend in his study.

3. Another qualification which a preacher should possess if he is to apply the truth effectively is an understanding of human nature.

Whenever a man addresses a congregation he faces a group of people with a composite of spiritual and emotional problems and personal cares. They are also in varied states of spiritual and emotional maturity, as well as physical and intellectual maturity.

It is of the utmost importance that the homilist have an understanding of human nature, with its many complexes. If he is to be successful in persuading people he must know how people are persuaded, and he must understand their varied dispositions, attitudes, ideals, and interests. Furthermore, he should be observant of the basic human drives and know how these dispositions are reflected in human behavior. In addition, he must be able to recognize the general characteristics of maturity. Of course, the preacher himself must be mature, with a well-balanced, integrated personality.

The minister should also have a sensitive understanding of the basic needs of various age groups—the needs of little children, of adolescents, of young people, of single men and women, of young married couples, of parents, and of older people as well. It would therefore be advisable for him to have an adequate course in psychology so that he may learn about and become cognizant of these human needs and the behavior patterns which relate to different age groups.

4. To be able to relate the truths of Scripture to the problems and circumstances of his people, the minister must acquaint himself with their conditions and involvements.

Paul could say to the Christians at Philippi, "I have you in my heart" (Philippians 1:7), and so with this attitude his epistle breathes the spirit of one who was vitally interested in them. The servant of the Lord who ministers His Word must show a like interest in his congregation, and by calling upon his people he will soon discover the circumstances and conditions which they face.

The sincere, dedicated pastor who thus keeps in sympathetic touch with the burdens and heart throbs of humanity and who lives at the same time in close touch with God, will be able to discern in the Scriptures those truths which have significance for the people whom he seeks to help.

The ability to see these vital relationships between the needs of people and the Bible will increase as the preacher's observations and knowledge of human nature increase. In fact, if the pastor plans wisely and prayerfully, every call which he makes may enable him to discover their joys and sorrows, their hopes and fears, their successes and their failures, and prepare him for the task of searching the Scriptures for the message and truths which might help them in their particular situations.

5. *A further qualification for a minister who wishes to communicate the Scriptures effectively is that he should speak naturally.*

It has not been our purpose in this book to deal with the subject of sermon delivery, but since so much depends upon the way the sermon is spoken, as well as its content, we feel that there is one particular feature in connection with the oral communication of the sermon about which we need to make special mention.

Because of the pressure of his duties and his zeal for proclaiming God's truth, the preacher may be unaware of the stress under which he is working. The result of such continuous pressure sometimes reveals itself when the man is in the pulpit. Instead of being at his best and speaking in a gracious and relaxed manner he may become tense and excited. His delivery is then apt to be unnatural and he may tend to speak too loudly or too emphatically.

When the messenger of the Gospel speaks in this manner he is unwittingly straining himself in the delivery of his discourse. At the same time he makes it difficult for his auditors to listen to him, for no matter how orthodox or important his message may be, it will be a strain for his congregation to give proper attention to his address.

Charles Haddon Spurgeon once declared that "the perfection of preaching is to talk." He meant, in other words, that the most effective manner of preaching is to speak in a normal conversational style as though the preacher were telling his message in the same natural manner in which he would speak if he were conversing with just one other individual.

When the speaker delivers his message without strain or force, not only does he put himself at ease but he also makes it easy for his congregation to listen to him. Such a style of delivery will also free the preacher from any tendency toward formal or artificial performance, for, if he would only remember it, the congregation always prefers to listen to a man who is simply his own natural self.

But this does not mean that the minister's delivery must be devoid of animation. On the contrary, the delight of sharing from the Word of God that which will prove an inspiration and uplift to the people should itself provide the stimulus the preacher needs to speak with enthusiasm. In fact, the earnestness and sincerity with which he delivers his address, and the very expression on his face and in his eyes, will show his auditors that he himself has experienced the truth which he seeks to impart to them. For, in the last analysis, there is no eloquence greater than the natural and gracious speech that flows from a warm and loving heart.

6. *Finally, for the minister to obtain the right response to his message, he must be completely dependent upon the working of the Spirit of God.*

After all we have said concerning application, it must ever be recognized that in the last analysis persuasion is entirely the work of the third Person of the Trinity. The minister may preach the Word with the utmost fidelity, he may make the most fervent appeals or warn with the deepest solemnity, but unless the Holy Spirit breathes upon the message and quickens the hearts of individuals, the sermon will of itself fail to accomplish anything. The Spirit of truth alone can stir the conscience, move the will, sanctify the soul, write God's law upon the heart, and stamp God's image upon the character. Even the Lord Jesus was dependent upon the Spirit of God to empower Him "in the days of His flesh," (NASB) for as He began His public ministry He said, "The Spirit of the Lord is on me, because he has anointed me to preach good news . . . to proclaim the year of the Lord's favor" (Luke 4:18-19). How necessary then that the man of God be controlled by the Holy Spirit so that as he stands in the pulpit to proclaim the Word of God, the Spirit Himself may empower his every word and work effectively in the hearts of men.

Such Spirit-endued preaching is usually closely associated with fervent prayer. The apostles said, "we will give our attention to prayer and the ministry of the word," and the Book of Acts is the inspired record of what the Spirit of God wrought through these men of prayer.

Before the great revival in New England which took place in the spring of 1735, Jonathan Edwards gave himself for three days and three nights to fervent supplication. As he paced up and down his room, he cried constantly to God, "Give me New England! Give me New England!" On the following Sunday morning, as he read his sermon on "Sinners in the Hands of an Angry God" the Spirit of God came mightily upon the congregation. Men and women were so deeply convicted of sin that they clung to the seats and pillars in the auditorium for fear that they would be cast into hell there and then. A great turning to God took place that day and the revival which began in that church quickly spread over all New England.

The Weymouth translation of James 5:16 reads, "The heartfelt supplication of a righteous man exerts a mighty influence." Surely this is the need of the hour—modern apostles, with the same infirmities perhaps as those men of old but who, like them, are men of prayer. Men of God are needed who so lay hold upon the power of God in the secret closet that as they proclaim the Word of God it will go forth with the anointing and quickening power of the Holy Spirit.

Principles for Making the Truth Relevant

1. Relate the sermon to basic human problems and needs.

We have already pointed out that if the homilist is to be successful in applying the truth, he must have an understanding of human nature and of the behavior patterns of various classes of individuals. In the communication of the Word of God, it is necessary not only to have a sensitive understanding of basic human problems and needs but also to relate the sermon to the perplexities and temptations which beset the man in the pew from day to day. We must find how the text is readily applicable to the conditions of the people we are addressing.

To assist the young preacher in discovering the relationship of the Scriptures to human needs we suggest that he make a list of characteristic human traits and behavior patterns and try to find the Scripture texts, as well as biblical examples, which deal with them. With the help of *Nave's Topical Bible* the student will soon discover an abundance of material in the divine revelation on such basic emotional problems as the sense of guilt, frustration, loneliness, fear, hatred, anger, and jealousy, and the more he learns of the relationship between the Book and the needs of men the more adequate he will be to minister to them.

We have also stated earlier in the chapter that it is the obligation of the sermonizer to acquaint himself with the day-to-day situations which face the individuals in the congregation and to understand their thinking. If the sermon is to be related to his hearers, the homilist should then introduce material which will immediately strike a responsive chord in the hearts of his audience as being peculiarly appropriate to their situations.

2. *Use your imagination in such a manner as to make the scenes and characters of the Bible alive today.*

As we have seen in a previous chapter, imagination can play a vital role in a sermon. This is particularly the case when it comes to the application of the truth to the hearers. But we must always be careful to use it judiciously, so that we are not carried away with highly fanciful mental images which may be either inappropriate or distasteful.

Observe in the illustration below how we have used imagination to draw on two characters of Scripture in order to relate the Word of God to the problems and needs of the individuals in the pew.

Suppose we are delivering an address on Genesis 45:1-15, and having expounded verses 4 through 8 we are now ready to make the application. We may then proceed as follows:

> What a wonderful spirit of forgiveness Joseph manifested to his brethren! Think of the years of unspeakable anguish, mental and physical, through which he passed, all because of the wickedness and hatred of his brethren, and yet he did not express a single word of remonstrance or harshness, neither was there a tinge of malice or bitterness toward them. On the contrary, he showed nothing but kindness and grace to these men who had wronged him so deeply. Surely, none of us can say that we have been wronged as much as Joseph was wronged, nor have we gone through anything like that which Joseph experienced. Has anyone ever forgiven us as much as Joseph forgave his brethren? If we are Christians we can say indeed, "In Christ God forgave" us all things. What should our attitude be then toward a brother who has wronged us? No doubt, one of the reasons why God turned all the evil in Joseph's life into good was that he never harbored any bitterness or ill-will toward those who were so greatly responsible for all his misfortunes. And the Lord will surely turn into good whatever ill may have befallen us through the thoughtlessness or unkindness of others if we, like Joseph, maintain a benevolent and forgiving spirit toward those who may have injured us

For our second example we choose Hebrews 11:24-27. In these verses we find that there were three allurements presented to Moses in Egypt—honor, riches, and pleasure, but he realized that if he was to be a true man of God he had to turn his back upon every one of them. We shall assume that we have expounded the text and have shown how each of these enticements was dangled before Moses to draw him into the world. We now present the application:

> Mind you, none of these things which were presented to Moses were wrong in themselves. God intends that we enjoy the respect of our fellow men, that we use our talents to the best advantage in this world, and that we take time for recreation and pleasure. But when any one of these things, perfectly right and legitimate in itself, hinders us from giving ourselves wholly to God, then it is evil. As Moses weighed the passing trivialities which the world could offer against his future reward, he made his decision. The best which the world could give paled into insignificance in contrast to the privilege of walking with God and being owned by God. He saw that what God wanted from him was not patronage, but fellowship. There are too many believers who will only give God their patronage—they are willing to give to the church, to support missions and missionaries, and to serve in some capacity or other in the work of the Lord. What God wants is not our patronage—He can do without our patronage —He wants us. He wants us—mind, heart, and soul. He wants our fellowship, but as the Apostle Paul wrote, it must be "the fellowship of His sufferings."

3. Employ illustrations which show how the truth can be applied to the lives of your people in the workaday world.

The individuals to whom the minister preaches on Sunday are men and women, boys and girls, who face the realities of life from day to day. They are confronted with pressures, frustrations, temptations, problems, and heartaches, and they need to be shown not only from the text of Scripture but also from life situations how the Bible has practical bearing upon their own encounters.

Illustrations, therefore, that are drawn from life and which are used appropriately can have a telling effect upon the auditors.

Consider the following incident which comes from a sermon on Luke 19:1-10 preached by J. Vernon McGee, former pastor of the Church of the Open Door in Los Angeles, California. Dr. McGee commented upon the fact that when Zacchaeus turned to the Lord, he immediately set about to make restitution for the wrongs which he had done to others. Then Dr. McGee quoted from an unpublished letter dated January 2, 1900, written by Frank DeWitt Talmage to Dr. R. A. Torrey which Dr. McGee came across quite accidentally while rummaging through some papers in a desk which once belonged to Dr. Torrey. The letter consisted of a confession by Dr. Talmage to Dr. Torrey and read in part:

Dear Torrey:

Today I am standing under the shadow of two griefs; first that of Mr. Moody's death. Second, the fact that I may have done you a very great injustice. . . .

(The confession of wrongdoing followed at this point, but because of the personal nature of the offense Dr. McGee did not wish to disclose it.)

If there is any way I can rectify the wrong, I will gladly do so . . . May the sweet spirit of him who has gone make me more and more preach the gospel of love.

Yours with sorrow,
(Signed) Frank DeWitt Talmage.

Then Dr. McGee made his application:

Tears came to my eyes when I read these words which had been hidden from the light for half a century. It was startling to realize how far we had come by midcentury. We retain the traditions of fundamentalism, but when was the last time you have seen such a sweet, humble and quiet confession of wrong? We in fundamental circles seem to have the idea that if a man's head is screwed on right, his feet may go in any direction they want to go and he is still a child of God. My friend, when your head goes in one direction and your feet in another, something is radically wrong. Zacchaeus did not say he was a fundamentalist—he did not have to say it, for he proved it by his works.

4. Draw from the text universal principles which are applicable for all time.

In the course of exegesis, striking truths may sometimes fairly leap at the homilist from the portion of the Scriptures which he is studying. Whenever such truths come to his attention, the exegete should write them down on his work sheet. Although he may not be able to use every one of these principles in the sermon which he is preparing, they may prove useful on some later occasion.

Here are five principles which Charles R. Swindoll extracted from the Lord's teaching on the subject of anxiety in Matthew 6:25-34:

> Worry keeps us from enjoying what we now have.
> Worry makes us forget our own worth.
> Worry is completely useless—it really solves nothing.
> Worry erases the promises of God from our minds.
> Worry is characteristic of the heathen, not the Christian.

It is easy to see that by the use of fundamental principles such as these we are able to relate Scriptures written centuries ago to people today.

Of course, it is not enough merely to state each principle as we proceed with our sermon. Wherever necessary we should also elaborate or enlarge upon each principle.

Sometimes a discourse in which we employ only one or two universal truths may be just as effective as one in which we use more, provided we take the time to expand or discuss them adequately.

For the benefit of the beginner, we show below six principles which we have derived from Psalm 23, one drawn from each successive verse in the Psalm.

> Every believer can rightfully claim that the Lord is his own personal guardian.
> The Lord provides perfect rest for the one who trusts in Him.
> I have a divine guide who is absolutely trustworthy.
> The Lord is present with His people when they need Him most.
> The Lord provides abundantly for His own, even under the most difficult circumstances.
> Because of the Lord's promises we can trust Him wholly for all that lies before us.

We may not only derive principles from individual verses in a text, but we may extract abiding truths from an entire section of Scripture. The following are drawn from Psalm 23 as a whole:

> A trusting believer has the assurance of the supply of every need throughout his life.
> The personal care of the Lord for each individual believer inspires great confidence.
> Contemplation upon the Lord's personal concern for each Christian produces a blessed assurance.

5. Make sure that every application is in line with the truth of the passage.

Correct application of Scripture is dependent upon accurate interpretation of the text. It is for this reason that we must make every effort to understand the meaning of Scripture. Although the work of exegesis may be a slow, painstaking task, it is of the utmost importance that we be able to speak with assurance of the true significance of the text. Not until we have learned the proper meaning of the passage can we be sure that our application runs parallel with the truth of the text before us.

The following statement, based on the narrative in Mark 16:1-4 concerning the women who went to the sepulchre to anoint the body of Jesus, was once turned in by a student in a Bible school: "The women came to the tomb prepared with the spices, just as we must come to Christ prepared to accept His will and lordship in our lives."

Anyone who is familiar with this account in Mark's Gospel will recognize that the student failed completely to understand the meaning of the text. Had he seen that the women acted with great courage and loving devotion by coming to the tomb at the break of day to anoint the body of Jesus, he would probably not have gone so far astray in his attempted practical application of the text. Instead of referring to the necessity of accepting Christ's will and lordship in our lives, the youthful Bible student might have spoken rather about the fact that where there is genuine love for the Savior there will be evidence of it by acts of sacrificial devotion to Him.

6. As a general rule, make the application specific or definite.

Too many times the appeal is expressed in such general terms or in such a vague, indirect manner that it fails to register upon the congregation as having any relevance to them. This is usually due to the fact that the preacher himself lacks definiteness in the objectives of his sermon, or it may be due to an unhealthy fear of being charged with fanaticism or narrowmindedness.

How different was Paul's attitude. He could affirm to the elders of the church at Ephesus, "I have not hesitated to proclaim to you the whole will of God" (Acts 20:27), and to the Thessalonians he could confidently assert, "for the appeal we make does not spring from error or impure motives, nor are we trying to trick you. On the contrary, we speak as men approved by God to be entrusted with the gospel. We are not trying to please men but God, who tests our hearts" (1 Thessalonians 2:3-4). Taking the great Apostle as our example, let us with holy boldness, but at the same time in a gentle and loving spirit, proclaim the Word in such a manner as to indicate clearly how its truths bear directly upon men.

One of the best means of addressing the appeal to a congregation is by the use of questions which apply specifically to them. We must be careful, however, that the questions are expressed in a courteous and appropriate manner, and the preacher should sometimes include himself in such interrogations with a "we" instead of "you."

For an example of specific application we use Joshua 5:13-15 which describes Joshua's vision of the Lord as he stood before the beleaguered city of Jericho. When Joshua saw the man with the sword drawn in his hand, he questioned, "Are you for us or for our enemies?" And the man answered, "Neither, but as commander of the army of the LORD I have now come." Verse 14 then reads, "Then Joshua fell facedown to the ground in reverence, and asked him, 'What message does my Lord have for his servant?' " We shall imagine that we have expounded the text and are now to apply the truth in relation to the effect of the vision upon Joshua:

> It is always the same when the Lord is seen by the Christian. The sight of our blessed Savior puts us in our rightful place—in the dust before God. This is the keynote of the kingdom of heaven—"He must become greater; I must become less." This was true of Joshua, of Job, of Isaiah, of Daniel, of Paul, and of John. Has this been our experience? Has it been our experience today? Have we seen Him afresh? The evidence will surely be shown in the condition of our souls before God, and like Joshua our response will be, "What message does my lord have for his servant?"

In a message on "Love's Behavior" drawn from 1 Corinthians 13, published in *Christian Economics,* April 4, 1967, Kyle M. Yates, professor of Bible at Baylor University in Waco, Texas, begins with a series of questions. Note how these interrogations direct the attention of the hearer to the relevancy of the text to his daily life:

> "How do you behave in your daily walk? Would you be considered a Christian by your pastor, your neighbor, your father or mother, your children, your wife, your husband? It would be tragic if any of these individuals should give a negative vote.

Honestly, what is your answer to the question? Do you actually believe that your behavior proves you are a Christian? It is a question of transcendent importance.

Paul comes to your rescue and puts down the definite, clear-cut picture of a Christian. You can find his portrait in 1 Corinthians 13:4-7. You cannot miss the point nor the verdict. The one essential ingredient is love."

In *The Calvary Pulpit* of March, 1960, Stephen F. Olford, pastor of the Calvary Baptist Church of New York City, has a sermon on "Abiding in Christ" with John 15:1-11 as the unit of exposition. Under his first main heading, "The Meaning of Abiding in Christ," Olford also uses interrogations as a means of making application:

"Look at verse 5. Jesus says, 'Apart from me (or severed from me) ye can do nothing.' My Christian friend, tell me, have you been working and struggling hard for years to do something, and have achieved nothing? Is it true that there is no fruitfulness in your life; no effectiveness in your life, no real joyfulness in your life? Are you still irritable? Provoked by your children? Attacked by paroxysms of temper? Defeated in moments of loneliness? Another week has gone by and you can't say with joy, 'Thank God, I have been the instrument of bringing yet another soul to Christ. The life of Jesus in me, flowing through me by the Holy Spirit, has quickened yet another one for whom Jesus died!' If you cannot say that, but instead, you are filled with a sense of futility, and defeat, then you don't know what it is to abide in Christ. 'Without me,' declared Christ, 'ye can do nothing.' "

The preceding paragraphs should be sufficient to enable the reader to see how the application may be made specific or definite. However, it should be noted that the application does not necessarily have to be done by direct exhortation or appeal. Sometimes it may be accomplished merely by implication. For instance, we can make the application by employing an apt illustration which serves by itself to apply the truth. But in whatever way the application is presented, the pulpiteer must be sure that the people are made aware of the fact that he is declaring the Word of God in its immediate relations to them.

The student should also bear in mind that it is never appropriate to make an application which is pointed to a specific individual or group in the congregation. To resort to such an unethical procedure is to exploit the sacred desk at the expense of a helpless people and will doubtless precipitate a bad reaction on the part of those toward whom the preacher's remarks are intended. On the other hand, when the truth is so presented that men of themselves make the application without feeling that the minister's statements are directed at them personally, it is apt to have a most salutary effect.

7. Spur the hearers with right motivation.

If the preacher has directed the sermon to the problems and needs of his hearers so that they are able to sense how the truth relates directly to them, it should be natural for the minister then to point them to a solution to their need. To do this, however, he will need to provide his hearers with adequate motivation or incentive. The minister may incite his congregation to action by appealing to the nobler instincts of men and women, as well as by warnings relating to the consequences of neglect or inaction. He may also motivate his hearers by citing some particular example of the truth or action which he is seeking to drive home to his people.

8. Relate the truth to the times.

We are all no doubt acutely conscious of the fact that we are living in a world of tremendous change—political, economic, social, religious, and moral. The standards and disciplines of the past are being held in contempt and more and more we see in every realm of society a drift from the restraints of law and order. The average man is vitally affected by these revolutionary changes as they touch upon every aspect of his daily life.

It is a sad commentary on some preachers that too much of what they preach is detached from the incisive biblical evaluation of the vital and current needs of people today. Their sermons cover a multitude of subjects, but in too many instances they are unrelated to modern life. This, in spite of the fact that whenever the Bible speaks, whether regarding the past or the future, it does so in order that it may be relevant to the present.

If the Word of God is to be made meaningful to an individual in the midst of the great upheavals taking place in society, he must be shown not only the meaning of the Bible but also how its truths are directly applicable to him in the face of all the bewildering situations in the world today. Preaching which relates the truth to the times and the conditions of the present is called interpretive preaching. It is the presentation of the facts of Scripture as they throw light upon current world affairs and their effect upon the man in the pew.

But while it is of vital importance to relate the Word of God to the times, there are certain pitfalls which beset interpretive preaching.

Some preachers, in an effort to be relevant, and in the face of the chaotic social conditions that are prevalent, equate the ministry of the Gospel with social service. Thus, instead of proclaiming the verities of the divine revelation they often major in social reform.

Many other clergymen become involved in political issues. They seem to feel that it is their responsibility to make pronouncements concerning political, economic, or world affairs. Some assume these prerogatives with the dubious idea that they have the last word on the perplexing issues which are puzzling and baffling the most astute statesmen and financiers, but when they impose their views on such matters they often hamper rather than enhance their own influence. We never read in the New Testament of the Apostles making pronouncements concerning the manner in which the Roman government ruled its empire, nor do we find that they ever adopted resolutions for the consideration of the senate at Rome. The pastor surely has a right as a private citizen to belong to the political party of his own choice, but as a representative of the church and in his pronouncements from the pulpit he should carefully preserve the distinction between political and moral issues, and studiously avoid anything which may involve his ministry in matters which "belong to Caesar."

The minister who seeks to bring the light of the Scriptures to bear upon current world affairs must therefore be a wise and discerning man. Not only should he stay clear of political issues but he should also be able to discriminate between truth and falsehood, between separation and compromise, and as a faithful pastor he must warn his people of religious movements or systems of doctrinal error which imperil the purity and orthodoxy of the church.

Vital Themes of the Interpretive Preacher

1. The Gospel

Three vital themes should especially engage the attention of the interpretive preacher. The first of these is the Gospel—God's good news for men. While the newspapers daily point to an ever increasing gravity in national and international affairs, the messenger of the Cross has good news indeed to bring to men in the midst of all the chaos and distress in the world today. The herald of the Gospel should therefore buy up his opportunities and proclaim with no uncertain sound the glorious news that Jesus saves.

2. Evangelism

Another relevant theme is evangelism. Not only should the minister proclaim the Gospel, but he should also encourage his people in every way possible to share the blessed news with others. The best means of promoting evangelism is for the pastor himself to be actively engaged in reaching the lost, and as he deals with unbelievers with whom he comes in contact he will be able to lead his congregation in a soul-winning ministry.

But evangelism should not be limited within the confines of one's own community. The true spirit of evangelism reaches out in ever-widening circles to embrace a world which is lost in sin. The minister who seeks to make the Scriptures relevant must admonish his parishoners in the light of world conditions to haste in carrying the message of saving grace to others before it is too late. The transmission of the Gospel must not be delayed, for if the world is to be reached for Christ we must go now. Therefore missions, both home and foreign, should have a prominent place in the ministry from the pulpit.

3. Prophecy

A third theme which should mark the ministry of the interpretive preacher is prophecy. At the present writing exciting news is coming out of the Middle East, so much so that hardly a day passes without some reference in the newspapers to names and places which are familiar to all Bible readers. In fact, the events taking place in Bible lands are so startling that they are arousing the interest even of the secular press in the promises of God to His ancient people Israel.

The homilist must not miss the unique opportunity which presents itself by these extraordinary events to direct the attention of the congregation to the signs of the times. Surely the cataclysmic judgments of the end of the age are drawing near, and it is the solemn obligation of the servant of God to set forth those portions of the Bible which foretell the things which are to come to pass upon the world. Sermons on prophecy will warn the ungodly of their danger, arouse the church to her responsibility, and enliven the saints concerning the blessed hope of the return of the Lord Jesus Christ. "And we have the word of the prophets made more certain, and you will do well to pay attention to it, as to a light shining in a dark place, until the day dawns and the morning star rises in your hearts" (2 Peter 1:19).

Example of an Interpretive Sermon Outline

We present below an example of an interpretive sermon outline in expanded form based on Hosea 10:12—"Sow for yourselves righteousness, reap the fruit of unfailing love, and break up your unplowed ground; for it is time to seek the LORD, until he comes and showers righteousness on you."

Title: "The Time to Seek the Lord"
Introduction: 1. Words of text addressed to Israel—immorality, vice, corruption, violence rampant in nation, and God used Hosea to call Israel to repentance. If ever time for Israel seek God, it was then.
2. Is the text applicable to us?
Proposition: The Lord makes clear the conditions when it is time to seek Him.
Interrogative sentence: What are those conditions?
Transitional sentence: There are at least three conditions shown in the Scriptures which when they exist indicate that it is time to seek the Lord.
I. When God's judgments threaten the land.
1. The reason for such threats of judgment.
Bible reveals God as moral Governor, taking note of nations.
Nothing escapes His eye—Prov. 15:3.
What must He see as looks upon our nation!
Note two conditions in U.S.
(1) Violence
The March 23, 1981, issue of *Time* magazine stated: "Every 24 minutes a murder is committed somewhere in the U.S., every 10 seconds a house is burglarized, and every 7 minutes a woman is raped. But . . . the curse of violent crime is rampant, not just in the ghettos of depressed cities . . . but everywhere in urban areas, in suburbs, and peaceful countrysides. More significant, the crimes are becoming more brutal, more irrational, more random—and therefore all the more frightening." (Reprinted by permission from Time, the Weekly Newsmagazine; copyright Time Inc. 1981.)
(2) Immorality.

The September 1, 1980, issue of *Newsweek* magazine declared: "Nearly half of the nation's 15 to 19 year old girls have had premarital sex, and the numbers are increasing." Commenting on the disastrous influence of TV on children, a professor of Communications Arts and Sciences at New York University was quoted in a leading U.S. magazine dated January 19, 1981 to have said: "It causes them (the children) to be increasingly impatient with deferred gratification. Even more serious, in my view, is that television is opening up all of society's secrets and taboos, thus erasing the dividing line between childhood and adulthood and leaving a very homogenized culture in its wake."

(3) Abortion.

A paragraph in the March 1, 1981, *Intercessors for America Newsletter* refers to "the unbelievable potential results from home do-it-yourself abortion kits" and grieves over a leading pharmaceutical company "which has has prostituted its historic pro-life values in spearheading this technology," and over a "marketing organization that encourages promiscuity and sells death services to unsuspecting teenagers."

Note 2 Peter 2:2-9, Proverbs 1:24-32.

2. The nature of God's judgments.

God punished Israel for her sin by allowing cruel, inhumane Assyrians to carry them away captive. Ancient monument shows king of Assyria gouging out eyes of captives taken in war. We do not know how God may judge our nation if persists in sin, but when God revealed His purpose to Abraham to destroy Sodom, Gomorrah for their guilt, Abraham "drew near" to God, and interceded for Sodom. Result—Gen. 19:29-30.

Should we wait till God's judgments fall, or follow example of Abraham and seek God now in behalf of our nation?

Transition: Not only do we need to seek the Lord when His judgments threaten the land, but we need also to seek Him

II. When our own spiritual condition is at a low ebb.

1. Indications of such a condition.

(1) Indifference to spiritual need of the lost.

Illus. Jonah in ship in storm. While heathen sailors cried every man to his god to save them from destruction, only man on ship who knew living God, asleep! Even after captain awoke him, begged him pray, did not do so. "There is no conscience so insensible as that

of a disobedient believer."
If we indifferent to the lost, then our spiritual
condition at low ebb.
(2) Following Jesus afar off.
Illus. Peter followed J. afar off, warmed himself by enemies' fire, finally denied Christ.
Is it true of us? Was there time when we were
fervent, devoted Christians, but now cold,
indifferent; lost desire for devotions, prayer,
spiritual things?
2. The effects of such a condition.
Chastisement. Someone once said: "God knows
how to 'spank.'"
Consider how God "spanked" Jonah—swallowed
by fish cf. Jonah 2:1—"Then inside the fish Jonah
prayed to the Lord his God."
If our spiritual condition at low ebb, should we
wait till God has to "spank" before we cry to Him?
If conscious of disobedience or following J. afar
off, let us seek God now before He has to chastise.
Note result on Peter—"he went outside and wept
bitterly."
Consider Rev. 2:4-5, 3:15-19.
Transition: We can surely discern that the first two
conditions about which we have spoken are
present today. There is, however, a third significant condition which indicates that it is time for us
to seek the Lord, namely,
III. When God is ready to pour out His blessings upon us.
1. The degree of blessing which God is ready to pour
out. Hos. 10:12—"It is time to seek the Lord,
until he comes and showers righteousness on
you." Hence, showers of blessing.
This what God waits to do—give abundant,
revival blessings. Mal. 3:10.
2. The conditions under which He pours out such
blessings.
(1) Repentance.
Hosea 10:12—"Break up your unplowed
ground."—Hence, allow Holy Spirit to
search, probe, reveal wrong; by God's grace,
to forsake evil.
(2) Fervent searching after Him.
Hosea 10:12—"It is time to seek the Lord,
until he comes and showers righteousness."
Thus, God desires us persist, be fervent in
seeking Him.
Jer. 29:13 and 2 Chron. 7:14.
Transition: Recognizing that the time has indeed
come for us to seek the Lord, let us delay no
longer to do so.
Conclusion: 1. Isaiah 55:6—"Seek the Lord while he may be
found; call on him while he is near." There may
come time when too late to seek Him.
2. Illus. Revival in country church.

EXERCISES

1. Make a list of Scripture passages which deal with the following emotional states or attitudes:

    (1) Love
    (2) Fear
    (3) Contentment
    (4) Self-confidence
    (5) Joy
    (6) Discontent
    (7) Trust
    (8) Callousness
    (9) Hope
    (10) Jealousy
    (11) Bitterness
    (12) Peace
    (13) Selfishness
    (14) Guilt
    (15) Frustration
    (16) Meekness

2. For each of the above emotional states or attitudes give at least one example of its manifestation by an individual in the Bible.

3. Prepare a topical message suitable for a group of college age young people. Give the title, introduction, proposition, interrogative sentence, transitional sentence, main divisions, subdivisions, and transitions between main divisions. Expand the outline, using brief phrases whenever possible as shown in the examples of expanded outlines at the conclusion of Chapters 9 and 11.

4. Construct a textual sermon which may be appropriate for delivery at a conference on Christian service. Follow the same instructions as contained in Exercise 3 above in the building of the outline.

5. Prepare an expository sermon suitable for an address before a Sunday school convention. Develop the outline in accordance with the instructions in Exercise 3.

6. Give four titles for a series of messages on evangelism. Select one of these titles and prepare an address on it. Use the rhetorical devices discussed in Chapters 9, 10, and 11 in the development of the discourse, and write the outline in expanded form like the expanded outlines at the close of Chapters 9 and 11.

7. Construct a sermon based upon one of the prophetic portions of the Old or New Testament. Give the title, introduction, proposition, main divisions, and subdivisions. Write out your application or applications word for word, showing the relevancy of the text to the times.

8. Secure from your school library or from some other source, published sermons by two well-known preachers of the past and the present, such as:

Charles Haddon Spurgeon	D. Martyn Lloyd-Jones
Alexander Maclaren	John R. W. Stott
G. Campbell Morgan	Stephen F. Olford
Joseph Parker	Paul S. Rees
George W. Truett	J. Sidlow Baxter
W. Graham Scroggie	Warren W. Wiersbe
Donald Grey Barnhouse	

Read one sermon from each author, and in the light of what you have learned in homiletics, make notes on the following items in each sermon:

(1) The qualities of the discussion.
(2) The sources of material used by the preacher.
(3) The rhetorical processes employed.
(4) The manner in which application is made.

9. Listen to sermons of well-known preachers on cassette tape (obtainable from Christian bookstores or directly from various radio ministries). Compare their sermons with your own recorded sermons and try to discover how you may improve your preaching skills.

BIBLIOGRAPHY

Ayer, William Ward. "Study Preparation & Pulpit Preaching," *Bibliotheca Sacra*, Vol. 124:494 (April June, 1967), pp. 106 116.

———. "Preaching to Combat the Present Revolution," *Bibliotheca Sacra*, Vol. 124:495 (July-September, 1967), pp. 206-217.

Baumann, J. Daniel. *An Introduction to Contemporary Preaching*. Grand Rapids, Michigan: Baker Book House, 1972, Chapters 2, 15, and 17.

Broadus, John A. *On the Preparation and Delivery of Sermons*. Revised by Jesse B. Weatherspoon. New York: Harper & Brothers, 1944, Part III, Chapter 4.

Caemmerer, Richard R. *Preaching for the Church*. St. Louis, Missouri: Concordia Publishing House, 1959, Chapters 40-45.

Davis, Henry Grady. *Design for Preaching*. Philadelphia, Pennsylvania; Fortress Press, 1958, Chapters 7, 8, 12, and 13.

Demaray, Donald E. *An Introduction to Homiletics*. Grand Rapids, Michigan: Baker Book House, 1976, Chapter 1.

DeWelt, Don. *If You Want to Preach*. Grand Rapids, Michigan: Baker Book House, 1957, Chapter 1.

Etter, John W. *The Preacher and His Sermon*. Dayton, Ohio: United Brethren Publishing House, 1902, Part II, Chapter 10.

Ford, D. W. Cleverley. *The Ministry of the Word*. Grand Rapids, Michigan: William B. Eerdmans Publishing Co., 1979, pp. 197-203.

Holmes, George. *Toward an Effective Pulpit Ministry*. Springfield, Missouri: Gospel Publishing House, 1971, Chapters 1-5, 13, and 14.

Jordan, G. Ray, *You Can Preach*. New York: Fleming H. Revell Company, 1958, Chapter 17.

Kaiser, Walter C., Jr. *Toward an Exegetical Theology, Biblical Exegesis for Preaching and Teaching*. Grand Rapids, Michigan: Baker Book House, 1981, Chapter 12.

Lane, Denis. *Preach the Word*. Welwyn, Hartfordshire, England: Evangelical Press, 1979, Chapters 1 and 12.

Lloyd-Jones, D. Martyn. *Preaching and Preachers*. Grand Rapids, Michigan: Zondervan Publishing House, 1972, pp. 256-264, and Chapters 1-3, 5-9, and 16.

Lockyer, Herbert. *The Art and Craft of Preaching*. Grand Rapids, Michigan: Baker Book House, Chapters 1 and 7.

Macpherson, Ian. *The Burden of the Lord*. Nashville, Tennessee: Abingdon Press, 1955, Chapters 1 and 3.

Miller, Donald G. *Fire in Thy Mouth*. Grand Rapids, Michigan: Baker Book House, 1976, entire book.

Pattison, T. Harwood. *The Making of the Sermon*. Philadelphia: The American Baptist Publication Society, 1941, Chapter 23.

Perry, Lloyd M. *A Manual for Biblical Preaching*. Grand Rapids, Michigan: Baker Book House, 1965, pp. 4-6.

Reu, M. *Homiletics, A Manual of the Theory and Practice of Preaching*. Minneapolis: Augsburg Publishing House, 1924, Chapter 13.

Robinson, Haddon W. *Biblical Preaching*. Grand Rapids, Michigan: Baker Book House, 1980, pp. 89-96, and 107-113.

Roddy, Clarence Stonelynn. *We Prepare and Preach*. Chicago: Moody Press, 1959, pp. 51-53, 67-69, 82-83, 182-184.

Skinner, Craig. *The Teaching Ministry of the Pulpit*. Grand Rapids, Michigan: Baker Book House, 1979, pp. 197-204.

Sleeth, Ronald E. *Persuasive Preaching*. New York: Harper & Brothers, 1956, Chapter 1.

Spurgeon, Charles Haddon. *Lectures to My Students*. Grand Rapids, Michigan: Zondervan Publishing House, 1965, Chapter 14.

Stewart, James S. *Heralds of God*. New York: Charles Scribner's Sons, 1946, entire book.

Weatherspoon, Jesse Burton. *Sent Forth to Preach*. New York: Harper and Brothers, 1954, entire book.

White, R. E. O. *A Guide to Preaching*. Grand Rapids, Michigan: William B. Eerdmans Publishing Co., 1973, Chapters 2, 5, 6, 12, and 20.

Whitesell, Faris Daniel. *Preaching on Bible Characters*. Grand Rapids, Michigan: Baker Book House, 1955, Chapter 4.

_____ . *Power in Expository Preaching*. New York: Fleming H. Revell Company, 1963, Chapter 7.

Wilson, Gordon. *Set for the Defense*. Western Bible and Book Exchange, 1968, entire book.

12. THE CONCLUSION

Definition of the Conclusion

We have learned that every sermon needs unity and purpose. At the beginning the preacher sets out to accomplish one aim in the sermon. That aim must always be clear and distinct and must control all the minister says in his discourse so that the various parts of the message move toward the same definite, specific end.

Therefore *the conclusion is the climax of the whole sermon in which the preacher's one constant aim reaches its goal in the form of a forceful impression.*

It should be clear that the conclusion is neither a mere appendage to the body of the sermon nor a series of platitudes unrelated to the message, but an integral part of the sermon. It is the final portion of the sermon in which all that has been previously stated is concentrated in force or intensity to produce a vigorous impact upon the congregation.

It follows that the conclusion is not the place for the introduction of any new ideas or arguments. Its purpose is solely to emphasize, reaffirm, establish, or finalize that which has already been declared in the sermon with the object of bringing home to the hearers the main thrust of the discourse.

The conclusion is undoubtedly the most potent element in the entire sermon. If it is poorly executed, it may weaken or even destroy the effect of the preceding parts of the discourse. But some preachers forget the importance of the conclusion with the result that their sermons, which otherwise are carefully and thoroughly prepared, fail at the crucial point. Instead of concentrating their material into a burning and powerful focus, they allow the current of thought to be dissipated by commonplace or feeble remarks at the close.

On the other hand, a good conclusion may somehow make up for the deficiencies of some other parts of the sermon or else serve to heighten the impression which the previous portions of the sermon may have made on the congregation.

Because of the vital importance of the conclusion the minister should give the utmost care to its preparation and seek in every possible way to make the final impression powerful and decisive.

Forms of the Conclusion

There are various forms for the conclusion. As we discuss these it should be remembered that the particular form employed will vary from one sermon to another, depending upon the kind of sermon to be preached and its contents, as well as upon the state or condition of the hearers. Again, there may be occasions when it is well to combine two of these forms in the same conclusion.

1. Recapitulation

A conclusion of this kind is usually used when the sermon is built upon a series of arguments or ideas where it is necessary for the congregation to give close attention if they are to follow the preacher's line of thought. The restatement of the main ideas of the sermon at the close serves to remind them of the basic features which have been discussed and prepares them for the final thrust of the message. Thus the recapitulation is not mere redundancy—an unnecessary repetition of the main divisions—but a reemphasis of the impression given during the message so as to bring the one main truth of the sermon to a focal point. The wise preacher will generally not state this résumé in the very words of the main divisions, but will use concise, pointed statements to express each one of these main ideas.

2. Illustration

The ideas or truths of a sermon can sometimes be brought to a climax most effectively by the use of a powerful or apt illustration. This is especially the case when the illustration itself is a summation of the main truth of the message. By this means the one great spiritual lesson of the sermon is brought home vividly to the congregation. When the preacher uses an illustration of this kind, it should be unnecessary for him to add many more words, if any, to the conclusion. The illustration, forceful and meaningful in itself, should generally be a sufficient conclusion.

A minister once delivered a sermon on Numbers 21:4-9 dealing with the stinging of the Israelites by the fiery serpents in the wilderness. After telling how the people who had been bitten were healed by looking at the serpent of brass which Moses lifted up on a pole, the preacher concluded his message with this well-known story of the conversion of Charles Haddon Spurgeon:

> When Spurgeon was a young man, he felt so much guilt over his sin that he went from one church to another all over town, trying to learn how he could be forgiven. One winter Sunday on his way to church, he struggled through a snowstorm which became so violent that he was forced to give up. He turned instead down a side street where he found a small chapel with only fifteen worshipers gathered together. Even the pastor had not been able to come because of the storm. In his place, a man from the congregation stood up to preach. He chose to speak on Isaiah 45:22: "Turn to me and be saved, all you ends of the earth; for I am God, and there is no other." Because the man knew very little about preaching, his sermon consisted for the most part of repeating the text in different ways. Finally, when he could say no more about the passage, he directed his attention toward Spurgeon sitting in the back of the church. He spoke directly to him. "Young man, you look very miserable, and you will never cease to be miserable —in life and in death—if you do not do as this text says. But if you will simply look to Jesus, you will be saved." Then he shouted, "Young man, look to Jesus." At that moment, Spurgeon ceased dwelling on his own guilt and inadequacy and began instead to trust in Christ for salvation. His despair dropped away and he was filled with joy. He knew now that his sins were forgiven, not by any effort on his part, but simply because he had looked to Christ and Christ alone for his salvation.

3. Application or appeal

As the message draws to a close, it should cause the individuals in the congregation to ask themselves, what has this truth to do with me, with my relationships in my home, my church, my business, and in my everyday life and conduct? For this reason the preacher should end many of his sermons with a direct application or appeal in which he makes a call for a response to the truths delivered in the message. Sometimes the most effective application is summing up the gist of the sermon by a repetition of the proposition or homiletical idea. At other times the minister may employ two or three principles from the passage which has been expounded to bring the discourse to its conclusion. Since these abiding principles are always related to life they need not be elaborated upon; a few brief remarks in connection with each of them will usually be adequate.

4. Motivation

In the conclusion, one must often not only impose a moral obligation upon men and women, but also provide them with an incentive to respond personally to the challenge presented. This incentive may take on a variety of forms.

In some instances the preacher will need to instill in the hearts of men a fear of divine disapproval for wrongdoing or evil-thinking. At other times he should appeal instead to such ideals as love for God and man, courage and fortitude, integrity and purity, nobility and self-respect. Whatever the approach, he should aim to persuade the people to respond affirmatively to the divine claims upon them.

Whatever the object of the sermon, the homilist should gather together in the conclusion all the main lines of thought in the discourse so as to produce a personal response. It is for this purpose that a biblical sermon is delivered—it demands a proper response by the individual either in attitude or in action. The minister should therefore give most careful thought to the conclusion so that in the vital moments of decision his words may be as direct and forceful as possible.

It is a mistake, however, to think that a sermon must end with an emotional or pathetic appeal in which the preacher works himself into a fever of excitement or strong feeling. On the contrary, a natural, simple, quiet ending is usually far more impressive and effective. It should also be noted that rebukes and solemn warnings are more apt to be received by the congregation if they are spoken in loving tenderness rather than with thundering denunciation and vehemence.

Principles for the Preparation of the Conclusion

1. The conclusion should generally be brief.

Although the conclusion is a vital part of the sermon and needs to be carefully and thoroughly prepared, it does not have to be lengthy. Instead, the conclusion should usually be fairly short. No specific amount of time can be indicated for the conclusion, but the homilist should see that due proportion is given to the main portion of the ser-

mon and that there is sufficient time to tie up the ideas of the message
or bring them forcibly to a focal point in the conclusion.

Some preachers have the habit of informing their congregations
that they are about to conclude, using such phrases as "in conclusion"
or "as I close," but instead of bringing the sermon immediately to an
end they often proceed for another ten or fifteen minutes. The congregation anticipates being dismissed within a reasonable time, and it is
the obligation of the sermonizer to respect the expectations of his
people. Therefore, when he has brought the message to the place
where it is proper to end and it is time to conclude, he should stop.

2. The conclusion should be simple.

The minister should not strive to make the conclusion elaborate or
ornate. Simple, plain, positive language which is at the same time
penetrating and vigorous is far more effective than high sounding
speech. The important factor in the conclusion is to speak with such
clarity that the aim of the sermon is unmistakable to the hearers.

3. The final words of the conclusion should be carefully and thought-
fully chosen.

These final words should be designed to impress the congregation
with the entire subject just discussed, or give a sense of the importance
or urgency of the message. In order to accomplish these objectives the
final words may consist of one of the following features:

a. A strong and vivid reproduction of the leading thought of the ser-
    mon.

Suppose, for example, that the preacher has spoken from John
15:1-8 on "The Fruitful Christian." His final words could be somewhat as follows: "Should we not each ask ourselves, 'Am I a fruitful
Christian?' Jesus said, 'If a man remains in me and I in him, he will
bear much fruit.' It has also been said, 'The branch draws all from the
root, and gives all in the fruit.' "

The appropriateness of these final remarks may be fully appreciat-
ed by noting the outline which follows:

> Title: "The Fruitful Christian"
> Text: John 15:1-8.
> Introduction: 1. The Bible contains many profound truths con-
>   cerning the Christian life.

                     2. To teach us some of these truths, Christ some-
                         times uses simple illustrations or parables, here
                         the vine and fruitful branches.

Proposition: One of the Lord's great purposes for His people is
                   that they become fruitful Christians.

Interrogative sentence: How can we become fruitful Christians?

Transitional sentence: As we examine the essential features in the
                   parable in John 15:1-8 we will learn how we may
                   become fruitful Christians.

         I. The vine, vv. 1, 5.
              1. This speaks of Christ, the True Vine, v. 1.
              2. This speaks of Christ in relation to us, v. 5.
        II. The branches, vv. 2-6.
              1. They speak of us through whom fruit is to be
                 borne, vv. 2, 4-5.
              2. They speak of us who are to abide in Christ in
                 order to bear fruit, vv. 4-6.
              3. They speak of us who are to bring forth plentiful
                 fruit, vv. 2, 5, 8.
       III. The husbandman, vv. 1, 2, 6, 8.
              1. This speaks of God who removes the fruitless
                 branches, vv. 1, 2a, 6.
              2. This speaks of God who prunes the branches,
                 v. 2b.
              3. This speaks of God who is glorified when we bear
                 much fruit, v. 8.

Conclusion: 1. Every believer may be a fruitful Christian.
               2. Final remarks—see above.

b. A quotation of the text itself.

If the preacher has chosen John 15:4 as his text, he may suitably finish the sermon with the exact words of his text: "Remain in me, and I
will remain in you. No branch can bear fruit by itself; it must remain in
the vine. Neither can you bear fruit unless you remain in me."

c. The quotation of another passage of Scripture appropriate to the
sermon.

Assuming once more that the text chosen for the discourse is John
15:4, the preacher may conclude with a parallel reference such as Galatians 5:22-23, "But the fruit of the Spirit is love, joy, peace, patience, kindness, goodness, faithfulness, gentleness and self-control.
Against such things there is no law."

In the topical outline shown below we have chosen to quote a single
verse as the conclusion to the message.

          Title: "What Makes a Christian Home?"
Introduction: 1. Definition: "A home is the father's kingdom, the

mother's world, the child's paradise."
2. Need today—more happy homes—more Christian homes.
3. Bible sets forth the ideals for a home.

Proposition: A Christian home is a home founded upon Christian ideals.

Interrogative sentence: What ideals can we find in the Scriptures for a Christian home?

Transitional sentence: There are at least three ideals which we may find in the Word of God for a Christian home.

    I. It is a home where love reigns.
       1. In the hearts of parents for each other, Titus 2:11, Colossians 3:19, Ephesians 5:25, 28-33, 2 Corinthians 13:4-7.
       2. In the hearts of parents for their children, Titus 2:4, Genesis 22:2.
    II. It is a home where parental authority is exercised.
       1. By the father as the ultimate authority, Ephesians 6:4, Ephesians 6:1-2.
       2. In the right spirit, Ephesians 6:4, Colossians 3:21
    III. It is a home where Christ is present.
       1. In the position of lordship, Ephesians 5:22-6:4.
       2. To manifest His power when He is obeyed, John 2:1-11.

Conclusion: John 14:21—"Whoever has my commands and obeys them, he is the one who loves me. He who loves me will be loved by my Father, and I too will love him and show myself to him "

d   The quotation of an appropriate poem or a stanza or two of a hymn.

As we have mentioned in Chapter 9, quotations of hymns or poetry should generally be very brief, usually a stanza or possibly two lines of a poem. A message on Matthew 11:28-29 could fittingly end with a poem such as the following:

> "Bear not a single care thyself,
> One is too much for thee,
> The work is mine, and mine alone,
> Thy work, to rest in Me."

e. A forceful challenge or appeal.

If the homilist delivers an evangelistic message on "Three Men Who Died at Calvary," in which he speaks of Christ on the central cross and the repentant and unrepentant thieves on the other two crosses, one on the left of Jesus and one on His right, his final words may be as follows: "Every man and woman stands today in the place of one of these two thieves. Either we are repentant or unrepentant, either we are forgiven or unforgiven, either we are saved or we are lost. In which place are you?"

We repeat the outline on Luke 15:11-24 given in Chapter 6 and call the student's attention to the conclusion, which consists of the use of an illustration, followed by an appeal. The appeal in this instance is somewhat similar to the one in the last paragraph.

Title: "Lost and Found"

Introduction: 1. At the World's Fair in Chicago, in order to assist parents to locate their children who had strayed on the grounds, the authorities established a "lost and found department" for children.

2. Luke 15 is the "Lost and Found Department" of Bible. Here Jesus tells of three things that were lost and found—a sheep, a silver coin, and a son.

3. The story of the son who was lost and found illustrates the history of a repentant sinner who is "lost and found."

Proposition: The Lord joyfully receives a repentant sinner.

Interrogative sentence: How does this truth emerge in the story of the prodigal who was "lost and found"?

Transitional sentence: This truth emerges in the four-fold history of a repentant sinner which the story of the prodigal depicts.

I. The sinner's guilt, vv. 11-13.
   1. In his self-will, vv. 11-12.
   2. In his shame, v. 13.
II. The sinner's misery, vv. 14-16.
   1. In his soul's hunger, v. 14.
   2. In his unavailing efforts to satisfy his hunger, vv. 15-16.
III. The sinner's repentance, vv. 17-20a.
   1. In the realization of his sinfulness, vv. 17-19.
   2. In his return to God, v. 20a.
IV. The sinner's restoration, vv. 20b-24.
   1. In the welcome given him by God, vv. 20b-21.
   2. In the favor bestowed upon him by God, vv. 22-24.

Conclusion: Illustration: There was another lost boy—the elder son. He was out in the field when his brother returned home. When entreated by his father to join in the feast taking place in the house for his brother, he refused. He claimed that he had lived righteously all his life and that he was worthy of reward rather than the prodigal. The elder son was lost and completely unrepentant. The prodigal returned home because he repented of his guilt. On the other hand, the elder son, in his pride and self-righteousness, so far as the story goes, never became reconciled to his father.

The two sons are typical of two classes of individuals —the one, the sinner who comes to God freely

> acknowledging his need for forgiveness; the other,
> the one who is so self-righteous that he regards him-
> self as needing no repentance.
>
> Have you, like the prodigal, gone to God admitting
> your guilt and finding the fullness of His forgiveness,
> or are you like the elder son, too good to need for-
> giveness from God? The Savior said, "Whoever
> comes to me I will never drive away." Won't you
> come to Him now?

Observe that in this last example, as well as in the previous one, the closing words in the appeal are an interrogation, leaving the hearer to supply his own response.

4. The conclusion should be expressed in the outline in a few brief sentences or phrases.

Like all the other parts of the sermon outline, the conclusion should be stated as briefly as possible, with each point or idea written on a separate line. The illustration below, which is the conclusion of the outline on "The Psalm of Contentment" given in previous chapters, shows how this should be done.

Conclusion: 1. John 10:4, 16, 27—Christ's sheep "hear
his voice."
2. If all that is said re sheep in this Psalm is to be true
in our experience, we must constantly hear
Christ's voice, follow Him.

In order that the student may see how the conclusion is related to the main body of the sermon, we now present the entire outline:

Title: "The Psalm of Contentment"
Text: Psalm 23.
Introduction: 1. Sheepherder in Idaho with band of 1,200 sheep
—unable to give individual attention to sheep.
2. Contrast Shepherd of this Psalm—as though He
has only one sheep for which to care.
3. Every child of God recognizes himself to be the
sheep spoken of in this Psalm.
Proposition: Contentment is the happy prerogative of every child
of God.
Interrogative sentence: Upon what is his contentment based?
Transitional sentence: The child of God learns from this Psalm
that as the Lord's sheep his contentment is based
on three facts in relation to the sheep.
I. The sheep's Shepherd, v. 1.
1. A divine Shepherd, v. 1.

        2. A personal Shepherd, v. 1.
    II. The sheep's provision, vv. 2-5.
        1. Rest, v. 2.
        2. Guidance, v. 3.
        3. Comfort, v. 4.
        4. Abundance, v. 5.
    III. The sheep's prospect, v. 6.
        1. A bright prospect for this life, v. 6.
        2. A blessed prospect for the hereafter, v. 6.
Conclusion: 1. John 10:4, 16, 27—Christ's sheep "hear
        his voice."
        2. If all that is said re sheep in this Psalm is to be true
        in our experience, we must constantly hear
        Christ's voice, follow Him.

With permission of its author, we show below an expository sermon outline prepared by James Morgan, a student in the homiletics class at Multnomah School of the Bible.

    Title: "Principles for Successful Missionary Outreach"
    Text: Acts 13:1-5.
Introduction: 1. Never in the history of the church has it had
        greater opportunity for evangelism.
        2. Much of the world is still open to us and, as we
        shall see, the church today need not fail to fulfill
        its divinely-given responsibility.
Proposition: God's principles for missionary outreach guarantee
        success.
Interrogative sentence: What are those principles?
Transitional sentence: Acts 13:1-5 reveals four effective
        principles for missionary outreach.
    I. There must be quality personnel available, v. 1.
        1. Men who are in active fellowship in the church,
        v. 1.
        2. Men who are spiritually equipped, v. 1.
    II. There must be a call from the Holy Spirit, v. 2.
        1. Men who are called by a specific choice, v. 2.
        2. Men who are called to a specific ministry, v. 2.
    III. The church must identify itself with the missionaries,
        v. 3.
        1. They must pray with them, v. 3.
        2. They must commission them, v. 3.
        3. They must accept responsibility in sending them,
        v. 3.
    IV. There must be diligent labor by those sent out,
        vv. 4-5.
        1. They must obey the leading of the Spirit, v. 4.
        2. They must preach God's Word, v. 5.
        3. They must work together, v. 5.
Conclusion: 1. These principles are not complex but are the ones
        God has chosen to use.
        Our response to Christ requires that we take our

place in putting these principles into action.
3. Each must ask himself:
"Am I qualified?"
"Am I listening for the voice of the Holy Spirit?"
"Am I truly identifying myself with those who
     have gone out?"
  "Am I willing to spend and be spent as God's
     Spirit may direct?"
4. God waits to hear our answer.

Another means of bringing this last outline to a proper conclusion may be through an illustration such as the following, which comes from Dr. John G. Mitchell, pastor emeritus of Central Bible Church in Portland, Oregon, and one of the founders of Multnomah School of the Bible:

> When Dr. Mitchell was pastoring a church in Grand Rapids, Michigan, he received a message from one of the young people of his church who was about to leave the United States for missionary service in China. Prior to the young man's departure by ship, he telegraphed Dr. Mitchell from San Francisco requesting his pastor to give him one final word of counsel before he sailed for the mission field. Dr. Mitchell wired back immediately, "Sit down at the feet of Jesus, and then tell the Chinese what you see."

The counsel which Dr. Mitchell gave this young man is applicable not only to a foreign missionary but also to every servant of Jesus Christ who is given the unspeakable privilege and honor of proclaiming "the unsearchable riches of Christ."

If we are to be worthy ministers of Christ, let us also sit at the feet of Jesus until our own hearts and characters are transformed into the likeness of our Lord.

> "And we, who with unveiled faces all reflect the Lord's glory, are being transformed into his likeness with ever-increasing glory, which comes from the Lord, who is the Spirit. Therefore, since through God's mercy we have this ministry, we do not lose heart" (2 Corinthians 3:18-4:1).

EXERCISES

1. Prepare a suitable introduction and conclusion for the topical sermon outline entitled "Can We Know God's Will for Us?" in Chapter 8.

2. Study the outline and remarks in Chapter 3 on the expository outline entitled "Wit's End Corner" and then formulate an appropriate introduction, proposition, interrogative sentence, transitional sentence, transitions between the main divisions, and the conclusion for the outline.

3. Instead of the conclusion shown at the close of Chapter 9 for the sermon entitled "Won by Love," provide an illustration which may form a fitting climax to the message.

4. By use of the rhetorical processes discussed in Chapters 9, 10, and 11, expand the outline on "The Psalm of Contentment" shown in this chapter.

5. Prepare a complete topical sermon outline suitable for a message on Father's Day, giving the title, introduction, proposition, interrogative sentence, transitional sentence, main divisions, subdivisions, transitions between the main divisions, and the conclusion. Expand the outline, using the rhetorical processes discussed in Chapters 9, 10, and 11. In your discussion, whenever possible, use brief phrases instead of complete sentences.

6. Construct a complete textual sermon outline on Acts 1:8, following the same directions as for Exercise 5.

Make a complete expository sermon outline on Philippians 4:4-9, folwing the same procedure as required in Exercise 5.

BIBLIOGRAPHY

Baird, John E. *Preparing for Platform and Pulpit*. Nashville, Tennessee: Abingdon Press, 1968, pp. 82-83.

Baumann, J. Daniel. *An Introduction to Contemporary Preaching*. Grand Rapids, Michigan: Baker Book House, 1972, pp. 142-145.

Blackwood, Andrew W. *The Fine Art of Preaching*. New York: The Macmillan Company, 1937, Chapter 9.

Brastow, Lewis O. *The Work of the Preacher*. Boston: The Pilgrim Press, 1914, Section IV, Chapter 5.

Broadus, John A. *On the Preparation and Delivery of Sermons*. Revised by Jesse B. Weatherspoon. New York: Harper & Brothers, 1944, Part II, Chapter 4.

Brown, H. C. Jr., H. Gordon Clinard and Jesse J. Northcutt. *Steps to the Sermon*. Nashville, Tennessee: Broadman Press, 1963, pp. 121-125.

Burrell, David James. *The Sermon, Its Construction and Delivery*. New York: Fleming H. Revell Company, 1913, Part III, Chapter 3.

Davis, Henry Grady. *Design for Preaching*. Philadelphia, Pennsylvania: Fortress Press, 1958, Chapter 11.

Demaray, Donald E. *An Introduction to Homiletics*. Grand Rapids, Michigan: Baker Book House, 1976, Chapter 6.

DeWelt, Don. *If You Want to Preach*. Grand Rapids, Michigan: Baker Book House, 1957, pp. 128-138.

Etter, John W. *The Preacher and His Sermon*. Dayton, Ohio: United Brethren Publishing House, 1902, Chapter 10.

Evans, William. *How to Prepare Sermons and Gospel Addresses*. Chicago: The Bible Institute Colportage Assn., 1913, Chapter 10.

Lane, Denis. *Preach the Word*. Welwyn, Hartfordshire, England: Evangelical Press, 1979, Chapter 11.

Macpherson, Ian. *The Burden of the Lord*. Nashville, Tennessee: Abingdon Press, 1955, pp. 114-118.

Pattison, T. Harwood. *The Making of the Sermon*. Philadelphia: The American Baptist Publication Society, 1898, Chapter 12.

Perry, Lloyd M. *A Manual for Biblical Preaching*. Grand Rapids, Michigan: Baker Book House, 1965, pp. 79-80.

Phelps, Austin. *The Theory of Preaching*. New York: Charles Scribner's Sons, 1892, Lectures 32-39.

Reu, M. *Homiletics, A Manual of the Theory and Practice of Preaching*. Minneapolis: Augsburg Publishing House, 1950, Chapter 18.

Robinson, Haddon W. *Biblical Preaching*. Grand Rapids, Michigan: Baker Book House, 1980, pp. 167-172.

Sangster, William Edwin. *The Craft of the Sermon*. Philadelphia: Westminster Press, n.d., Part I, Chapter 6.

Skinner, Craig. *The Teaching Ministry of the Pulpit*. Grand Rapids, Michigan: Baker Book House, 1979, pp. 173 175.

Sleeth, Ronald E. *Persuasive Preaching*. New York: Harper & Brothers, 1965, Chapter 6.

White, R. E. O. *A Guide to Preaching*. Grand Rapids, Michigan: William B. Eerdmans Publishing Co., 1973, Chapter 10.

Whitesell, Faris Daniel and Lloyd M. Perry. *Variety in Your Preaching*. Westwood, New Jersey: Fleming H. Revell Company, 1954, Chapter 9.

13. Summary

Basic Steps in the Preparation of a Sermon Outline

Because of the multiplicity of rules about sermon construction which we have proposed in the preceding chapters, we shall show below the basic processes, step by step, in the preparation of a Bible message.

1. Choice of a passage.

If we were preaching through a book in the Bible, the task of selecting a unit of Scripture for exposition would be eliminated. We would simply choose as our next passage the one immediately following our last passage. This is indeed the ideal plan as it not only saves the pastor searching from week to week for a suitable text, but it also enables him to teach through a book. If the series of sermons on any one book is not too extensive it gives the people a well-rounded view of the book and also makes it possible for the preacher to touch on numerous sensitive subjects which relate to the lives of his congregation without appearing in any way to be purposely directed at them.

The difficulty in the selection of a passage arises when we are not following a prescribed plan, and the passages which we employ do not therefore follow any special order. We are then obliged to depend upon various circumstances to give us an indication of the direction we should take in the choice of the Scripture passage upon which we are to preach. The spiritual and temporal needs of the congregation, special times of festivity, difficulty or stress, particular goals or plans of the church, as well as the regular days of celebration in the church calendar, will make it necessary for us to find a text which is appropriate to the occasion. But whatever the circumstance upon which we are to bring God's message to His people, we need to rely upon the leading of the Holy Spirit to direct us to the particular portion which it is His purpose for us to use. As we wait upon Him, He will undoubtedly lead us by various means to the choice of the right text.

While meditating one day in his study on the story of the prodigal son, a pastor was suddenly arrested by the words in Luke 15:17 which read in the King James Version, "and when he came to himself." These words so gripped the minister's soul that for the following Sunday morning service he prepared a message entitled, "Return to Spiritual Sanity." That Sunday morning a Christian woman who lived in another city visited the church. She had wandered from the Lord and was so burdened with guilt that she thought that she was about to go insane. When she was seated in a pew and read the sermon title in the bulletin which the usher had handed her, she realized at once that the message which the minister was about to preach was just for her. That sermon was given by the Lord to His faithful servant and was used to the restoration of the backslidden woman to her Lord and to spiritual sanity.

2. Thorough exegetical study of the passage.

There are times when the Spirit of God may reveal like a flash the message He wishes us to deliver; the basic features and truths of the text which we are to proclaim may come to us in such a remarkable way that we may put the entire discourse together in a matter of minutes or within an hour or so. As a general rule, however, the preparation of a sermon requires prayerful and diligent research.

3. Discovery of the main thrust of the passage.

We discussed at some length in Chapter 7 how we may discover the subject and complement of the text and express these in the form of an exegetical idea in a single complete sentence. This sentence indicates the main thought of the text.

We also learned from the same chapter that the exegetical idea leads to a statement of the proposition or homiletical idea in which the basic truth of the passage is expressed in the form of an abiding principle which is true for all time and applicable to all men everywhere. This truth becomes the main thrust of the passage, and that which the preacher must seek to bring home to the hearts of his hearers throughout the message.

But an expository unit may be regarded from more than a single point of view, depending upon the approach which we may be led by the Spirit of God to make. We have referred to this in Chapter 3 in connection with the method of multiple approach to a passage. Nevertheless, we must always remember that our main objective should be stated so that it will relate the Scripture passage to the people in the pew.

4. Construction of the sermon outline.

By the time the preacher has completed his exegetical study of the passage, he often has a good idea of the structure of the passage and the natural divisions of the text. These natural divisions may provide the verse divisions for the sermon outline, but this is not always the case. Only after the homilist has stated his proposition is he ready to proceed with building the sermon outline, for, as we have stated previously, the thesis is the foundation upon which the sermon is constructed, and, with its accompanying transitional sentence, indicates the direction in which the discourse will proceed. The main divisions unfold, develop, or explain the concept expressed in the proposition.

If the preacher purposes to build his sermon by the inductive approach, he will state his points in an orderly sequence, culminating with the statement of the proposition at the close of his address. Or, depending upon the aim which the minister has in mind for his discourse, the sermon may not contain a formal expression of the thesis at all.

We have also learned that the main divisions should be stated clearly so that they will be immediately intelligible to the hearers, and that the points in the outline should progress step by step to an apex. One of the advantages of a clear-cut, logical outline is that it makes it easier for the sermonizer to think through the message as he delivers it to his congregation, thus avoiding the distraction to himself and to his auditors which results when the preacher glances frequently at his notes. At the same time, the people in the pew find it much easier to follow a discourse which is plainly set before them in an orderly sequence, with smooth transitions helping them to recognize the movement of ideas from one unit of thought to the next.

5. Filling in the sermon outline.

Once he has drawn up the mainheads and subheads of his sermon, the preacher must then fill in his outline with such material as will adequately convey to the hearers the ideas represented by the main divisions of his outline.

Inasmuch as one of the chief objects of the sermon is to explain the meaning of the text, the material which the minister should employ in filling in the outline must come first from the data he has gathered in his exegesis of the Biblical passage. In addition to this, he may include facts drawn from various sources such as other forms of literature, his own personal experiences, the experiences of others, and his observation of things around him. By the use of his imaginative faculties, he may also conjure up mental images to add delightful freshness to his presentation of the truth, provided he exercises his imagination judiciously.

In the expansion of the sermon outline the preacher needs to employ more than one of the following rhetorical processes: explanation, argumentation, quotation, illustration, and application. As we have said, explanation of the text is basic in the interpretation of any passage of Scripture. However, the order in which we use the various other rhetorical processes will depend upon the circumstances and conditions which may arise as we proceed with the development of the sermon, point by point.

Having gathered a considerable amount of material for the expansion of his outline, the beginner may be in danger of including too much in his communication. If he were to attempt to present this accumulation of ideas to his people he would get lost in a profusion of concepts and facts and his auditors would become confused by the mass of material set before them.

To avoid this situation, the preacher should aim at simplicity. He must keep before him the one central truth which he is seeking to impart, and carefully but ruthlessly eliminate all extraneous material. A discourse which has a clearly-directed aim and which moves rapidly and steadily toward its climax is generally far more effective and forceful than one in which both speaker and hearer get bogged down in a quantity of details, or one which is too heavy for the people in the pew to assimilate.

Throughout the entire message the minister must gauge the amount of time he should spend on each point. Some parts of the sermon may require more attention than others, depending upon the importance of each section and the response from the audience.

6. Preparation of the conclusion, introduction, and title.

While the thoughts which have occupied him in the development of the body of his discourse are still fresh in his mind, the preacher should prepare the conclusion. Once he has brought the message to its climax in the conclusion, he should stop. The attention span of the average listener is limited. Therefore, the minister should not prolong the conclusion of the sermon.

The introduction and title of the sermon are often the last items to be prepared, not because they are unimportant, but because the homiletical craftsman usually has a clearer idea of how he ought to introduce his theme after he has constructed the main part of this message and knows what he is going to discuss throughout the discourse.

7. Prayerful dependence upon the Spirit of God.

Although we have mentioned it before, we cannot stress it enough: Along with all the time and effort which we put into the preparation and delivery of a sermon, our ministry must always be carried out in prayerful dependence upon the Spirit of God. He alone can put the right thought in our minds, the right words on our lips, and fill us with a loving and gracious spirit in which to deliver the message, so that the blessing of God may attend our communication of His truth. Then we will be able to preach in the power of the Holy Spirit to needy men and women, and to the uplifting of weary souls to the glory of our blessed Lord and Savior Jesus Christ.

> "We do not preach ourselves, but Jesus Christ as Lord, and ourselves as your servants for Jesus' sake" (2 Corinthians 4:5).

"But we have this treasure in jars of clay to show that this all-surpassing power is from God and not from us" (2 Corinthians 4:7).

> The glory of love is brightest
>   When the glory of self is dim,
> And they have the most impelled me
> Whom most have pointed to Him.
>
> They have held me, stirred me, swayed me,
> I have hung on their every word
> Till I fain would arise and follow,
> Not them, not them, but their Lord
>
>   Ruby Weyburne

Scripture Index

Subject Index